THE PLEASURES OF
GOD

THE PLEASURES OF
GOD

JOHN PIPER

MULTNOMAH
Portland, Oregon

Edited by Steve Halliday
Cover design by Bruce DeRoos
Cover photo by Galen Rowell/Mountain Light

THE PLEASURES OF GOD
© 1991 by John Piper
Published by Multnomah Press
10209 SE Division Street
Portland, Oregon 97266

Multnomah Press is a ministry of
Multnomah School of the Bible
8435 NE Glisan Street
Portland, Oregon 97220

Printed in the United States of America.

Library of Congress Cataloging-in-Publication Data

Piper, John, 1946—
    The pleasures of God : meditations on God's delight in being God / John Piper.
    p.   cm.
    Includes bibliographical references and indexes.
    ISBN 0-88070-436-5 (hd)
    ISBN 0-88070-537-X (pa)
    1. God.   I. Title.
BT102.P534 1991
231—dc20   91-11364
                                                    CIP

98 99 - 10 9 8 7

To My Sons

Karsten Luke Piper
Benjamin John Piper
Abraham Christian Piper
Barnabas William Piper

Contents

Preface   9

Introduction: How the Book Was Born   13

1. The Pleasure of God in His Son   23

2. The Pleasure of God in All He Does   47

3. The Pleasure of God in His Creation   79

4. The Pleasure of God in His Fame   101

5. The Pleasure of God in Election   123

6. The Pleasure of God in Bruising the Son   161

7. The Pleasure of God in Doing Good
   to All Who Hope in Him   187

8. The Pleasure of God in the Prayers of the Upright   211

9. The Pleasure of God in Personal Obedience
   and Public Justice   241

Epilogue: Almost Too Good to Be True—
   A Final Word of Hope   269

Appendix: Letter to a Friend Concerning the So-called
   "Lordship Salvation"   279

Scripture Index   307

Person Index   319

Subject Index   323

Preface

This is a book about the good news of God's gladness in being God. It's about what the apostle Paul called "the gospel of the glory of the happy God" (1 Timothy 1:11). It is not mainly about us. But it is about what we were made for.

In one sense this book should have come before *Desiring God*.[1] Fathers come before sons. But sometimes it is good for sons to go first. They sound more up-to-date. They get a hearing more easily in the modern world. A chip off the old block seems less imposing than the whole block. So it may look like *The Pleasures of God* is the offspring of *Desiring God*, but in this case "the child is father of the man."

Desiring God can be summed up in one sentence: God is most glorified in us when we are most satisfied in him. *The Pleasures of God* adds this foundational truth: We will be most satisfied in God when we know why God himself is most satisfied in God. Therefore this is a book about the unimaginably good news that God delights fully in being God.

To put it another way, this is a book about grace. I almost used the subtitle: "Meditations on God-centered Grace." It would have been true. The book is a passionate defense of the freedom of grace—that because God is supremely happy in the fellowship of the Trinity, "he is not served by human hands as though he needed anything, since he himself gives to everyone life and breath and all things" (Acts 17:25). Instead of being served, God magnifies the fullness of his own self-replenishing joy by overflowing freely with grace. Jesus came not to be served but to serve. I have tasted the river of his delights in a thousand ways. It fills me again and again with longing to move up the river nearer and nearer to the spring.

Along the way this overflowingly gracious God has brought into my life some very precious people. For over ten years I have savored the listening and the love of an amazingly patient congregation. In the summer of 1990 they entrusted me with three months free to write. They were hard to leave and easy to come back to.

Shelley Solin, my ministry assistant, has carried more burdens for me than anyone knows. She is a brilliant administrator. We fight the fight of faith together in a very broken world.

Carol Steinbach has again given her keen editorial eye to the work and made the book triply useful by painstakingly producing, with the aid of Becky Osterhus, two of the indexes.

My wife, Noël, with whom I have just celebrated our twenty-fifth Valentine's Day together, rejoiced with me to watch the birthing of the book. She read every page again and again as the revisions came off the printer. Noël, thanks for the early morning walks down Atlanta Street. These lines are as true today as when I wrote them on our twentieth anniversary:

Although the fig tree blossom not,
And all the vines of our small plot
Be barren, and the olive fail,
The sheep grow weak and heifers frail,
We will rejoice in God, my love,
And take our pleasures from above:
The Lord, our God, shall be our strength
And give us life, whatever length
On earth he please, and make our feet
Like mountain deer, to rise and cleat
The narrow path for man and wife
That rises steep and leads to life.

Finally, a word to my sons. The book is dedicated to you, Karsten and Benjamin and Abraham and Barnabas. If there is any legacy I want to leave you, it is not money or house or land; it is a vision of God—as great and glorious a God as one could ever see. But more than that, I want to leave the legacy of passion for this God. A passion far beyond what any human can produce. A passion for God flowing from the very heart of God. Never forget that God is most glorified in you when you are most satisfied in him. But even more—and this is my prayer for you—in God's time, may your satisfaction in him be without measure, as it becomes the very pleasure of God in God.

John Piper
Minneapolis, Minnesota
February 1991

Note

1. John Piper, *Desiring God* (Portland: Multnomah Press, 1986).

"The Worth and Excellency of a soul
is to be measured by the object of its love."

Henry Scougal

Introduction

How the Book Was Born

Where I Found the Key

For the second time I was reading through *The Life of God in the Soul of Man*, by Henry Scougal. It was one of those times which I call "going out to pasture"—some Monday morning, perhaps, when a pastor feels more like a lame sheep than a leading shepherd. I wanted food—solid, rich, root-deepening, thirst-wakening, life-giving food for a spent soul.

I remembered back seven years to the first time I read *The Life of God* and pulled it down from the shelf. Virtually every page was marked with lines and notes and exclamation points. It started to come back how deeply this book had moved me. Even the notes in the margins awakened old affections.

There are some books whose vision is so deep and clear that truth rings from the page like the toll of a large bell, perfectly obvious, but rare and precious. They unfold the heart of man and God with such forceful illumination that the truth is not just shown to my mind but created in my heart.

I read again that "the soul of man . . . hath in it a raging and inextinguishable thirst . . ."[1]

And there was thirst!

I read, "Never doth a soul know what solid joy and substantial pleasure is till, once being weary of itself, it renounces all property [and] gives itself up to the Author of its being."[2]

And there was in me an immense longing to give myself up to God, for the quenching of this "raging thirst."

So it went as I grazed in the green pasture of this remarkable book.

Not everybody responds this way to a three-hundred-year-old book. But I have to admit that most of my soul's food comes from very old books. I find the atmosphere of my own century far too dense with man and distant from the sweet sovereignty of God.

Not so with Henry Scougal. He was remembered as one whose "whole soul seemed to be swallowed up in the contemplation of Jesus Christ."[3] He wrote *The Life of God in the Soul of Man* in 1677 when he was only twenty-seven years old.

He had come to the University of Aberdeen in Scotland at the age of fifteen. At nineteen he was appointed instructor of philosophy, and then, after four years of teaching, he left the university for a one-year pastorate in Auchterless about twenty miles away. He was called back to Kings College in the university to teach divinity and died of tuberculosis on June 13, 1678, before he was twenty-eight years old. It's one of the dark strains in the melody of God's providence that the likes of Henry Scougal (twenty-seven years), David Brainerd (twenty-nine years), Henry Martyn (thirty-one years), and Robert Murray McCheyne (twenty-nine years) should all die at such an early age.

But they all did more for God's kingdom in their short lives than most others have done with three score and ten. Scougal's achievement was beyond all his expectations. *The Life of God in the Soul of Man* was not written for publication. It was written as a letter to a friend in spiritual need. The friend began to circulate it privately, until Bishop Gilbert Burnet published it. For three hundred years it has been reprinted at the request of God's hungry people, and today ranks as a classic of Christian devotion.

I'm obviously not the first to feed on this little book. George Whitefield, the great evangelist of the eighteenth century, paid the book a remarkable tribute:

> Though I had fasted, watched, and prayed, and received the sacrament so long, yet I never knew what true religion was till God sent me that excellent treatise by the hand of my never-to-be-forgotten friend.

The never-to-be-forgotten friend was Charles Wesley. Whitefield had come to him in deep spiritual perplexity and Wesley had given him a copy of Scougal's *Life of God.* Whitefield's experience confirms the power of this book:

> O what a ray of divine life did then break in upon my soul! I fell awriting to all my brethren and to my sisters. I talked to the students as they came into my room. I laid aside all trifling conversation. I put all trifling books away, and was determined to study to be a saint, and then to be a scholar. From that moment God has been carrying on His blessed work in my soul.[4]

If Scougal's little book (105 pages in the Bethany edition, 160 pages in the Sprinkle edition) touched the great Whitefield so deeply, it's not surprising that I was helped. About thirty pages into the book, I reached the section titled "The Excellency of Divine Love." One sentence riveted my attention. It took hold of my thought life in early 1987 and became the center of my meditation for about three months. What Scougal said in this sentence was the key that opened for me the treasure house of the pleasures of God. He said, "The worth and excellency of a soul is to be measured by the object of its love."[5]

Beholding as a Way of Becoming

In the context of this key sentence Scougal is referring to the *human* soul. But what occurred to me as I meditated on these words was the question: If this is true for man, may it not also be true for God? Is it not also the case that the worth and excellency of *God's* soul is to be measured by the object of his love?[6]

How else do we assess the beauty of an invisible heart than by what it loves? Someone might suggest, "By what it *thinks.*" But clear and accurate thought is beautiful only in the service of right affections. The devil himself is quite an able intellect. But he loves all the wrong things. Therefore his thinking serves evil and his soul is squalid.

Or perhaps someone would suggest that we can assess the beauty of a soul by what it *wills.* Yes, but there is half-hearted willing and whole-hearted willing. You don't judge the glory of a soul by what it wills to do with lukewarm interest, or with mere teeth-gritting determination. To know a soul's proportions you need to know its passions. The true dimensions of a soul are seen in its delights. Not what we dutifully will but what we passionately want reveals our excellence or evil.

> The soul is measured by its flights,
> Some low and others high,
> The heart is known by its delights,
> And pleasures never lie.

This is clearly what Scougal means by love when he says, "The worth and excellency of a soul is to be measured by the object of its *love*." He means the delights and pleasures that we take in what we love. For example, he says,

The love of God is a *delightful and affectionate sense* of the divine perfections which makes the soul resign and sacrifice itself wholly unto him, desiring above all things to please him, and *delighting in nothing so much as in fellowship and communion with him*, and being ready to do or suffer any thing for his sake or at his pleasure.[7]

Therefore when love is well-placed, the soul's pleasures are unsurpassed:

The most ravishing pleasures, the most solid and substantial delights that human nature is capable of, are those which arise from the endearments of a well-placed and successful affection.[8]

And when the pleasures of a "well-placed" affection are unsurpassed, its excellency is revealed. For "the excellency of a soul is to be measured by the object of its love."

Without doubt, for human beings the affection of love is "well-placed and successful" when placed in God. For this is the first and greatest commandment: "You shall love the Lord your God with all your heart" (Matthew 22:37). So the most excellent soul is the soul that loves God most. And to the degree that such love is openly manifest, to that degree is the loving soul revealed in its worth and beauty.

So it is with God. The worth and excellency of *God's* soul is to be measured by the object of his love. It is even more true for him than for us that love is that powerful and prevalent passion of the soul on which both its perfection and happiness depend. So if God's love is his powerful and prevalent passion—the omnipotent energy of his approval and enjoyment and delight—then "the pleasures of God" are the measure of the excellency of his soul.

The more I thought about it the more important Scougal's insight seemed. If he is right, I thought, then one way to meditate on the excellency of God is to meditate on his pleasures. One way to see the glory of God is to see his joy. This was a thrilling thought to me because I knew from experience and from Scripture that the more I focus on the glory of God, the more I am changed into his likeness. We tend to become like what we admire and enjoy. And the stronger our admiration, the greater the influence. Henry Scougal put it like this:

> He who loveth mean and sordid things doth thereby become base and vile; but a noble and well-placed affection doth advance and improve the spirit unto a conformity with the perfections which it loves.[9]

If the excellence of God could be admired in his pleasures, and if we tend to conform to what we admire, then focusing on the pleasures of God could help me be conformed to God. This made sense not only from experience but also from Scripture.

For example, in 2 Corinthians 3:18 Paul says, "We all, with unveiled face, *beholding* the glory of the Lord, are *being changed into his likeness* from one degree of glory to another."[10] Beholding is a way of becoming. So if the pleasures of God are the mark of his excellency, or his glory, then meditating on these pleasures holds out great hope for being changed into his likeness. This was a tremendous incentive for me to press on in thinking about Scougal's sentence: "The worth and excellency of a soul is to be measured by the object of its love."

Where the Book Was Born

Once I saw this plainly, I knew what I had to do. I took a four-day study leave from my duties at the church and went to northern Minnesota with my Bible and a concordance. As I looked up all the places in the Bible where God's delights and pleasures and joys are mentioned, I saw a series of sermons emerging. I preached those sermons in early 1987. Not only that, I saw emerging a major biblical study on the character of God. I saw that the pleasures of God were in fact a portrait of God. Every pleasure was another feature in the glory of his countenance. This book is the result of that discovery in northern Minnesota.

I regard this book as a vision of God through the lens of his happiness. What the church and the world need today, more than anything else, is to know and love God—the great, glorious, sovereign, happy God of the Bible. Very few people think of God as supremely happy in the fellowship of the Trinity and in the work of creation and redemption. The volcanic exuberance of God over the worth of his Son and the work of his hands and welfare of his people is not well-known. God's delight in being God is not sung the way it should be, with wonder and passion, in the worship places of the world. And we are the poorer and weaker for it.

My hope and prayer in writing this book is that more and more people would meditate with me on the pleasures of God; and that in doing so we would focus our attention on his excellency and glory. In this way our souls would be increasingly satisfied with God and changed gradually into his likeness. Thus, more and more, would God's glory be manifest in the world through the mission of his church.

The Book's Flow of Thought

The order of the chapters is intentional, each building on the other. The first six chapters are entirely God-focused. The spotlight is not on what kind of human attitudes and actions God delights in, but rather on God's pleasure in his own nature and work. We begin with the most fundamental truth, namely, that from all eternity God has been supremely happy in the fellowship of the Trinity. From this inexhaustible fountain of self-replenishing joy flows the freedom of God in all his sovereign work, creating the universe, spreading his fame, choosing a people, and bruising his Son.

At this point there is a turning point in the book. With chapter 7 we begin to focus on God's pleasure in the responses of his people. This order is very important. We need to see first and foremost that God is God—that he is perfect and complete in himself, that he is overflowingly happy in the eternal fellowship of the Trinity, and that he does not need us to complete his fullness and is not deficient without us. Rather *we* are deficient without *him*; the all-sufficient glory of God, freely given in fellowship through his sacrificed Son, is the stream of living water that we have thirsted for all our lives.

Unless we begin with God in this way, when the gospel comes to us, we will inevitably put ourselves at the center of it. We will feel that *our* value rather than *God's* value is the driving force in the gospel. We will trace the gospel back to God's need for *us* instead of tracing it back to the sovereign grace that rescues sinners who need *God.*

But the gospel is the good news that God is the all-satisfying end of all our longings, and that even though he does not need us, and is in fact estranged from us because of our God-belittling sins, he has, in the great love with which he loved us, made a way for sinners to drink at the river of his delights through Jesus Christ. And we will not be enthralled by this good news unless we feel that he was not obliged to do this. He was not coerced or constrained by our value. *He* is the center of the gospel. The exaltation of *his* glory is the driving force of the gospel. The gospel is a gospel of *grace*! And grace is the pleasure of God to magnify the worth of God by giving sinners the right and power to delight in God without obscuring the glory of God.

So for the first six chapters we focus on the pleasures that God has directly in himself and in the freedom of his work, so that it will be unmistakable that God is the center of the gospel. Now we will be able to see why the human responses, which God demands and enjoys, come as good news to sinners, and yet keep God at the center of his own affections. If the gospel demands a response from sinners, then the demand itself must be good news instead of an added burden, otherwise the gospel would not be gospel. And if the true biblical gospel always has God at the center, then the response it demands must magnify him and not us.

The last three chapters take up three human responses which satisfy the human heart and glorify the name of God. Chapter 7 is a bridge because it starts with God's delight in doing good to us and ends with his delight in our response of *hope.* "The Lord takes pleasure in those who hope in his steadfast love" (Psalm

147:11). In turn, the response of hope comes to verbal expression in *prayer* and active expression in *obedience*. When we hope in God, we glorify God as the fountain of deep and lasting joy. When we pray, we give expression to that God-glorifying hope. And when we obey with joy, we prove that the God of all-satisfying hope is real in our lives. Obedience is the irrepressible public relations project of those who have tasted and seen that the Lord is good (Matthew 5:16).

Finally, the epilogue tries to express the inexpressible—the truth that God delights to give us the very delight that he has in himself. "Enter into the joy of your Master," is a command that I am eager to obey. But what is that joy? That is the crucial question before us in this book. What is the Master's joy? In what does God find "the most ravishing pleasures, the most solid and substantial delights"? What is "a well-placed and successful affection" for the everlasting God? What are *The Pleasures of God?*

Notes

1. Henry Scougal, *The Life of God in the Soul of Man* (Harrisonburg, Virginia: Sprinkle Publications, 1986), 108.
2. Ibid., 71-72.
3. Ibid., xxvi.
4. Quoted in Henry Scougal, *The Life of God in the Soul of Man*, ed. Winthrop S. Hudson (Minneapolis: Bethany Fellowship, Inc., 1976), 13. A fuller statement of Whitefield's response to Scougal's book is found in Arnold Dallimore, *George Whitefield*, 1 (Edinburgh: The Banner of Truth Trust, 1970), 72-73.
5. Scougal, *The Life of God*, 62.
6. When I refer to God's soul I do not mean to imply anything like the distinction we see in Matthew 10:28, between body and soul, as though God had a body from which his soul was distinguished. I am using the term very loosely of God's inner person or character the way it is used, for example, in Jeremiah 32:41, where God says, "I will rejoice over them to do good to them, and I will truly plant them in this land, with all my heart and *with all my soul*," or in Isaiah 42:1, "Behold my servant . . . in whom *my soul* delights."
7. Scougal, *The Life of God*, 46-47 (my emphasis).
8. Ibid., 66.
9. Ibid., 62-63.
10. The Greek word translated "beholding" (*katoptrizomenoi*) can mean "reflecting" and some interpreters take it to mean that here: "And we all

with unveiled face, reflecting the glory of the Lord . . ." But the preceding and following contexts lead me to think "beholding" is correct. Just before verse 18, Paul describes the unbelieving Israelites as having "hardened" minds and thus being "veiled" so that when they read the books of Moses they do not behold what is really there (vv. 14-15). Thus the unveiling of the mind is to enable it to behold truly what is there. This is the sense of verse 18: the veil has been lifted from our minds and we now behold the glory of the Lord for what it really is. Moreover, in the following context Paul speaks again of the glory of the Lord revealed in the gospel (4:3-4). Whether we behold it or not depends on whether it is "veiled" and whether our minds are "blinded". So again the issue in being unveiled is first an issue of being able to *behold*, not first an issue of being able to *reflect*. The reflecting is what comes second in "being changed from one degree of glory to another" (v. 18).

*"This is my beloved Son
with whom I am well pleased."*

Matthew 17:5

Chapter 1

The Pleasure of God
in His Son

Entering the Joy of God

There is a beautiful phrase in 1 Timothy 1:11 buried beneath the too-familiar surface of Bible buzzwords. Before we dig it up, it sounds like this: "The gospel of the glory of the blessed God."[1] But after you dig it up, it sounds like this: "The good news of the glory of the happy God."[2]

A great part of God's glory is his happiness. It was inconceivable to the apostle Paul that God could be denied infinite joy and still be all-glorious. To be infinitely glorious was to be infinitely happy. He used the phrase, "the glory of the happy God," because it is a glorious thing for God to be as happy as he is. God's glory consists much in the fact that he is happy beyond our wildest imagination.

And this is the *gospel*: "The gospel of the glory of the happy God." It is good news that God is gloriously happy. No one would want to spend eternity with an unhappy God. If God is unhappy then the goal of the gospel is not a happy goal, and that means it would be no gospel at all. But in fact Jesus invites us to spend eternity with a happy God when he says, "Enter into the *joy* of your master" (Matthew 25:23). Jesus lived and died that *his* joy—God's joy—might be in us and our joy might be full (John 15:11; 17:13). Therefore the gospel is "the gospel of the glory of the happy God."

What I want to try to show in this chapter is that the happiness of God is first and foremost a happiness in his Son. Thus when we share in the happiness of God we share in the very pleasure that the Father has in the Son. This is why Jesus made the Father known to us. At the end of his great prayer in John 17 he said to his Father, "I made known to them your name, and I will make it known, *that the love with which you have loved me may be in them,* and I in them" (v. 26). He made God known so that God's pleasure in his Son might be in us and become our pleasure.

Imagine being able to enjoy what is most enjoyable with unbounded energy and passion forever. This is not now our experience. Three things stand in the way of our complete satisfaction in this world. One is that nothing has a personal worth great enough to meet the deepest longings of our hearts. Another is that we lack the strength to savor the best treasures to their maximum worth. And the third obstacle to complete satisfaction is that our joys here come to an end. Nothing lasts.

But if the aim of Jesus in John 17:26 comes true, all this will change. If God's pleasure in the Son becomes our pleasure, then the object of our pleasure, Jesus, will be inexhaustible in personal worth. He will never become boring or disappointing or frustrating. No greater treasure can be conceived than the very Son of God. Moreover, our ability to savor this inexhaustible treasure will not be limited by human weaknesses. We will enjoy the Son of God with the very enjoyment of his Father. God's delight in his Son will be in us and it will be ours. And this will never end, because neither the Father nor the Son ever ends. Their love for each other will be our love for them and therefore our loving them will never die.

Loved for Shining like the Sun

God's pleasure is first and foremost a pleasure in his Son. The Bible reveals this to us while showing us the face of Jesus shining like the sun. In Matthew 17 Jesus takes Peter, James, and John up on a high mountain. When they are all alone something utterly astonishing happens. Suddenly God pulls back the curtain of the incarnation and lets the kingly glory of the Son of God shine through. "His face shone like the sun, and his garments became white as light" (v. 2). Peter and the others were stunned. Near the end of his life Peter wrote that he had seen the Majestic Glory on the holy mountain, and that he had heard a voice from heaven, "This is my beloved Son, with whom I am well pleased; listen to him" (2 Peter 1:17-18; Matthew 17:5).

When God declares openly that he loves and delights in his Son, he gives a visual demonstration of the Son's unimaginable glory. His face shown like the sun, his garments became translucent with light, and the disciples fell on their faces (Matthew 17:6). The point is not merely that humans should stand in awe of such a glory, but that God himself takes full pleasure in the radiance of his Son. He reveals him in blinding light, and then says, "This is my delight!"

As I write this, a memory is fresh in my mind that makes the radiance of God's Son very real. Our staff took a two-day retreat for prayer and planning at the beginning of 1991. The retreat center was a former mansion now made into simple accommodations by the Maryhill sisters for people who want to seek God. Our second day there I got up early and took my Bible to the garden porch, a glassed-in nook of the house overlooking a steep drop-off and the Mississippi River to the east. The sun was not yet up, but there was light.

My appointed reading for that morning was Psalm 3. I read, "You, O Lord, are my glory, and the lifter of my head." And as I pondered this, the red pinpoint of the sun pierced the horizon straight in front of me. It startled me because I hadn't realized I was facing east. I watched for a moment as the pinpoint became a fingernail of fire. Then I read on. "Arise, O Lord!" And I looked up to see the whole red-gold ball blazing just over the river. Within moments there was no more looking at it without going blind. The higher it rose the brighter it got.

I thought of John's vision of Christ in Revelation 1: "His face was like the sun shining in full strength" (v. 16). My glimpse that morning lasted maybe five minutes before the strength of the rising sun turned my face away. Who can look upon the sun shining in *full* strength? The answer is that God can. The radiance of the Son's face shines first and foremost for the enjoyment of his Father. "This is the Son whom I love; he is *my* pleasure. You must fall on your face and turn away, but I behold my Son in his radiance every day with love and never-fading joy."

I thought to myself, surely this is one thing implied in John 17:26—that the day is coming when I will have the capacity to delight in the Son the way the Father does. My fragile eyes will get the power to take in the glory of the Son shining in his full strength just the way the Father does. The pleasure God has in his Son will become my pleasure, and I will not be consumed but enthralled for ever.

Loved for Serving like a Dove

Again, the Father speaks words of endearment and delight about his Son on another occasion. At Jesus' baptism the Spirit of God descends like a dove while the Father says from heaven, "This is my beloved Son, in whom I am well pleased" (Matthew 3:16-17). The image is very different. Not a flaming sun of intolerable brightness, but a soft, quiet, vulnerable dove—the kind of animal poor people offered for sacrifices in the temple. God's pleasure in his Son comes not only from the brightness of his majesty but from the beauty of his meekness.

The Father delights in his Son's *supremacy* and in his *servanthood.* "The Father loves the Son and has given *all things* into his hand" (John 3:35). "Behold *my servant,* whom I uphold, my chosen, in whom my soul delights" (Isaiah 42:1). Matthew quotes this Old Testament testimony of the Father's joy and connects it with the anointing of the Holy Spirit and the meekness of Jesus' ministry.

> Behold, my Servant whom I have chosen,
> my beloved in whom my soul delights.
> I will put my Spirit upon him,
> and he shall proclaim justice to the Gentiles.
> He will not wrangle or cry aloud,
> nor will anyone hear his voice in the streets;
> he will not break a bruised reed
> or quench a smoldering flax (Matthew 12:18-20).

The Father's very soul exults with joy over the servant-like meekness and compassion of his Son. When a reed is bent and about to break, the Servant will tenderly hold it upright until it heals. When a wick is smoldering and has scarcely any heat left, the Servant will not pinch it off, but cup his hand and blow gently until it burns again. Thus the Father cries, "Behold, my Servant in whom my soul delights!"

The worth and beauty of the Son come not just from his majesty, nor just from his meekness, but from the way these mingle in perfect proportion. When the angel cried out in Revelation 5:2, "Who is worthy to open the scroll and break its seals?" the answer came back, "Weep not; look, *the Lion of the tribe of Judah*, the Root of David, has conquered, so that he can open the scroll and its seven seals" (5:5). God loves the strength of the Lion of Judah. This is why he is worthy in God's eyes to open the scrolls of history and unfold the last days. But the picture is not complete. How did the Lion conquer? The next verse describes his appearance: "And between the throne and the four living creatures and among the elders, I saw *a Lamb standing, as though it had been slain.*" Jesus is worthy of the Father's delight not only as Lion of Judah, but also as the slain Lamb.

One of the sermons of Jonathan Edwards that God used to kindle the Great Awakening in New England in 1734-1735 was titled "The Excellency of Christ." In it Edwards unfolds the glory of God's Son by describing the "admirable conjunction of diverse excellencies in Christ." His text is Revelation 5:5-6, and he unfolds the union of "diverse excellencies" in the Lion-Lamb. He shows how the glory of Christ is his combining of attributes that would seem to be utterly incompatible in one Person.

In Jesus Christ, he says, meet infinite highness and infinite condescension; infinite justice and infinite grace; infinite glory and lowest humility; infinite majesty and transcendent meekness; deepest reverence toward God and equality with God; worthiness of good and the greatest patience under the suffering of evil; a great spirit of obedience and supreme dominion over heaven and earth; absolute sovereignty and perfect resignation; self-sufficiency and an entire trust and reliance on God.[3]

Loved as Happy Co-Creator

Although the qualities of lowliness and meekness were not manifest until the incarnation, they were nevertheless part of the

Son's character from all eternity. He did not undergo a conversion before he submitted to the Father's will that he die for sinners. This is why the love that the Father has for the Son goes back before creation. "Father . . . *you loved me before the foundation of the world*" (John 17:24). There never was a time when the Father was denied the pleasure of delighting in the glory of his Son.

God also loved his Son *in* the very act of creating the universe. He enjoyed his Son as his own Word of Wisdom and creative Power in the act of creation. "In the beginning was the Word, and the Word was with God, and the Word was God. He was in the beginning with God. All things were made through him, and without him was not anything made that was made" (John 1:1-3). The Son was the Wisdom of God creating, with God, all that is not God. And, as the Proverbs say, "A wise son makes a glad father" (Proverbs 10:1; 15:20). God was glad in the wisdom of his creative Son.

In fact, the Proverbs are even more specific concerning God's Wisdom. Proverbs 8 personifies Wisdom at the beginning of creation as a Master Workman delighting the heart of God. "When he [God] established the heavens, I [Wisdom] was there . . . beside him, like a Master Workman; and I was daily his delight, rejoicing before him always" (Proverbs 8:27,30).[4] The Son of God was the Father's delight as he rejoiced with the Father in the awesome work of making a million worlds.

I wonder if there was a faint resemblance of this creative camaraderie between Father and Son when Joseph and Jesus worked together in the carpenter's shop in Nazareth. I picture Jesus about fifteen years old, humming as he worked. The plank is cut with masterful strokes, carved with three small posts protruding in their appointed places, and then fitted perfectly into the joining board to make a solid bench. Jesus smiles as he smacks the wood with pleasure. All the while Joseph has been standing at the door watching the hands of his son. He sees the image of his own workmanship and his own life. The skill of his son is the evidence of the father's skill. The humming of his son is the endorsement of the father's joy. And when they put their energy together to lift a finished table for the synagogue, their eyes meet with a flash of delight that says, "You are a treasure to me, and I love you with all my heart."

I have four sons. Though I have not heard any of them preach, I have seen them make A's in school, and letter in varsity soccer, and memorize long portions of Scripture, and slay dragons with plastic swords. And when I see their skill, I think of all the hours we have played and prayed and thought and fought (the dragons!) together over the years. And my heart fills with a sense of wonder that I am creating things through my sons. And when they rejoice in this, and when they smile at me on the sidelines or in the audience, they are a pleasure to me almost as great as anything in the world.

Perhaps we may be allowed to see in this a faint echo of the shout of joy the Father had in the Son when together they created the universe out of nothing. Imagine the look they gave each other when a million galaxies stood forth at their command.

Infinite Intimacy

No other relationship comes close to this one. It is utterly unique. The Son is absolutely unique in the affections of the Father. He is the "only begotten" (John 1:14, 18; 3:16, 18; 1 John 4:9). There is *the* Son, by eternal generation, and there are other "sons" by adoption. "When the fullness of time came, God sent forth his *Son* . . . to redeem those who were under the law, so that we might receive *adoption as sons*" (Galatians 4:4-5). Only in "receiving" Jesus as *the* Son are others empowered to become "children of God" (John 1:12). Jesus often referred to God as "my Father" and "the Father," but he never referred to God as "our Father" except once, when teaching the disciples how *they* should pray (Matthew 6:9). Once he used the remarkable expression, "my Father and your Father . . . my God and your God" (John 20:17). The relationship between God the Father and his eternal Son is utterly unique.

Their intimacy and communion are incomparable. "No one knows the Son except the Father and no one knows the Father except the Son" (Matthew 11:27). "No one has ever seen God; the only begotten Son, who is *in the bosom of the Father*, he has made him known" (John 1:18). Jesus spoke with such unprecedented endearment and intimacy concerning the Father that his enemies sought to kill him "because . . . he called God his own Father, making himself equal with God" (John 5:18). The

Father's intimacy with the Son was such that he opened all his heart to him. "The Father loves the Son, and shows him all that he himself is doing" (John 5:20). He withholds no blessing from the Son but pours out his Spirit on him without measure. "He whom God has sent utters the words of God, for it is *not by measure* that he gives the Spirit; the Father loves the Son, and has given all things into his hand" (John 3:34-35). And as the Son carries out the redeeming plan of the Father, the Father's heart abounds with increasingly intense expressions of love for the Son. "For this reason the Father loves me, because I lay down my life" (John 10:17). This overflowing esteem that the Father has for his only Son spills over onto all who serve the Son: "If anyone serves me," Jesus says, "the Father will honor him" (John 12:26). Thus the Father seeks every means possible to manifest his infinite delight in the Son of his love—including the converse: "How much worse punishment do you think will be deserved by the man who has spurned the Son of God!" (Hebrews 10:29).

No angel in heaven ever received such honor and affection as the Son has received from all eternity from his Father. As great and wonderful as angels are, they do not rival the Son. "For to what angel did God ever say, 'You are my Son, today I have begotten you'? Or again, 'I will be to him a Father, and he shall be to me a Son'?" (Hebrews 1:5). "To what angel has he ever said, 'Sit at my right hand, till I make your enemies a stool for your feet'?" (Hebrews 1:13). The point is clear. The Son of God is not an angel—not even the highest archangel. Rather God says, "Let God's angels worship him!" (Hebrews 1:6). The Son of God is worthy of all the worship that the hosts of heaven can give—not to mention ours. Nor will God himself be excluded from the celebration of the Son. He is thrilled over the greatness and the goodness and the triumph of the Son. He gives him a name which is above every name (Philippians 2:9); he crowns him with honor (Hebrews 2:9); and he glorifies him in his own presence with the glory that he had before the world was made (John 17:5).

Unimaginable Fervency

It is impossible to overstate the greatness of the fatherly affection God has for his one and only Son. We see this unbounded affection behind the logic of Romans 8:32. "He who did not spare *his own Son*, but gave him up for us all, how shall he not also with him freely give us all things?" The point of this unspeakably precious verse is that if God was willing to do the hardest thing for us (give up his cherished Son to misery and death), then surely that which looks hard (giving Christians all the blessings that heaven can hold) will not be too hard for God. What makes this verse work is the immensity of the Father's affection for the Son. Paul's assumption is that "not sparing his own Son" was the hardest thing imaginable for God to do.[5] Jesus is, as Paul put it simply in Colossians 1:13, "the Son of his love."

If there ever was a passion of love in the heart of God it is a passion for his Son. A. W. Tozer once said, "God never changes moods or cools off in his affections or loses enthusiasm."[6] If there is any enthusiasm in God of which this is true, it is his enthusiasm for the Son. It will never change; it will never cool off. It burns with unimaginable fervency and zeal. Therefore, I affirm with Jonathan Edwards, "The infinite happiness of the Father consists in the enjoyment of His Son."[7]

So when we say that God loves his Son, we are not talking about a love that is self-denying, sacrificial, or merciful. We are talking about a love of delight and pleasure. God is not stooping to pity the undeserving when he loves his Son. That is how God loves *us*. It is not how he loves his Son. He is well-pleased with his Son. His soul delights in the Son! When he looks at his Son he enjoys and admires and cherishes and prizes and relishes what he sees. The first great pleasure of God is his pleasure in the Son.

The Fullness of Deity Dwells in a Body

To avoid a harmful mistake about God's love for his Son, we need to go further now and show that the Son of God has the fullness of deity. A person might agree with the affirmation that God has pleasure in the Son, but then make the mistake of thinking that the Son is merely an extraordinarily holy man that the Father somehow adopted to be his Son because he delighted in him so much. From as early as the second century the Christian church has distinguished true biblical faith from different forms of this kind of teaching called adoptionism.[8]

Colossians 2:9 gives us a very different angle on things. "In [Christ] the whole *fullness of deity* dwells bodily." The Son of God is not merely a holy and faithful man. He has the fullness of deity. God did not look for a holy man whom he could somehow take up into the Godhead by putting deity in him. Rather "the Word became flesh" in an act of incarnation (John 1:14). God sought a humble, faithful woman, and, through the virgin birth, united the fullness of his deity with a child of his own conceiving. "And Mary said to the angel, 'How can this be, since I have no husband?' And the angel said to her, 'The Holy Spirit will come upon you and the power of the Most High will overshadow you; therefore the child to be born will be called holy, the Son of God'" (Luke 1:34-35). God did not take a holy man up into deity. He clothed the fullness of deity with a virgin-born human nature, Jesus of Nazareth the Son of God, the God-Man, in whom "the whole fullness of deity dwells bodily."

This is why Jesus' friends and enemies were staggered again and again by what he said and did. He would be walking down the road, seemingly like any other man, then turn and say something like, "Before Abraham was, I am." Or, "If you have seen me, you have seen the Father." Or, very calmly, after being accused of blasphemy, he would say, "The Son of Man has authority on earth to forgive sins." To the dead he might simply say, "Come forth," or, "Rise up." And they would obey. To the storms on the sea he would say, "Be still." And to a loaf of bread he would say, "Become a thousand meals." And it was done immediately. And in response to the high priest's question, "Are you the Christ, the Son of the Blessed?" he said, "I am; and you will see the Son of Man seated at the right hand of Power, and coming with the clouds of heaven." No man ever spoke like this man. No man ever lived and loved like this man. For in this man God himself had made all the fullness of deity dwell bodily.

And God did this with all his heart. It was his *pleasure* to make the Word flesh. Colossians 1:19 puts it like this: "In him all the fullness (of deity) *was pleased* to dwell." This translation seems to say that "fullness" was pleased, or had pleasure. That's an unlikely statement, because *persons* are usually pleased, not abstract things like "fullness." The NIV seems closer to the meaning when it paraphrases like this: "*God was pleased* to have all his fullness dwell in [Christ]."[9] In other words, it was God's *pleasure* to do this.[10] We have seen that God loved his Son before the foundation of the world (John 17:24), and that he loved him in his incarnate state (John 10:17). Now we see that, when God the Father and God the Son engaged to unite deity and humanity in Jesus, the Father rejoiced over this act. He delighted in his Son's readiness to redeem the world. Therefore it says, "It pleased [God] for the fullness of deity to dwell in [Christ]."

Begotten Not Made

Now again we should press on a step farther to guard against misunderstanding and to enlarge the vista of the glory of God's gladness in the Son. The fullness of deity, which now dwells bodily in Jesus (Colossians 2:9), already existed in personal form before the God-Man, Jesus Christ, existed as a Jewish teacher on the earth. This pushes us back further into the happiness of the triune God. *The Son, in whom God delights, is the eternal image and radiance of God and is thus himself God.*

In Colossians 1:15-16 Paul says, "[Christ] is the image of the invisible God, the firstborn of all creation; for in him all things were created in heaven and on earth."

Historically this has been a very controversial text. And still today there are sects like the Jehovah's Witnesses that give it a meaning contrary to the meaning understood by historic Christian orthodoxy. About A.D. 256 a man named Arius was born in Libya who became one of the most famous heretics of the Christian church. He put this text to use for his doctrine. He was educated by a teacher named Lucian in Antioch and became a prominent elder in the church of Alexandria in Egypt. He was described as "a tall, lean man, with a downcast brow, very austere habits, considerable learning, and a smooth, winning address, but quarrelsome disposition."[11]

The so-called Arian controversy began about 318 in Alexandria when Arius disputed with Bishop Alexander concerning the eternal deity of Christ. Arius began to teach that the Son of God was different in essence from the Father and that he was created by the Father rather than co-eternal with the Father. Socrates, a church historian who lived in Constantinople between A.D. 380 and 439, tells the story of how this controversy began:

> Alexander (Bishop of Alexandria) attempted one day, in the presence of the presbyters and the rest of his clergy, too ambitious a discourse about the Holy Trinity, the subject being "Unity in Trinity."
>
> Arius, one of the presbyters under his jurisdiction, a man possessed of no inconsiderable logical acumen, thinking that the bishop was introducing the doctrine of Sabellius the Libyan [who stressed Jewish monotheism to the extent of denying a true Trinity], from love of controversy, advanced another view diametrically opposed to the opinion of the Libyan, and, as it seemed, vehemently controverted the statements of the bishop. "If," said he, "the Father begat the Son, He that was begotten has a beginning of existence; and from this it is evident, that there was when the Son was not. It therefore necessarily follows that He had His essence from the non-existent."[12]

It is easy to see how Colossians 1:15 could be made to support Arius's position. Paul said that Christ is "the firstborn of all creation." One could easily take this to mean that Christ was himself part of creation and was the first and highest creature. Thus he would have a beginning; there would be a time when he had no existence at all. And thus his essence would not be the essence of God but would be created out of nothing like the rest of creation. This is in fact what Arius taught.[13]

The next seven years after this first dispute in 318 saw the controversy spread across the entire empire. Constantine, the emperor, was forced to become involved for the sake of the unity of the church. He called a great Council in 325 to deal with these weighty matters, and designated the city to be Nicea "because of the excellent temperature of the air, and in order that I may be present as a spectator and participator in those thing which will be done."[14] The Council produced a creed that left no doubt that it considered Arius's ideas heretical.

The Nicene Creed that we know and recite today is based on the one I will quote which is technically called "The Creed of Nicea." It will be plain to every reader which parts of the creed are intended to distinguish orthodoxy from Arianism.

> We believe in one God the Father All-sovereign, maker of all things visible and invisible;

And in one Lord Jesus Christ, the Son of God, begotten of the Father, only-begotten, that is, of the substance of the Father, God of God, Light of Light, true God of true God, begotten not made, of one substance with the Father, through whom all things were made, things in heaven and things on the earth; who for us men and for our salvation came down and was made flesh, and became man, suffered, and rose on the third day, ascended into the heavens, is coming to judge living and dead. And in the Holy Spirit.

And those that say "There was when he was not,"
    and, "Before he was begotten he was not,"
   and that, "He came into being from what-is-not,"
or those that allege, that the Son of God is
       "Of another substance or essence"
    or "created,"
    or "changeable,"
    or "alterable,"
these the Catholic and Apostolic Church anathematizes.[15]

This has remained the orthodox understanding of Scripture throughout all church history to our own day. I feel compelled to defend this understanding here because if Arianism (or the Jehovah's Witnesses) proved right, then the pleasure of God in his Son would be a radically different thing than I take it to be. And the foundation of everything else in this book would be shaken. Everything hangs on the unbounded joy in the triune God from all eternity. This is the source of God's absolute self-sufficiency as a happy Sovereign. And every true act of free grace in redemptive history depends on it.

How then are we to understand Paul when he says in Colossians 1:15, "[Christ] is the image of the invisible God, the *firstborn of all creation*"? What does firstborn mean? And does not "of all creation" mean that he is part of creation?

First, we should realize that "of all creation" does not have to mean that Christ was part of creation. If I said, "God is ruler *of all creation*," no one would think I meant God is part of creation. I mean that he is ruler *"over* all creation." There is a good clue in the next verse (Colossians 1:16) which helps us understand whether Paul means something like this. He says, "[Christ] is the image of the invisible God, the firstborn of all creation; *because in him all things were created*." In other words, the *reason* Paul calls Christ the firstborn "of all creation" is "because in him *all things* were created." The reason is *not* that he was the first and greatest created thing. The reason is that *every* created thing was created by him. This does not incline us to think then that "firstborn of all creation" means "firstborn *among* all created things," but rather "firstborn *over* all created things."

The second thing to realize is that the term "firstborn" (*prōtotokos*) can have a strictly biological meaning: "And she gave birth to her *firstborn* son and wrapped him in swaddling cloths" (Luke 2:7). But it can also have a non-biological meaning of dignity and precedence.[16] For example in Psalm 89:27 God says of the one who will sit on David's throne, "I will make him *the firstborn*, the highest of the kings of the earth." The meaning here is that this king will have preeminence and honor and dignity over all the kings of the earth. Other non-biological uses are found in Exodus 4:22 where Israel is called God's "firstborn son;" and Hebrews 12:23 where all believers are called the "firstborn who are written in heaven."

So there are four reasons we can give now why Arius and the Jehovah's Witnesses are wrong to say that Colossians 1:15 means that Christ was part of God's creation. First, the word "firstborn" can very naturally mean "preeminent one" or "one with superior dignity" or "one who is first in time and rank." It does not have to imply that Christ was brought forth as part of the creation.[17] Second, verse 16 (as we have seen) implies clearly that Christ was the Creator of all things and not part of the creation ("because in him *all things* were created"). Third, Chrysostom (A.D. 347- 407) pointed out that Paul avoided the word that would have clearly implied that Christ was the first creation (*prōtoktistos*)[18] and chose to use instead a word with connotations of parent-child, not Creator-creation (firstborn, *prōtotokos*).

This leads to the fourth reason for rejecting the Arian interpretation of Colossians 1:15. In using the term "firstborn," Paul speaks in remarkable harmony with the apostle John who calls Christ God's "only begotten Son" (John 1:14,18; 3:16;18; 1 John 4:9) and teaches clearly that this does not make him a creature but rather makes him God: "In the beginning was the Word and the Word was with God and *the Word was God*" (John 1:1-2).[19] C.S. Lewis shows why the use of the term "begotten" (and we could add Paul's term, "firstborn") implies the deity of Christ and not his being a creature.

> When you beget, you beget something of the same kind as yourself. A man begets human babies, a beaver begets little beavers, and a bird begets eggs which turn into little birds. But when you make, you make something of a different kind from yourself. A bird makes a nest, a beaver builds a dam, and man makes a wireless set—or he may make something more like himself than a wireless set, say, a statue. If he's clever enough a carver he makes a statue which is very much like a man indeed. But, of course, it's not a real man; it only looks like one. It can't breathe or think. It's not alive.[20]

For these reasons, then, I take my stand gladly with the great tradition of Christian orthodoxy and not with ancient or modern Arianism. Christ is the image of the invisible God, the firstborn *over* all creation. "He is *the radiance of the glory of God and the very stamp of his nature*" (Hebrews 1:3). "Though *he was in the form of God*, [he] did not count *equality with God* a thing to be grasped" (Philippians 2:6). "In the beginning was the Word, and the Word was with God, and *the Word was God*" (John 1:1).

So the Son in whom the Father delights is the image of God and the radiance of the glory of God. He bears the very stamp of God's nature and is the very form of God. He is equal with God and, as John says, is God.

From all eternity, before creation, the one reality that has always existed is God. This is a great mystery, because it is so hard for us to think of God having absolutely no beginning, and just being there forever and ever and ever, without anything or anyone making him be there—just absolute reality that everyone of us has to reckon with whether we like it or not. But this ever-living God has not been "alone." He has not been a solitary center of consciousness. There has always been another, who has been one with God in essence and glory, and yet distinct in personhood so that they have had a personal relationship for all eternity.

The Bible teaches that this eternal God has always had a perfect *image* of himself (Colossians 1:15), a perfect *radiance* of his essence (Hebrews 1:3), a perfect *stamp* or *imprint* of his nature (Hebrews 1:3), a perfect *form* or expression of his glory (Philippians 2:6).

We are on the brink of the ineffable here, but perhaps we may dare to say this much: as long as God has been God (eternally) he has been conscious of himself; and the image that he has of himself is so perfect and so complete and so full as to *be* the living, personal reproduction (or begetting) of himself. And this living, personal image or radiance or form of God *is God*, namely God the Son. And therefore God the Son is coeternal with God the Father and equal in essence and glory.[21]

God's Delight in Being God

We may conclude that the pleasure of God in his Son is pleasure in himself. Since the Son is the image of God and the radiance of God and the form of God, equal with God, and indeed *is* God, therefore God's delight in the Son is delight in himself. The original, the primal, the deepest, the foundational joy of God is the joy he has in his own perfections as he sees them reflected in the glory of his Son. Paul speaks of "the glory of God in the face of Christ" (2 Corinthians 4:6). From all eternity God had beheld the panorama of his own perfections in the face of his Son. All that he is he sees reflected fully and perfectly in the countenance of his Son. And in this he rejoices with infinite joy.

At first this sounds like vanity. It *would* be vanity if we humans found *our* deepest joy by looking in the mirror. We *would* be vain and conceited and smug and selfish if we were like God in this regard. But why? Aren't we supposed to imitate God (Matthew 5:48; Ephesians 5:1)? Yes, in some ways. But not in every way. This was the first deceit of Satan in the garden of Eden: he tempted Adam and Eve to try to be like God in a way that God never intended them to be like him—namely self-reliant. *Only* God should be self-reliant. All the rest of us should be God-reliant. In the same way we were created for something infinitely better and nobler and greater and deeper than *self*-contemplation. We were created for the contemplation and enjoyment of *God*! Anything less than this would be idolatry toward him and disappointment for us. God is the most glorious of all beings. Not to love him and delight in him is a great loss to us and insults him.

But the same is true for God. How shall God not insult what is infinitely beautiful and glorious? How shall God not commit idolatry? There is only one possible answer: God must love and delight in his own beauty and perfection above all things.[22] For *us* to do this in front of the mirror is the essence of vanity; for *God* to do it in front of his Son is the essence of righteousness.

Is not the essence of righteousness to place supreme value on what is supremely valuable, with all the just actions that follow? And isn't the opposite of righteousness to set our highest affections on things of little or no worth, with all the unjust actions that follow? Thus the righteousness of God is the infinite zeal and joy and pleasure that he has in what is supremely valuable, namely, his own perfection and worth. And if he were ever to act contrary to this eternal passion for his own perfections he would be unrighteous, he would be an idolater.

This is not irrelevant speculation. It is the foundation of all Christian hope. This will become increasingly obvious especially in chapter 6, but let me point the way here. In this God-centered, divine righteousness lies the greatest obstacle to our salvation. For how shall such a righteous God ever set his affection on sinners like us who have scorned his perfections? But the wonder of the gospel is that in this divine righteousness lies also the very foundation of our salvation. The infinite regard that the Father has for the Son makes it possible for me, a wicked sinner, to be loved and accepted in the Son, because in his death he vindicated the worth and glory of his Father. Now I may pray with new understanding the prayer of the psalmist, "*For your name's sake*, O Lord, pardon my guilt, for it is great" (Psalm 25:11). The new understanding is that Jesus has now atoned for sin and vindicated the Father's honor so that our sins are forgiven "on account of *his* name" (1 John 2:12). We will see this again and again in the chapters to come—how the Father's infinite pleasure in his own perfections is the fountain of our everlasting joy. The fact that the pleasure of God in his Son is pleasure in himself is not vanity. It is the gospel.

Boundless Joy vs. Broken Cisterns

If Henry Scougal is right—that the worth and excellency of a soul is measured by the object and intensity of its love—then God is the most excellent and worthy of all beings. For he has loved his Son, the image of his own glory, with infinite and perfect energy from all eternity. How glorious and happy have been the Father and the Son and the Spirit of love flowing between them from all eternity![23]

Let us then stand in awe of this great God! And let us turn from all the trivial resentments and fleeting pleasures and petty pursuits of materialism and merely human "spirituality." And let us be caught up into the gladness that God has in the glory of his Son, who is the radiance and image of his Father. There is coming a day when the very pleasure that the Father has in the Son will be in us and will be our own pleasure. May God's enjoyment of God—unbounded and everlasting—flow into us even now by the Holy Spirit! This is our glory and our joy.

That millions "exchange their glory for that which does not profit" is an appalling thing.

> Be appalled, O heavens, at this
>> be shocked, be utterly desolate,
>>> says the Lord,
> for my people have committed two evils:
>> they have forsaken me,
>>> the fountain of living waters,
> and hewed out cisterns for themselves,
>> broken cisterns,
>>> that can hold no water." (Jeremiah 2:12-13)

There is only one fountain of lasting joy—the overflowing gladness of God in God. Without beginning and without ending, without source and without cause, without help or assistance, the spring is eternally self-replenishing. From this unceasing fountain of joy flow all grace and all joy in the universe—and all the rest of this book. Let everyone who is thirsty come.

Notes

1. Most versions (NIV, NASB, RSV, KJV) treat the phrase, "of the glory," as an adjective and translate like this: "the *glorious* gospel of the blessed God." But this is not necessary because all these versions translate a similar phrase in 2 Corinthians 4:4 as, "the gospel of the *glory of Christ*," not as, "the *glorious gospel* of Christ." I agree with Henry Alford that the versions should follow the same literal principle in 1 Timothy 1:11 that they follow in

2 Corinthians 4:4. "All propriety and beauty of expression is here [in 1 Timothy 1:11], as always, destroyed by this adjectival rendering. The gospel is 'the glad tidings of the glory of God,' as of Christ in 2 Corinthians 4:4, inasmuch as it reveals to us God in all His glory." Henry Alford, *The Greek Testament*, 3 (Chicago: Moody Press, 1958), 307.

2. The word translated "blessed" in this phrase (*makarios*) is the same one used in the beatitudes. "*Blessed* are the poor in spirit for theirs is the kingdom of Heaven. *Blessed* are those who mourn, for they shall be comforted. *Blessed* are the meek, for they shall inherit the earth." And so on. It means "happy" or "fortunate." Paul himself uses it in other places to refer to the happiness of the person whose sins are forgiven (Romans 4:7) or the person whose conscience is clear (Romans 14:22). So 1 Timothy 1:11 is referring to "the gospel of the glory of the *happy* God."

3. Jonathan Edwards, "The Excellency of Christ," *The Works of Jonathan Edwards*, 1, ed. Sereno Dwight (Edinburgh: Banner of Truth Trust, 1976), 680-683.

4. The Hebrew does not have the word "his" in the phrase "his delight" and so some versions and commentators interpret the delight to be Wisdom's and not God's (for example, NIV, Keil and Delitzsch). But "I was delights" (literal rendering) is a very unusual way to say, "I was filled with delight" (NIV). Moreover in verse 31 the same word is used with the personal pronoun "my" attached to it to make clear when the delight of Wisdom is in view. I follow the RSV and NASB. But in any case the principle of a father being made glad by a wise son holds even if it is not made explicit about God's gladness over his Son in creation.

5. See chapter 6, "The Pleasure of God in Bruising the Son" for a discussion of how God can take pleasure in something that is so hard for him to do.

6. A. W. Tozer, *A. W. Tozer: An Anthology* (Camp Hill, Pennsylvania: Christian Publications, 1984), 89.

7. Jonathan Edwards, "An Essay on the Trinity," *Treatise on Grace and other Posthumously Published Writings*, ed. Paul Helm, (Cambridge: James Clarke and Co. Ltd., 1971), 105.

8. See William Cunningham, *Historical Theology*, 1 (Edinburgh: Banner of Truth Trust, 1960), 275. On Theodotus, the first to teach this heresy in the second century, see *A New Eusebius*, ed. J. Stevenson (London: SPCK, 1968), 157-159, 165.

9. Alford agrees with this on the analogy of Paul's use of *eudokeō* (be pleased with) elsewhere. "The subject here is naturally understood to be God, as expressed in 1 Corinthians 1:21 and Galatians 1:15." *The Greek Testament*, 3, 205.

10. The word *eudokeō* can carry more or less connotation of strong delight. The lexicon of Bauer, Arndt, and Gingrich gives two clusters of usage for the word. One is "consider good, consent, determine, resolve." The other is "be well pleased, take delight." *A Greek-English Lexicon of the New Testament and Other Early Christian Literature* (Chicago: The University of Chicago Press, 1957), 319. Only the context can determine whether the connotation of delight is more or less present. The reason I think it carries

the connotation of delight here in Colossians 1:19 is, first, because at least six of Paul's other ten uses of the word almost certainly carry this connotation (1 Corinthians 10:5; Romans 15:26-27 [compare 2 Corinthians 8:2]; 2 Corinthians 5:8; 12:10 [compare Romans 5:3]; 2 Thessalonians 2:12); second, the other uses in the New Testament outside Paul seem to have this connotation (Matthew 3:17 = Mark 1:11 = Luke 3:22; Matthew 17:5 = 2 Peter 1:17; Matthew 12:28; Luke 12:32; Hebrews 10:6,8,38); third, the four other uses in Paul (not yet mentioned) can carry this connotation (1 Corinthians 1:21; Galatians 1:15; 1 Thessalonians 2:8; 3:1); and fourth, it is inconceivable to me, in view of all we have seen of the Father's delight in the Son and his profound joy over the incarnate obedience of the Son, that he could act in the incarnation with less than immense enthusiasm and joy. (See note 5.)

11. *A Religious Encyclopedia: Or Dictionary of Biblical, Historical, Doctrinal, and Practical Theology*, 1, ed. Philip Schaff (New York: The Christian Literature Co., 1888), 139.

12. *A New Eusebius*, 340.

13. There are two letters from Arius that state these views in Ibid., 344-347.

14. Ibid., 358.

15. The creed is taken from *Documents of the Christian Church*, 2d Ed., ed. Henry Bettenson (London: Oxford University Press, 1967), 25.

16. J. B. Lightfoot, *St. Paul's Epistle to the Colossians* (Grand Rapids: Zondervan Publishing House, 1959), 146-150.

17. The use of *prōtotokos* in Colossians 1:18 (firstborn from the dead) does not contradict this. His being part of the dead is determined by the preposition "from" (*ek*), not merely by the word *prōtotokos*. This preposition is not used in verse 15.

18. Cited in Henry Alford, *The Greek Testament*, 3, 203.

19. The attempt by the Jehovah's Witnesses to make this verse mean, "And the Word was a god," is shown to be grammatically and contextually erroneous by Bruce Metzger, "The Jehovah's Witnesses and Jesus Christ," *Theology Today*, April 1953, 65-85.

20. C. S. Lewis, *Beyond Personality* (New York: Macmillan Co., 1948), 5.

21. For how the personal, divine Holy Spirit fits in to this conception of the Trinity see note 23. Jonathan Edwards develops this view of the Son's deity in an essay entitled *An Essay on the Trinity* (note 7 above). He first considers a human analogy:

> If a man could have an absolutely perfect idea of all that pass'd in his mind, all the series of ideas and exercises in every respect perfect as to order, degree, circumstance etc. for any particular space of time past, suppose the last hour, he would really, to all intents and purpose, be over again what he was that last hour. And if it were possible for a man by reflection perfectly to contemplate all that is in his own mind in a hour, as it is and at the same time that it is there, in its first and direct existence; if a man, that is, had a perfect reflex or contemplative idea of every thought at the same moment or moments that that thought was, and of every exercise

at and during the same time that that exercise was, and so through a whole hour, a man would really be two during that time, he would be indeed double, he would be twice at once. The idea he has of himself would be himself again (p. 102).

Edwards then carries the analogy over to God and says,

Therefore as God with perfect clearness, fullness and strength, understands Himself, views His own essence (in which there is no distinction of substance and act but which is wholly substance and wholly act), that idea which God hath of Himself is absolutely Himself. This representation of the Divine nature and essence is the Divine nature and essence again: so that by God's thinking of the deity, [deity] must certainly be generated. Hereby there is another person begotten, there is another infinite eternal almighty and most holy and the same God, the very same divine nature.

And this person is the second person of the Trinity, the only begotten and dearly beloved Son of God; He is the eternal, necessary, perfect, substantial and personal idea which God hath of Himself; and that it is so seems to me to be abundantly confirmed by the word of God (p. 103).

Here Edwards begins a lengthy meditation on Scripture to demonstrate that this view is not merely the result of rational speculation but also the fruit of biblical meditation.

22. I have tried elsewhere to show that this is not merely, or even mainly a logical deduction but a clearly revealed truth of Scripture. See *Desiring God,* Appendix 1, (Portland: Multnomah Press, 1986), 227-238.

23. Here it will be appropriate to mention how the Holy Spirit is conceived of in the view of the Trinity that I have developed, depending largely on Jonathan Edwards. In note 21 I quoted his view of how the Father begets the Son. Here I will quote the key passage on the "procession" of the Holy Spirit.

The Godhead being thus begotten by God's loving an idea of himself and shewing forth in a distinct subsistence or person in that idea, there proceeds a most pure act, and an infinitely holy and sacred energy arises between the Father and Son in mutually loving and delighting in each other, for their love and joy is mutual, Proverbs 8:30—"I was daily his delight, rejoicing always before him"—This is the eternal and most perfect and essential act of the divine nature, wherein the Godhead acts to an infinite degree and in the most perfect manner possible. The Deity becomes all act, the Divine essence itself flows out and is, as it were, breathed forth in love and joy. So that the Godhead therein stands forth in yet another manner of subsistence, and there proceeds the third person in the Trinity, the Holy Spirit, viz. the deity in act, for there is no other act but the act of the will. (Edwards, *An Essay on the Trinity,* 108)

Edwards proceeds to develop an extended biblical defense of this view of the Holy Spirit (Edwards, *An Essay on the Trinity,* 108-118). He sums up his view like this:

And this I suppose to be the blessed Trinity that we read of in
the Holy Scriptures. The Father is the deity subsisting in the
prime, unoriginated and most absolute manner, or the deity in
its direct existence. The Son is the deity generated by God's
understanding, or having an idea of Himself and subsisting in
that idea. The Holy Ghost is the deity subsisting in act, or the
divine essence flowing out and breathed forth in God's infinite
love to and delight in Himself. And I believe the whole Divine
essence does truly and distinctly subsist both in the Divine idea
and Divine love, and that each of them are [sic] properly distinct
persons (Edwards, *An Essay on the Trinity*, 118).

*"Whatever the Lord pleases he does,
in heaven and on earth,
in the seas and all deeps."*

Psalm 135:6

Chapter 2

The Pleasure of God
in All He Does

My Heart's Desire

The basic goal of my life and the reason for writing this book is to direct the attention of more and more people to the pleasures of God revealed in Scripture; that we might see in the pleasures of God some of the infinite measure of his worth and excellency; and, in seeing this glory, be transformed to the likeness of his Son; and give ourselves so passionately to the work of mercy and missions, that all the nations will see and give glory to our Father in heaven.

When I preached on the pleasures of God back in 1987 I jotted down in my notes one Sunday this summary aim and prayer:

> Portray his pleasures in preaching.
> Behold his glory in listening.
> Approach his likeness in meditation.
> Display his worth in the world.

Whether in preaching or in writing, this is my heart's desire. I long for all God's people to be able to say, "My eyes are ever toward the Lord . . . I keep the Lord always before me . . . My heart says to [the Lord], Your face, Lord, do I seek. Hide not your face from me" (Psalm 25:15; 16:8; 27:8-9). I long for them to seek God with the heartfelt yearning of Moses when he prayed, "Show me, I pray, your glory" (Exodus 33:18), and then to come forth from this encounter into a dark and desperate world with their faces shining because they have seen the majesty of God (Exodus 34:29).

In chapter 1 we focused on the pleasure that God the Father has in his Son. The most important lesson to be learned from that truth is this: God is and always has been an exuberantly happy God. From all eternity, even before there were any human beings to love, God has been overflowingly happy in his love for the Son. He has never been lonely. He has always rejoiced, with overflowing satisfaction, in the glory and the partnership of his Son. The Son of God has always been the landscape of God's excellencies and the panorama of God's perfections, so that from all eternity God has beheld, with indescribable satisfaction, the magnificent terrain of his own radiance reflected in the Son.

A second lesson to learn from God's pleasure in the Son is that God is not constrained by any inner deficiency or unhappiness to do anything he does not want to do. If God were unhappy, if he were in some way deficient, then he might indeed be constrained from outside in some way to do what he does not want to do, in order to make up his deficiency and finally to be happy. This is what distinguishes us from God. We have an immense void inside that craves satisfaction from powers and persons and pleasures outside ourselves. Yearning and longing and desire are the very stuff of our nature. We are born deficient and needy and dissatisfied. We come into the world knowing almost nothing, and have to spend years and years going to classes or learning in the school of hard knocks, in order to fill up a little of this void of ignorance. Parents and teachers tell us to do things that we don't like to do because we need to do them to overcome some weakness in ourselves—to increase our knowledge or strengthen our bodies or refine our manners or sharpen our intellect.

But God is not like that. He has been complete and overflowing with satisfaction from all eternity. He needs no education. No one can offer anything to him that doesn't already come from him.

> For who has known the mind of the Lord,
> or who has been his counselor?
> Or who has given a gift to him that he might be repaid?
> For from him and through him and to him are all things.
> To him be glory for ever. Amen. (Romans 11:34-36)

So no one can bribe God or coerce him in any way. Whatever you or I or anyone or any circumstance offers to God, it is only the reflex of something he has already given or already done. The source of all things cannot be enriched or tempted with angelic or human service. "He is not served by human hands as though he needed anything, since he himself gives to all men life and breath and everything" (Acts 17:25). If anyone offers God anything—and aims to offer it rightly—he must say with David, "Who am I, and what is my people, that we should be able thus to offer willingly? For all things come from you, and we have given only what comes from you" (1 Chronicles 29:14; cf. 1 Corinthians 4:7). In other words, all that is, including the ability to offer willingly, is a gift from the overflowing, all-sufficient, ever-happy God.

What Brainerd Taught the Indians

The picture that comes to my mind when I think of this great truth is not the lecture hall or the debating chamber or even the place where I preach week in and week out. The picture that comes to my mind is a clearing in the woods of New Jersey. The year is 1745 near a village called Crossweeksung. David Brainerd, the twenty-seven-year-old missionary to the Indian people, coughs up blood every day because he is dying of tuberculosis. He will live barely two more years. He is preaching to 130 Indians whom God has called out of darkness by an amazing awakening under Brainerd's preaching. According to Brainerd's own testimony, his message this day concerns the all-sufficiency and everlasting happiness of God. He tells us what he was burdened to teach these pre-literate Indians in the wilderness:

> It is necessary, in the first place, to teach them, that God is from everlasting, and so distinguished from all creatures; though it is very difficult to communicate anything of that nature to them, they having no terms in their language to signify an eternity *a parte ante* [that is, eternity past]. . . . The divine all-sufficiency must also necessarily be mentioned, in order to prevent their imagining that God was unhappy while alone, before the formation of his creatures.[1]

By "alone" Brainerd does not mean that God had no fellowship with his Son in the Holy Spirit before creation. He only means that there were no creatures with whom to relate. Yet God was not unhappy, because in the fellowship of the Trinity he is all-sufficient. Brainerd believed with all his heart that this was good news. It was not to be kept from the simplest believers. It was a great part of God's glory, and God's glory was the heart of all true religious experience.[2]

When my mind returns from that scene in the woods of New Jersey I am encouraged to press the truth more earnestly than ever. God does what he does, not begrudgingly or under external constraint as though he were boxed in or trapped by some unforeseen or unplanned situation. On the contrary, because he is complete and exuberantly happy and overflowing with satisfaction in the fellowship of the Trinity, all he does is free and uncoerced. His deeds are the overflow of his joy. This is what it means when the Scripture says that God acts according to the "good pleasure" of his will (Ephesians 1:5). It means that nothing outside God's own pleasure—the pleasure he has in himself—has constrained his choices and his deeds.

All That the Lord Pleases

This brings us to the focus of the present chapter, "The Pleasure of God in All He Does." If God is not under constraint by forces outside himself to act contrary to his good pleasure, but rather only acts out of the overflow of the joy of his boundless self-sufficiency, then all his acts are the expression of joy and he has pleasure in all that he does. We begin our biblical reflections at Psalm 135. It begins by calling us to praise the Lord: "Praise the Lord. Praise the name of the Lord, give praise, O servants of the Lord." Then, starting in verse 3 the psalmist gives us reasons why we should feel praise rising in our hearts toward God. He says, for example, that the Lord is "good and gracious" (verse 3), and that he has "chosen Jacob for himself" (verse 4), and that he is great above all gods (verse 5). Then in verse 6 this list of reasons for praise climaxes with the great affirmation,

> *All that the Lord pleases, he does,*
> in heaven and on earth,
> in the seas and all deeps.

Similarly in Psalm 115 this note is sounded with clarity and force. It begins by calling for God to glorify himself and reaches up to declare his sovereign freedom in the heavens:

> Not to us, O Lord, not to us,
> but to your name give glory,
> for the sake of your steadfast love and your faithfulness!
> Why should the nations say,
> "Where is their God?"
> Our God is in the heavens;
> *All that he pleases he does* (verses 1-3).

What these two verses (Psalm 135:6; 115:3) teach is that everything God takes pleasure in doing, he does, and cannot be hindered from doing. Or to put it somewhat differently, all that he does he takes pleasure in. He cannot be kept back from doing what he delights most to do. And he cannot be forced to do what he does not delight in. And this is true everywhere in the universe. That's the meaning of "in heaven and on earth, in the seas and all deeps" (Psalm 135:6).

Another witness to this truth is the prophet Isaiah. God speaks through him and says,

> I am God and there is no other;
> I am God, and there is none like me,
> declaring the end from the beginning
> and from ancient times things not yet done,
> saying, "My counsel shall stand,
> *and I will accomplish all my pleasure.*"
> Isaiah 46:9-10

The word translated "pleasure" (*hēphetz*) is the noun form of the verb "he pleases" (*haphētz)* in Psalm 135:6 and 115:3. It is the word used in Psalm 1:2 ("His *delight* is in the law of the Lord"), and Psalm 16:3 ("They are the noble in whom is all my *delight*"), and Isaiah 62:4 ("You shall be called My *delight* is in her, and your land Married; for the Lord delights in you and your land shall be married").

Sovereign Freedom

The point is that God acts in sovereign freedom. His acts do not spring from the need to make up deficiencies but from the passion to express the abundance of his delight. This is the meaning of his freedom. I have called it *sovereign* freedom because this is the note struck in all three texts we have looked at—God does in fact do all his pleasure. He is free in that he has no deficiencies that make him dependent, and he is sovereign in that he can act on his delights without being stopped by powers outside himself. "All that he pleases he does." Thus his freedom is a sovereign freedom.

What God the Father beholds as he looks out across the panorama of his own perfections in the Person of his Son is an all-satisfying scene of infinite wisdom, love, and power. Thus his happiness flows from his perfections, including the perfection of his infinite power. It is this immeasurable power that guarantees the freedom of God's delight in all that he does. His delight is the joy that he has in the reflection of his own glory in the person of his Son. But part of that glory is infinite power. And the unique function of his power is to make way for the overflow of his joy in the work of creation and redemption. It is his power that removes (in God's time and God's way) any obstacles to the accomplishment of his good pleasure. Thus the declaration that God does all that he pleases is a declaration of his power. This is what we mean by sovereignty—God's power always makes way for his perfections to be expressed according to his good pleasure.

I love the image that C. S. Lewis gives of God's sovereign freedom in creation. It shows how the good pleasure of his heart to create and save is the happy overflow of his all-sufficiency. Lewis says,

> To be sovereign of the universe is no great matter to God . . . We must keep always before our eyes that vision of Lady Julian's in which God carried in His hand, a little object like a nut, and that nut was "all that is made." God who needs nothing, loves into existence wholly superfluous creatures in order that He may love and perfect them.[3]

In a Class By Himself

This connection between power and pleasure is behind 1 Timothy 6:15-16, where the apostle Paul calls God, "the *blessed* and only Sovereign, the King of kings and Lord of lords, who alone has immortality." We saw in chapter 1 (p. 41, note 2) that "blessed" (*makarios*) means "happy" (1 Timothy 1:11). Thus Paul is speaking of the "happy and only Sovereign." Notice what is stressed in calling God "blessed" or "happy." God's sole and unique power over all other powers is stressed. First, he is called the "only Sovereign"—not just the Sovereign, but the *only* Sovereign. In other words he has no serious competitors for his power. He is the *only* "powerful one."

Then Paul says that this happy God is "King of kings." Again the point is that he is over all other royal authorities that might seem to challenge his power and his freedom to act as he pleases. Then Paul says that he is "Lord of lords." If there are any gods or lords (and there are!), Paul emphasizes that there is none that can successfully overthrow the power and freedom of the Lord of lords (1 Corinthians 8:5-6). Finally Paul says that "he alone has immortality." God is in a class by himself. All other beings depend upon his creative power for existence and life (Acts 17:25). He depends upon no one.

All of this teaches that the happiness of God is rooted in his utterly unique power and authority in the universe. He is the "*only* Sovereign," and therefore he is the *happy* Sovereign, because there is none that can frustrate what he aims to do according to his good pleasure. C. S. Lewis put it like this: "The freedom of God consists in the fact that no cause other than Himself produces His acts and no external obstacle impedes them—that His own goodness is the root from which they all grow and His own omnipotence the air in which they all flower."[4]

Is God Our Model Risk-Taker?

In the summer of 1987 I attended a young leaders conference sponsored by the Lausanne Committee for World Evangelization called "Singapore '87." One of the speakers there sounded a note that shows the immense relevance of what I am saying here in this chapter. Among all the excellent things I heard at the conference, this note, however, was, in my judgment, a misleading one. It was by no means the dominant note of the conference, for which I am glad, because I think the cause of world evangelization would suffer if it became a dominant note in the music of missionary preaching.

This particular speaker developed a vision of God as our model "risk-taker." He portrayed God as taking great risks, and said that this is why we should be willing to take great risks for the cause of world evangelization. Now, make no mistake, I love to hear leaders call for radical, risk-taking allegiance to the global cause of the gospel. So I was emotionally primed to say amen to this speaker's conclusions. But when he was done I felt like the very foundations of Christian risk-taking had been weakened rather than strengthened—namely, the truth that "God is in heaven; he does all that he pleases."

I failed to meet the speaker to talk with him personally, and so I wrote him a letter to express my concern. I think quoting my letter at length might be the most engaging way I could explain why I think the sovereignty and freedom of God to do all his pleasure is so important. I have made only slight changes to conceal identities and clarify at a few spots. The letter is dated July 6, 1987.

Dear [friend],

My main reason for writing is to offer a perspective on one of the brief talks that you made concerning God as our model risk-taker. I wanted to speak to you in person about this, because it sets forth a view of God that is so different than the one I have. It seemed to me from what others said in our small group, as well as over lunch, that your view of God as a risk-taker was not typical of what others were thinking.

I'm perfectly willing to admit that perhaps I am reading too much into the term "risk-taker" and that the differences that I perceive are simply a matter of semantics. But just in case that's not so, let me spell out my response . . .

I seems to me that the dimension of God's character which frees me to be a risk-taker for his glory is precisely the truth that God does not and cannot take any risks.[5] In my own life the greatest obstacle to risk-taking is unbelief—unbelief in the promises and love and power and wisdom of God; or to put it another way, that God has the power, authority, wisdom, and willingness to make us "more than conquerors" through our injuries and loss. This is the confidence that frees me to take a risk for Christ.

But the God that you described as a risk-taker does not inspire that kind of confidence. To describe God as a risk-taker and gambler, as you did, suggests 1) that he cannot foresee what will come of his decisions; and 2) that he is not in control of things so as to make his counsel stand. But it seems to me that Scripture presents a very different portrait of God.

Let me take a few of the examples that you used to illustrate God as a risk-taker.

1. Did God take a risk in putting the Great Commission into our hands? I don't think so. He did not put it into our hands to such an extent that it is out of his own hands. John 10:16 says that Jesus must and will gather his sheep that are not yet in the fold! ("I have other sheep, that are not of this fold; *I must bring* them also, and they will heed my voice.") He is the one who opens the hearts of men (Acts 16:14). He draws people to the Son, overcoming their resistance to his sovereign grace (John 6:44,65). He calls his messengers, and they accomplish their mission only by his power (Romans 15:15-18; 1 Corinthians 15:10).

The Great Commission is not in question. "This gospel of the kingdom *will* be preached throughout the whole world, as a testimony to all nations; and then the end will come" (Matthew 24:14). "All the ends of the earth shall remember and turn to the Lord; and all the families of the nations shall worship before him. For dominion belongs to the Lord and he rules over the nations" (Psalm 22: 27-28). The full number of the gentiles shall come in (Romans 11:25). "The earth shall be filled with the glory of the Lord" (Numbers 14:21). All of Scripture affirms the victory of God in world missions. It is not in question. God has promised. God is sovereign! Because he rules over the hearts of men and is the Lord of his church, his purpose cannot fail! Therefore, giving the Great Commission to the church was not a risk.

Perhaps before looking at the other points you made I should try to define "risk." I would define it this way: A person takes a risk when he performs an action that exposes him to the uncertain possibility of injury or loss. This means that if you know that an action will hurt you and you choose it anyway, you do not call it a risk. You may call it foolishness. You may call it sacrifice. Or you may call it love. But risk implies uncertainty: maybe I will lose, and maybe I won't; I'm not sure.

The same thing is true of gambling. If you know the outcome of the dice when you roll them, it is not gambling. It is sure loss or sure gain. Uncertainty is at the heart of risk and gambling.

But God is not uncertain about anything![6] "I am God, and there is none like me, declaring the end from the beginning and from ancient times things not yet done" (Isaiah 46:9-10). God knows from ancient times what is yet to happen in the future. "Behold, the former things have come to pass, and new things I now declare; before they spring forth I tell you of them" (Isaiah 42:9). God knows how all his plans will turn out. In what sense, then, can we speak of him taking risks, that is, acting with uncertainty about how things will turn out?

2. You said that God took a risk at the incarnation when he sent Jesus Christ into the world. You illustrated this with the possibility that Jesus may have been killed by Herod's soldiers when he was yet a baby in Bethlehem.

But do you really believe that God had surrendered control of circumstances so that all the Old Testament promises of Christ's crucifixion and teaching and resurrection could have come to nought? Was God's word of promise, which came to fulfillment in the life and death and resurrection of Jesus Christ, really so uncertain?

What becomes of Acts 2:23—that Jesus was delivered up to be crucified (not with risk, but) "according to the definite plan and foreknowledge of God"? How can the incarnation be called a risk when it was God's precise intention and will (at least seven hundred years before it happened) to bruise his Son (Isaiah 53:10)? How can it be a risk for God to send his Son into the world when it was his plan that the Son be crucified (Acts 4:28)? It seems to me that we should not call the incarnation a risk, but rather a definite, planned sacrifice of the Son.

3. The same thing seems to be true of our individual conversion. Acts 13:48 says, "When the Gentiles heard this, they were glad and glorified the word of God; and as many as were ordained to eternal life believed." God does not leave even the issue of conversion finally in the hands of man—as though the makeup and size of the eternal worshiping community would be designed by the minds of sinful men and not by the infinite wisdom of God. The Lord knows those who are his (2 Timothy 2:19). He is the one who grants repentance (2 Timothy 2:25-26). He will call his own sheep by name and they will hear and come (John 10:3-4).

Nor does God leave to uncertain risk our growth and perseverance in holiness. Rather, he says, "I will put my Spirit within you, and will cause you to walk in my statutes and be careful to observe my ordinances" (Ezekiel 36:27). It is the Lord himself who works in us to will and to do his good pleasure (Philippians 2:12-13; Hebrews 13:21). This is not mechanical or forced. But it is sure for God's true people. Festo Kevengere, who served with African Enterprise, described the ineluctable, sovereign work of the Spirit in our lives like this:

> He keeps struggling with our reluctancies and hesitations. He comes and convicts me over something, and I begin to fidget.

We are real tough to handle, aren't we? The gracious Holy
Spirit does not push. He just does some gentle nudging.

When you fidget and become restless, He stops for awhile
and lets you go on. Then He comes again and catches you in
a corner where you won't fidget so much. In the corner, He
does His beautiful work of turning you around. And what do
you see? The Lamb of God.

The cutting of the stone is done and you have been fitted in!
That is how He is taking us, stones of all races and backgrounds,
and fitting us together into a beautiful dwelling place of God.[7]

My conclusion from these reflections is that we should indeed take
risks for the cause of Christ. In fact, before coming to Singapore I
had gotten myself ready by preaching three sermons under the
theme, "Risk and the Cause of God." But the reason we humans
can take risks is because we are ignorant of our *earthly* future. We
are uncertain how things will turn out here. But God is in heaven
and does whatever he pleases (Psalm 115:3). His counsel always
stands and his purposes are accomplished (Isaiah 46:9-10). He
knows the end from the beginning, and therefore cannot take
risks. He can sacrifice himself, and he can love. But he never rolls
dice. Nothing that he does is ever a gamble.

For his own wise purposes, He can allow his cause to suffer
temporary setbacks (both individually and globally). He can love at
the price of his Son's life. But to describe him as a risk-taker calls
into question his omniscience and sovereignty, and therefore takes
away the very foundation of our confidence, and thus the power
that enables us to take risks for God.

I thank you so much for taking the time to read this. Please know
that it is written with the great hope that I have misunderstood
your view of God. It comes with the great expectation that
whatever remnants of disagreement may lie between us after this
letter, will not hinder our allegiance to Jesus Christ and our
willingness to lay down our lives for his honor.

Your friend and partner in the great Work,

John Piper

There is much in Scripture to show the vision of God's
sovereign freedom to do all his pleasure. I have laid out many
more texts in *Desiring God* (pp. 24-28). But I hope we have seen
enough already in this chapter to know that we should bow
before God and praise his sovereign freedom—that he always acts
according to his own "good pleasure," following the dictates of

his own delights. He never becomes the victim of circumstance. He is never forced into a situation where he must do something in which he cannot rejoice.

Perhaps the glory of God's greatness in this regard will shine brighter if we see it in the confidence and courage it has given to thousands of risk-taking missionaries. Consider just one example, William Carey.[8]

William Carey's Awesome God

William Carey is known as the father of modern missions. He gave forty years of his life in India from 1793 to 1834, and never went home on furlough. The vision of God that inflamed his heart for the nations was the free and sovereign God of warm-hearted, evangelical Calvinism—the God of George Whitefield the evangelist who had died when Carey was nine years old, and the God of Augustus Toplady (1740-1778), who wrote the hymn "Rock of Ages," and the God of John Newton (1725-1807), author of "Amazing Grace." Carey is often remembered for his strong opposition to the hyper-Calvinists of his day who were reputed to have told him to cool down in his enthusiasm for world missions because if God wanted to reach the heathen he would do it without Carey's help.[9]

Carey did indeed oppose this unbiblical view of God's sovereignty. But what is not as well known is that he opposed it not with an Arminian vision of God's limited power, but with a biblically balanced vision of God's free and sovereign grace. This is evident in the way he balanced the biblical teaching of God's sovereign work in conversion with the responsibility we have for persuading people to exercise their wills to believe. He wrote,

> We are sure that only those who are ordained to eternal life will believe [Acts 13:48], and that God alone can add to the church such as shall be saved [Acts 2:47]. Nevertheless we cannot but observe with admiration that Paul, the great champion for the glorious doctrines of free and sovereign grace, was the most conspicuous for his personal zeal in the work of persuading men to be reconciled to God.[10]

Carey did not believe that God could be frustrated in his designs for the world, but that "all the Lord pleases he does." This was the confidence that kept him going through incredible hardships for forty years. He shows us his view of God's freedom to act in his own good pleasure by answering one of the hardest questions that a missionary can be asked on the mission field. In 1797, four years after he came to India, Carey tells us of being confronted by a Brahman. Carey had preached on Acts 14:16 and 17:30 and said that God formerly allowed all men everywhere to go their own way, but now he commands all men everywhere to repent.

The Brahman responded, "Indeed I think God ought to repent for not sending the gospel sooner to us."

It is not an easy objection to answer. Carey's answer is awesome, like the God he loved and served:

> To this I added, suppose a kingdom had been long overrun by the enemies of its true king, and he though possessed of sufficient power to conquer them, should yet suffer them to prevail, and establish themselves as much as they could desire, would not the valor and wisdom of that king be far more conspicuous in exterminating them, than it would have been if he had opposed them at first, and prevented their entering the country? Thus by the diffusion of gospel light, the wisdom, power, and grace of God will be more conspicuous in overcoming such deep-rooted idolatries, and in destroying all that darkness and vice which have so universally prevailed in this country, than they would have been if all had not been suffered to walk in their own ways for so many ages past.[11]

What an answer! The free and sovereign God rules the nations in such a way that even the ages of unbelief will redound to his glory in the most pagan of countries when the gospel victory comes! Carey did not say that God's good pleasure was so frustrated by a stubborn and disobedient people whom he just couldn't sanctify enough to act the way they should. It is absolutely true that disobedience to the Great Commission violates God's word. And it is true that many generations of professing Christians will have to give an account for this sin.

But it does not follow (all Arminian logic notwithstanding) that God was handcuffed and unable to give his people a new heart of obedience (Ezekiel 11:19-20) or unable to cause them to walk in his statutes (Ezekiel 36:27). Whatever the cause of the church's disobedience to the Great Commission, Carey knew he could not lay it to the charge of God's impotence. This is why he answered the way he did. God has his wise and holy purposes in all that he does and he does all that he does according to his own good pleasure. Carey shared the vision of God I have tried to describe in these chapters. I learned much of it from him! God is in heaven and he is doing all his good pleasure, no matter how mysterious this may seem. This was the power behind the first era of modern missions.

The Vision Behind Operation World

And we should not think that the spirit of Carey is dead today. It is still driving large segments of the great missionary movement of our day to complete the Great Commission in this generation. One of the books that God is using around the world to mobilize the church in missionary passion and prayer is Patrick Johnstone's *Operation World.*[12] It gives a status report on the circumstances relating to the spread of the gospel and the growth of the church in each country of the world. I cannot help but wonder whether its updated re-publication in 1986 was one of the crucial factors in God's plan to bring about such amazing changes in Eastern Europe at the end of the 1980's. What is the spirit and conviction behind this mountain-moving book? Patrick Johnstone expresses it with fervor:

> Only the Lamb could open the seals. All the earth-shaking awesome forces unleashed on the world are released by the Lord Jesus Christ. He reigns today. He is in the control room of the universe. He is the only Ultimate Cause; all the sins of man and machinations of Satan ultimately have to enhance the glory and kingdom of our Saviour. This is true of our world today—in wars, famines, earthquakes, or the evil that apparently has the ascendancy. All God's actions are just and loving. We have become too enemy-conscious, and can over-do the spiritual warfare aspect of intercession. We need to be more God-conscious, so that we can laugh the laugh of faith knowing that we have power over all the power of the enemy (Luke 10:19). He has already lost control because of Calvary where the Lamb was slain. What confidence and rest of heart this gives us as we face a world in turmoil and in such spiritual need.[13]

Does God Have Pleasure in the Death of the Wicked?

This is a glorious picture of God in his sovereign freedom—to do whatever he pleases and to accomplish all his pleasure. But it would be a fuzzy picture, a bit out of focus, if we stopped here. To bring it into focus and sharpen it, we have to ask this question: "How can God say in Ezekiel 18:23 and 32 that he does not have *pleasure* in the death of any impenitent person, if in fact he accomplishes all his *pleasure* and does whatever he *pleases?*"

In Ezekiel 18:30, God is warning the house of Israel of impending judgment: "Therefore I will judge you, O house of Israel, every one according to his ways, says the Lord." And he is urging them to repent: "Repent and turn from all your transgressions." At the end of verse 31 he says, "Why will you die, O house of Israel? For I do not have pleasure in the death of any one, says the Lord God; so turn, and live."

This seems to be a very different picture than the one we saw in Psalm 135, where God does all that he pleases. This is the kind of text that causes people to jump to the conclusion (too quickly!) that William Carey had not read all of his Bible. Here God seems to be cornered. It seems that he is forced into judging them when he really doesn't want to. He seems to be about to do something that he is not pleased to do.[14] Is he going to accomplish all his pleasure or not? Is God really free to do everything according to his good pleasure? Or does his sovereign freedom have its limits? Can he do whatever he pleases up to a point, and then after that is he forced into doing things he only grieves to do?

We might try to solve the problem by going back to Psalm 135 and saying that God does whatever he pleases in the *natural* sphere but not in the *personal* sphere. After all it says in Psalm 135:7: "He it is who makes the clouds rise at the end of the earth, who makes lightnings for the rain and brings forth the wind from his storehouses." Might this not imply that God does all his pleasure in nature but not in the lives of persons?

This effort to limit God's freedom to the sphere of nature will not work for two reasons.

One reason is that if God controls the wind and makes it blow whenever and wherever he pleases—which is certainly true ("He makes the wind to blow and the waters flow," Psalm 147:18; and remember Jesus' "Peace! Be still!")—then God is somehow responsible for the destruction of thousands of lives by drowning because of the storms and hurricanes and tornadoes and monsoons and typhoons which God has "brought forth from his storehouses" over the centuries.

Do we charge God with wrong when we say this? Might it not be Satan who makes destructive wind blow? This is a good question. The answer is not simple. I don't mean the answer is hard to find. I mean that the answer is complex. Satan does have great power in this world to do harm. (See note 16.) We know that he can cause sickness (Luke 13:16; Acts 10:38) and, since he is called a "murderer from the beginning" (John 8:44), we may infer that he can indeed kill, whether by sickness or by stirring up people to kill or in other ways as well. It is hard not to see his hand in the tragic deaths, for example, of missionary children. The reason I think of this is because two hours ago I received a phone call that the son of a missionary friend was killed in a car accident. A year ago another missionary family I had met in Cameroon lost two of their three children in one day to malaria within days after coming home on furlough. And such stories are multiplied almost every day.

I hope no one will think that what I am saying here is written in some detached atmosphere, untouched by the pain and heartache of tragedy. I am not suggesting that such things are easy to bear or that they can be overcome with a few simple theological observations. For everything there is a season: "a time to weep, and a time to laugh; a time to keep silence, and a time to speak" (Ecclesiastes 3:4,7). In the moment of tragedy and world-shattering grief it is time to embrace and be silent. But the time for questions and answers will come. And when they come, it is a shortsighted compromise with the father of lies to say that Satan is stronger than God and that the hands of the Almighty were tied. This has never been the answer of the deepest saints. I have wept with many of them, and prayed and waited to see what their response would be. And, though they are not all as eloquent as Sarah Edwards, they all, sooner or later, say something like what she said.

Sarah Edwards's Sovereign God

Her husband Jonathan Edwards had been away from home for some weeks in 1758 to assume the presidency of Princeton College. On February 13 he was inoculated for smallpox; but the cure became the killer, and he died from the inoculation on March 22, 1758. He was fifty-four years old and left his wife with ten children. When Sarah heard of her husband's death, the first letter she wrote was to her daughter Esther:

> My very dear child!
>
> What shall I say? A holy and good God has covered us with a dark cloud. O that we may kiss the rod, and lay our hands on our mouths! The Lord has done it. He has made me adore his goodness, that we had him so long. But my God lives; and he has my heart. O what a legacy my husband, and your father, has left us! We are all given to God; and there I am, and love to be.
>
> Your affectionate mother,
>
> Sarah Edwards[15]

I believe with all my heart that the biblical teaching of God's sovereignty over Satan is the greatest answer in the world when the very meaning of life is threatened by the horrors and tragedies of death and disease. It is the answer of Scripture and it is true and full of hope.

The Bible does not teach that Satan has the highest control in the world. God is shown to be the controller of the wind in Genesis 8:1; Exodus 14:21; 15:10; Psalm 78:26; 107:25; 148:8; Isaiah 11:15; and Jonah 1:4; 4:8. There is a possible exception in the book of Job. In Job 1:11-12 God gives Satan the freedom to attack all that Job has, including his family. Then in Job 1:19 "a great wind" levels the house where Job's children are and kills them all. The text doesn't say who caused the wind to blow. But in Job 1:21 Job himself says, "The Lord gave and the Lord has taken away; blessed be the name of the Lord." So even if Satan has a hand in making the wind blow, Job knows that behind Satan is the real Ruler of the world and the wind, namely, the Lord.[16] So he says, "The Lord has taken away." Should Job have said this? The writer takes away all doubt that Job is right to say this, because in the next verse (1:22) he says, "In all this Job did not sin or charge God with wrong." Neither did Isaiah when he quoted God as saying, "I form light and create darkness, I make comfort and create calamity, I am the Lord, who does all these things" (Isaiah 45:7). Nor did Jeremiah err when he said, "Is it not from the mouth of the Most High that good and evil (i.e. calamity) come" (Lamentations 3:38). Nor Amos when he said, "Does evil befall a city, unless the Lord has done it?" (Amos 3:6).

So when Psalm 135 says that the Lord does whatever he pleases it has to include the taking of personal life through wind and sea which he alone controls. The Lord gives and the Lord takes away. He is the source of all life (Acts 17:25) and he appoints the time for its return (1 Samuel 2:6; Deuteronomy 32:39). James takes this for granted when he tells us that we should reckon with the sovereign control of God even in our ordinary business plans.

> Come now you who say, "Today or tomorrow we will go into such and such a town and spend a year there and trade and get gain," whereas you do not know about tomorrow. What is your life? For you are a mist that appears for a little time and then vanishes. Instead you ought to say, "If the Lord wills, we shall live and we shall do this or that." As it is you boast in your arrogance. All such boasting is evil" (James 4:13-16).

James assumes that it is the will of the Lord that determines whether anyone gets from one town to another. For him it is a matter of humility to give God this right and a matter of arrogance to act, not to mention teach, that it is not so.

But there is a second reason we can't limit the freedom of God in Psalm 135 to the natural realm. The psalm goes farther than just saying that God causes wind and lightning. In verses 8-10 it says that God's sovereign freedom was shown most vividly in the Exodus when he delivered Israel from Egypt: "He it was who smote the firstborn of Egypt, both of man and of beast . . . who smote many nations and slew mighty kings. . . ." Therefore when the Psalmist says in verse 6 that "whatever the Lord pleases he does," he doesn't just refer *implicitly* to the tragedies owing to wind; he also refers *explicitly* to the destruction of rebellious Egyptians, and nations and kings. This is the scope of what God does when he does all he pleases.

So in Ezekiel it says that God is *not pleased* with the death of unrepentant people, and in Psalm 135 it says that God does whatever he pleases including the slaying of unrepentant people, for example, the enemies of his people in Egypt. And the very same Hebrew verb is used in Psalm 135:6 ("he pleases") and Ezekiel 18:32 ("he does not have pleasure").

Making the Problem Worse

Before I suggest a solution to this problem let me make it worse.

Many Christians today have a conception of God that isn't troubled by his being cornered into doing things he doesn't want to do. And I can easily imagine that one response to what we have seen so far would be to say that we have created an artificial problem because Psalm 135 doesn't actually say that God takes delight in destroying the Egyptians. Perhaps someone would say that "doing whatever he pleases" in Psalm 135:6 is just a figure of speech and doesn't carry the sense of pleasure or delight. And so they would say that God only grieves when he must judge unrepentant sinners, and there is no sense in which he is doing what he is pleased to do.

In answer to this I would say again that the same word used in Psalm 135:6 for God's being "pleased" in all that he does is used in Ezekiel 18:32 for God's not being "pleased" with the death of unrepentant sinners. And I would refer to the discussion of this word (*haphētz*) earlier in the chapter. Then I would direct attention to Deuteronomy 28:63 where Moses warns of coming judgment on unrepentant Israel. But this time it says something strikingly different from Ezekiel 18:32:

And as the Lord took delight in doing you good and multiplying you, *so the Lord will take delight in bringing ruin upon you and destroying you.*

So we are brought back to the inescapable fact that in some sense God does not delight in the death of the wicked (that is the message of Ezekiel 18), and in some sense he does (that is the message implicitly of Psalm 135:6-11 and explicitly of Deuteronomy 28:63). In other words, one cannot simply oppose the thesis of this chapter (that God has pleasure in all that he does) by quoting texts like Ezekiel 18:32. The Bible shows (in Deuteronomy 28:63; Proverbs 1:24-26; Revelation 18:20; Ezekiel 5:13; and Isaiah 30:31-32) that even acts of judgment which in one sense do not please God in another sense do please him. Our method is not to choose between these texts, or to cancel out one by the other, but to go deep enough into the mysterious mind of God to see (so far as possible) how both are true. How shall we account for this apparent tension?

The Infinitely Complex Emotional Life of God

The answer I propose is that God is grieved in one sense by the death of the wicked, and pleased in another.[17] God's emotional life is infinitely complex beyond our ability to fully comprehend. For example, who can comprehend that the Lord hears in one moment of time the prayers of 10 million Christians around the world, and sympathizes with each one personally and individually as a caring Father (as Hebrews 4:15 says), even though among those 10 million prayers some are broken-hearted and some are bursting with joy? How can God weep with those who weep and rejoice with those who rejoice when they are both coming to him at the same time—in fact are always coming to him with no break at all? Or who can comprehend that God is angry at the sin of the world every day (Psalm 7:11), and yet every day, every moment, he is rejoicing with tremendous joy because somewhere in the world a sinner is repenting (Luke 15:7,10,23)? Who can comprehend that God continually burns with hot anger at the rebellion of the wicked and grieves over the unholy speech of his people (Ephesians 4:29-30), yet takes pleasure in them daily (Psalm 149:4), and ceaselessly makes merry over penitent prodigals who come home? Who of us could dare say what complex of emotions is not possible for God? All we have to go on here is what he has chosen to tell us in the Bible. And what he has told us is that there is a sense in which he does not experience pleasure in the judgment of the wicked, and there is a sense in which he does.

The Painful Joy of Justice

From this I conclude that the death and misery of the unrepentant is in and of itself no delight to God. God is not a sadist. He is not malicious or bloodthirsty. Instead when a rebellious, wicked, unbelieving person is judged, what God delights in is the exaltation of truth and righteousness, and the vindication of his own honor and glory.[18] (For further discussion of God's heart in judgment see chapter 5, "How Is God like George Washington?" pp. 145-146.)

When Moses warns Israel that the Lord will take delight in bringing ruin upon them and destroying them if they do not repent (Deuteronomy 28:63), he means that those who have rebelled against the Lord and moved beyond repentance will not be able to gloat that they have made the Almighty miserable. God is not defeated in the triumphs of his righteous judgment. Quite the contrary. Moses says that when they are judged they will unwittingly provide an occasion for God to rejoice in the demonstration of his justice and his power and the infinite worth of his glory (Romans 9:22-23).[19]

Let this be a warning to us. God is not mocked. He is not trapped or cornered or coerced. Even on the way to Calvary he had legions of angels at his disposal. "No one takes my life from me; I lay it down of my own accord"—of his own good *pleasure*, for the *joy* that was set before him. At the one point in the history of the universe where God looked trapped, he was in charge, doing precisely what he pleased—dying to justify the ungodly like you and me.

My Own Experience of the Sovereignty of God

The sovereignty of God is a precious reality for me and for many people in my church. How many times have we gotten word of some heart-wrenching calamity in one of our church families! We have gone to our knees before the Lord and cried out to him for their help and comfort. Time and again I have heard my people submit themselves to the sovereign will of God and seek his good purposes in it. Once a tornado ripped through our area destroying homes and stores and uprooting huge trees. It was a Sunday afternoon. That evening we prayed. Even today, years later, I can recall a woman calling on God for mercy for the victims, and then lifting her voice to extol God for his power in the roaring wind, and asking him that we all be humbled and brought to repentance before such majestic authority.

Not long ago the son of one of our church leaders was run over by a motor boat. He lived, but his knees were badly damaged, and there were superficial nicks on his chest and neck from the propeller. When his father testified in a deacon meeting, he said that his main comfort and lesson was the sovereignty of God. "God has his purposes for the life of my son," he said, "and for the whole family. This will turn out for the good of all of us as we trust in him. God could have taken my son with another half-inch difference. But instead he said to the blade: 'Thus far and no farther.' "

God does not always stop the blade. On December 16, 1974, he did not save my mother's life. She was riding with my father on a touring bus heading toward Bethlehem in Israel. A van with lumber tied on the roof swerved out of its lane and hit the bus head on. The lumber came through the windows and killed my mother instantly. The death certificate said, "lacerated medulla oblongata." When we saw her body ten days later, after the funeral home did the best it could, my sister fainted. We left my father to weep alone over the coffin for a long time.

Then I went in and shut it for the last time. We used pictures at the visitation.

What was my comfort in those days? There were many. She suffered little. I had her for twenty-eight years as the best mother imaginable. She had known my wife and one of my four children. She was now in heaven with Jesus. Her life was rich with good deeds and its good effects are lasting long after she is gone. And underneath all these comforts, supporting all my unanswered questions, and calming my heart, there is the confidence that God is in control and God is good. I take no comfort from the prospect that God cannot control the flight of a four-by-four. For me there is no consolation in haphazardness. Nor in giving Satan the upper hand. As I knelt by my bed and wept, having received the dreaded phone call from my brother-in-law, I never doubted that God was sovereign over this accident and that God was good. I do not need to explain everything. That he reigns and that he loves is enough for now.

So let us stand in awe and wonder of God—eternally happy in the fellowship of the Trinity; infinitely exuberant in the wisdom of his work; free and sovereign in his self-sufficiency. "Our God is in heaven; he does all that he pleases." Let us humble ourselves under his mighty hand, and rejoice that his counsel will stand, and that one day all the families of the nations shall worship before him; for dominion belongs to the Lord, and he rules over the nations!

Notes

1. *Second Appendix to Mr. Brainerd's Journal,* in *The Works of Jonathan Edwards,* 2 (Edinburgh: Banner of Truth Trust, 1974), 426.

2. He wrote in his journal four months before he died, "I saw with no less clearness that the essence of religion consisted in the soul's conformity to God . . . and this from a clear view of his infinite excellency and worthiness in himself, to be loved, adored, worshiped, and served by all intelligent creatures. Thus I saw that when a soul loves God with a supreme love, he therein acts like the blessed [happy] God himself, who most justly loves himself in that manner: So when God's interest and his are become one, and he longs that God should be glorified, and rejoices to think that he is unchangeably possessed of the highest glory and blessedness [happiness], herein also he acts in conformity to God." *The Life of David Brainerd,* compiled by Jonathan Edwards, ed. Norman Pettit (New Haven: Yale University Press, 1985), 449.

3. Quoted from *The Four Loves* in *A Mind Awake: An Anthology of C. S. Lewis,* ed. Clyde Kilby (New York: Harcourt, Brace and World, 1968), 85.

4. Quoted from *The Problem of Pain* in Ibid., 80.

5. In saying there is something God cannot do, I am not limiting his sovereignty, because all I am saying is that God cannot use his sovereignty to make himself unsovereign. We have all heard the question: Can God make a rock big enough so that he cannot lift it? If we say yes, then he can't lift the rock. If we say no, then he can't make the rock. Heads he loses, tails he loses. The problem with this question is that it is a word trick and not a weakening of God. C. S. Lewis described the trick like this:

   You may attribute miracles to him but not nonsense. This is no limit to his power . . . you have not succeeded in saying *anything* about God: meaningless combinations of words do not suddenly acquire meaning simply because we prefix to them the two words "God can." It remains true that all *things* are possible with God: the intrinsic impossibilities are not things but nonentities. It is no more possible for God than for the weakest of His creatures to carry out both of two mutually exclusive alternatives; not because His power meets an obstacle, but because nonsense remains nonsense even when we talk it about God (from *The Problem of Pain* in *A Mind Awake,* 79).

   I could wish we were dealing here only with the word games of sophomore philosophy students just discovering such conundrums. But this is not the case. There are serious scholarly attempts being made today to argue that

God's omnipotence and knowledge do in fact include the ability to make a human creature, for example, whose choices he *cannot* know in advance. In other words, it seems that God's knowledge is great enough to create something that exceeds his knowledge. Richard Rice, professor of theology at Loma Linda University, argues this way: "Can [God] create beings with a capacity to surprise and delight him, as well as disappoint him, as they choose, and not know in advance what all their choices will be? If he cannot, then there is something significant that God cannot do. And this means that his power is limited." [From "Divine Foreknowledge and Free-Will Theism," in *A Case for Arminianism: The Grace of God, the Will of Man*, ed. Clark H. Pinnock (Grand Rapids: Zondervan Publishing House, 1990), 137.] But the question we should ask professor Rice is this: Is it a "significant thing" for an omniscient and omnipotent God to create a being whose choices are beyond his foreknowledge? Or is it a "nonentity" or "nonsense" as, I believe, Lewis would suggest? See the following footnote for more on this issue.

6. We saw in footnote 5 that not all Christians believe this. In fact there is renewed effort today, from within the household of faith, to refute the truth of God's knowledge of all future events. Recently Clark Pinnock edited a book of essays entitled *A Case for Arminianism: The Grace of God, the Will of Man*, in which he and others defend God's limited foreknowledge. Pinnock himself, after a pilgrimage from Calvinism to Arminianism (and beyond, since classical Arminianism still affirmed that God knows all future actions), now declares, "Decisions not yet made do not exist anywhere to be known even by God. They are potential—yet to be realized but not yet actual. God can predict a great deal of what we will choose to do, but not all of it, because some of it remains hidden in the mystery of human freedom . . . God too faces possibilities in the future, and not only certainties. God too moves into a future not wholly known because not yet fixed" (pp. 25-26).

   Pinnock was pressed to this position first by neo-Arminian logic, not Scripture. This is ironic because of how persistently he accuses others of silencing Scripture with "Calvinian logic" (pp. 19, 21, 22, 25, 26, 28). The neo-Arminian logic goes like this: "A total omniscience would necessarily mean that everything we will ever choose in the future will have been already spelled out in the divine knowledge register, and consequently the belief that we have truly significant choices to make would seem to be mistaken" (p. 25). Thus the philosophical presuppositions that foreknowledge is incompatible with "significant choices" and that the reality of what he calls "significant choices" is more sure than the total foreknowledge of God—these two neo-Arminian (not classical Arminian) presuppositions lead him logically to reject the total foreknowledge of God. Only then does he say, "Therefore, I had to ask myself if it was biblically possible to hold that . . . free choices would not be something that can be known even by God because they are not yet settled in reality" (p. 25). In another place he says, "Let me explain five of the doctrinal moves that *logic required* and I believed *Scripture permitted* me to make . . ." (p. 18-19, italics added). Scripture was searched as a confirmation of what neo-Arminian logic demanded.

On the surface Pinnock's basic argument against God's foreknowledge of free human choices looks like C. S. Lewis's argument against limiting God's omnipotence by saying he can't make a rock big enough so that he can't lift it (see note 5). Lewis says that the idea of a being with total ability creating something *beyond* its ability is logical nonsense. It is saying yes and no about the same thing in the same way at the same time. This is no-thing. And to say God can't do a no-thing is not to limit his ability at all. Pinnock attempts something similar with God's foreknowledge. He says, "Decisions not yet made do not exist anywhere to be known even by God." In other words, they are a no-thing. And so to deny that God can know a no-thing is not to limit his knowledge at all. On the surface the arguments look similar. But they are not.

There is a profound difference. God's omnipotence is preserved by Lewis because non-omnipotent omnipotence is a self-contradiction. This however is not the logical structure of Pinnock's argument. He is not preserving the omniscience of God by rejecting non-omniscient omniscience, but by redefining omniscience so as to exclude knowledge of future human choices. Logic does not require this, and so it is not like Lewis's argument. Rather, a philosophic presupposition requires it, namely, the presupposition that future choices have no knowable reality. They are a no-thing. The ground of this statement is not the law of non-contradiction—like saying (with Lewis) that a non-omnipotent omnipotence is a self-contradiction. Rather, the ground of that statement is an ontological or metaphysical judgment: future choices do not have a standing in reality that allows them to be the object of knowledge, not even God's. It is not logic that demands this. It is a philosophic neo-Arminian system that demands it.

Pinnock calls this system, as he sketches it, "free will theism." He says it is a "doctrine of God that treads the middle way between classical theism, which exaggerates God's transcendence of the world, and process theism, which presses for radical immanence" (p. 26). One of the most puzzling things about Pinnock's presentation of the system is his description of it as a creative and courageous new insight drawn out by a responsible interaction with our modern culture. He believes that this new shift away from classical theism began "because of a fresh and faithful reading of the Bible in dialogue with modern culture, which places emphasis on autonomy, temporality, and historical change" (p. 15). He suggests that the developers of this neo-Arminian "free will theism" are like Augustine in his generation: "If an Augustine had the courage to deal with the culture of his day and come up with some dazzling new insights, then we can do the same in our own setting" (p. 29). "Just as Augustine came to terms with ancient Greek thinking, so we are making peace with the culture of modernity. Influenced by modern culture, we are experiencing reality as something dynamic and historical and are consequently seeing things in the Bible we never saw before" (p. 27).

I say this is puzzling. If what we have here in this "free will theism" are "dazzling new insights" under the influence of modern culture, why is it that I read the same thing in the Socinians of the seventeenth century? I read in an eighteenth century Encyclopedia that, according to Socinius (1539-1604), "God's omniscience is defined in such a way that it does not conflict with the contingency of events and the freedom of the will. God does not know in such a way that whatsoever he knows will surely come to pass. If God's knowledge . . . were to make everything to happen necessarily, which does happen, then there would be no real sin, or guilt of sin." *A Religious Encyclopedia: Or Dictionary of Biblical, Historical, Doctrinal, and Practical Theology,* ed. Philip Schaff (New York: The Christian Literature Co., 1988), 2209.

And if this system is owing to a biblically faithful, creative and courageous interaction with our modern culture, why do I turn to Stephen Charnock (1628-1680), the Puritan pastor and chaplain to Oliver Cromwell, and find him treating virtually every modern argument against the omniscience of God which were all alive and well in his day three hundred years ago? I suspect that the reason for this is that there is nothing significantly new about Pinnock's "free-will theism" but that this system is owing to the same impulses that are present in every generation to resist (however unwittingly!) the absolute Creator rights over his creature, and to make a place for human autonomy and self-determination through the limitation of God—either his power or his knowledge or both.

Charnock poses this utterly relevant question for Pinnock and his neo-Arminian colleagues, "But what if the foreknowledge of God, and the liberty of the will, cannot be fully reconciled by man? Shall we therefore deny a perfection in God to support a liberty in ourselves? Shall we rather fasten ignorance upon God, and accuse him of blindness, to maintain our liberty?" *Discourses upon the Existence and Attributes of God* (Grand Rapids: Baker Book House, 1979), 450. The new Arminians, against the wisdom even of their Arminian ancestors, have given a fatally wrong answer to this question.

If any reader has gotten this far in this note you are probably the kind of person who would like to see the evidences for God's foreknowledge laid out in the way Charnock gives them. Among the ninety-two pages on God's knowledge, there is a section with this thesis: "God knows all future contingencies, that is, God knows all things that shall accidentally happen, or, as we say, by chance; and *he knows all the free motions of men's wills that shall be to the end of the world*" (p. 439, italics added). He lays out his compelling arguments biblically and logically in the following twenty-six pages.

For example, he shows that "the Scripture gives so large an account of contingents, predicted by God, no man can certainly prove that anything is unforeknown to him. It is as reasonable to think he knows every contingent, as that he knows some that lie as much hid from the eye of any creature, since there is no more difficulty to an infinite understanding. to know all, than to know some" (pp. 442-443). God predicted in advance, by name and before they were born, that Cyrus would help rebuild Jerusalem (Isaiah 44:28), and that Josiah would destroy Jeroboam's altar (1 Kings 13:2). "What," Charnock asks, "is more contingent, or is more the effect of the liberty of a man's will, than the names of their children?" (p. 441). Yet God foreknew this human choice of Cyrus's and Josiah's parents, not to mention their own choices to do what God had predicted they would do.

God predicted Pharaoh's choice to honor the butler and hang the baker (Genesis 40:13,19). He predicted the decisions of sinful men to pierce Jesus and not break a bone (Psalm 34:20; Zechariah 12:10; John 19:36-37) and the decisions to divide his garments (Psalm 22:18; John 19:24). He foreknew the decision of the Egyptians to oppress Israel (Genesis 15:13); and the decision of Pharaoh to harden his heart (Exodus 3:19); and the decision of Isaiah's hearers to refuse to hear his message (Isaiah 6:9); and the decision of the Israelites to rebel after Moses's death (Deuteronomy 31:16); and the decision of Judas to betray Jesus (John 6:64).

He foreknew that the Amorites' voluntary sin would be "full" by the fourth generation, and he promised Abraham that only after this filling up of their sins will his posterity come and inhabit the land (Genesis 15:16). Charnock asks the barbed question, "If Abraham had been a Socinian (we could say, neo-Arminian), to deny God's knowledge of the free acts of men, had he not a fine excuse for unbelief? What would his reply have been to God? 'Alas, Lord, this is not a promise to be relied upon, the Amorites' iniquity depends upon the acts of their free will, and such thou canst have no knowledge of; thou canst see no more than a likelihood of their iniquity being full, and therefore there is but a likelihood of thy performing the promise, and not a certainty!' Would not this be judged not only a saucy, but a blasphemous answer?" (p. 444). (For other texts describing God's foreknowledge of future voluntary acts see 1 Samuel 23:10-13; 2 Kings 13: 19; Jeremiah 38:17-20; Ezekiel 3:6-7. See also Matthew 11:21 for God's knowledge of decisions that certainly would have happened under different circumstances.)

I would only add one more observation concerning Clark Pinnock's rejection of the orthodox doctrine of God's omniscience. I have found it typical on several fronts that as people move away from a long-cherished view of truth, they try to make their move look more attractive by caricaturing the older view in various unappealing ways. For example, Pinnock describes the God I am presenting in this book as "having to control everything like an oriental despot" (p. x), and "forcing [people] to enact the pre-programmed decrees" (p. 20), and guiding history in a "coercive" way (p. 21), and being "virtually incapable of responsiveness" (p. 24). All this negative caricature is then put over against a God who works in terms remarkably amiable to the contemporary, modern mindset, for example, "giving salvation and eternal life *under the conditions of mutuality*" (p. xi, italics added). Pinnock attempts to give the impression that those who believe in the sovereign God of Jonathan Edwards and George Whitefield and William Carey and J. I. Packer relate to him in a kind of philosophical way that is fatalistic and impersonal, while the new Arminians enjoy "a dynamic personal relationship between God, the world, and God's human creatures" (p. 15).

In response to this I am tempted to ask if the vision of God that I have portrayed in *Desiring God: Meditations of a Christian Hedonist* (1986) and *The Pleasures of God* is a lifeless, fatalistic, impersonal vision of the God I love and worship. But I would rather respond by letting A. W. Tozer speak for thousands of us who know the God of total omniscience and total omnipotence, not as some lifeless philosophic idea, but as the all-satisfying Wonder and precious Father and Friend of our lives.

> Omnipotence is not a name given to the sum of all power but an
> attribute of a personal God whom we Christians believe to be the

Father of our Lord Jesus Christ and of all who believe on Him to life eternal. The worshiping man finds this knowledge a source of wonderful strength for his inner life. His faith rises to take the great leap upward into the fellowship of Him who can do whatever he wills to do, for whom nothing is hard or difficult because He possesses power absolute." *A. W. Tozer: An Anthology* (Camp Hill, Pennsylvania: Christian Publications, 1984), 94.

7. *Outlook*, xv, 1 (January 1978): 1.

8. For many more examples see Iain Murray, *The Puritan Hope* (Edinburgh: Banner of Truth Trust, 1971).

9. This was supposed to have been said by the elder John Ryland at the Northampton Association of Ministers. But his son, John Ryland, Jr., disputed that the story was true: "I never heard of it till I saw it in print, and cannot give credit to it at all." Quoted in Ibid., 280, note 14.

10. Quoted from his "Form of Agreement" written by him to guide the life of the Brethren of the Mission of Serampore. Quoted in Ibid., 145.

11. Quoted in Tom Wells, *A Vision for Missions* (Edinburgh: Banner of Truth Trust, 1974), 13.

12. Patrick Johnstone, *Operation World* (Kent, England: STL Books, 1987). The book may be ordered from Send The Light (Operation Mobilization), P.O. Box 28, Waynesboro, Georgia 30830, USA; or WEC Publications, Bulstrode, Gerrards Cross, Bucks SL9 8SZ, England.

13. Ibid., 21.

14. Similarly there are texts that tell us God is kept back from doing things he has a desire to do (e.g. Matthew 23:37) as well as texts that express God's grief over things he has done (e.g. Genesis 6:7; 1 Samuel 15:11).

15. Sereno Dwight, Memoirs, in *The Works of Jonathan Edwards*, ed. S. Dwight, 1 (1834: repr. ed., Edinburgh: Banner of Truth, 1974), clxxix.

16. It is true that Satan has remarkable freedom to "rule" this world. He is called the "ruler of this world" (John 12:31); and "the god of this world" (2 Corinthians 4:3-4); and "the prince of the power of the air" (Ephesians 2:2). He offers Jesus "all the kingdoms of the world" if he would bow down to him (Luke 4:5-7). Nevertheless God is clearly pictured in the Bible as holding sway over the world, even though Satan is called the "god of this world." For example, the authority of governing rulers in the world is from God (Romans 13:1) including Pilate's as he condemns Jesus (John 19:10-11); it is God who "removes kings and sets up kings" (Daniel 2:20-21); "he does according to his will in the host of heaven and among the inhabitants of the earth; and none can stay his hand or say to him, 'What are you doing?'" (Daniel 4:34-35); and "the king's heart is a stream of water in the hand of the Lord; he turns it wherever he will" (Proverbs 21:1; see also Ezra 1:1; 6:22).

Even though Luke 22:3 says that Satan entered into Judas and brought about the final betrayal to the Jews, nevertheless Peter asserts that behind Satan, God was guiding all things: "This Jesus [was] delivered up according to the definite plan and foreknowledge of God" (Acts 2:23); indeed, "Herod and Pontius Pilate, with the Gentiles and the peoples of Israel, [did] whatever [God's] hand and plan had predestined to take place" (Acts

4:27-28). But all these satanically influenced, and divinely guided leaders, failed in their opposition to God. For "the Lord brings the counsel of the nations to naught; he frustrates the plans of the peoples. The counsel of the Lord stands forever, the thoughts of his heart to all generations" (Psalm 33:10-11; Isaiah 43:13). Of every attack on God's people in the world it can be said, "Who has commanded and it came to pass, unless the Lord has ordained it? Is it not from the mouth of the Most High that good and calamity come?" (Lamentations 3:37-38). "Does evil befall a city, unless the Lord has done it?" (Amos 3:6). Yet we must always be aware that in his mysterious dealings with the world and with his own people the principle stands sure: "As for you, you meant evil against me; but God meant it for good" (Genesis 50:20).

Behind Satan's limited freedom to act is the hand of a sovereign God guiding all things for the good of his people (Romans 8:28). Compare the activity of God and Satan in these three pairs of texts: 1 Chronicles 21:1 and 2 Samuel 24:1; Luke 22:31 and 22:32; 2 Corinthians 4:4 and Romans 11:25.

The defeat and downfall of Satan is decisively accomplished in the death and resurrection of Jesus and will come to pass without fail. This is seen in Matthew 8:29; 16:18; 25:41; Luke 10:17-18; 11:21-22; John 17:15; 1 John 2:14; 3:8; 5:18; Romans 8:37-39; 16:20; Hebrews 2:14-15; Colossians 1:13; 2:15; and Revelation 20:10. Therefore in the present age we are called to resist Satan by our faith in the triumph over him that has been accomplished and assured by Jesus. This is seen in James 4:7; 1 Peter 5:8-9; Ephesians 6:10-13; Acts 26:18; 2 Timothy 2:24-26; Romans 16:19-20; and 2 Corinthians 11:3.

17. A fuller description of this proposed solution, especially as Jonathan Edwards worked it out, is given in *Desiring God*, 28-31.

18. This is the way Jonathan Edwards tackled the problem of how God and the saints in heaven will be happy in heaven for all eternity knowing that many millions of people are suffering in hell forever. It is not that suffering is pleasant to God and the saints in itself, but that the vindication of God's infinite holiness is cherished so deeply. See John Gerstner, *Jonathan Edwards on Heaven and Hell* (Grand Rapids: Baker Book House, 1980), 33-38.

19. I have tried to give a careful, exegetical account of this interpretation of Romans 9:22-23 in *The Justification of God* (Grand Rapids: Baker Book House, 1983). From the one passing reference to this study in *A Case for Arminianism The Grace of God, the Will of Man* (see note 5 above) it seems that serious attention has not been paid to the arguments I gave there. Pinnock has a legitimate concern that Romans 9 be interpreted with an awareness of Romans 10 and 11 in view. He said, "I believe that if Piper had moved forward in Romans beyond Romans 9, he would have encountered Paul's earnest prayer to God that the lost be saved (10:1) and his explanation of how it happens that any are actually included or excluded—through faith or the lack of it (11:20). Romans 9 must be read in the context of the larger context of Romans 9-11" (p. 29, note 10). I certainly don't want to disagree that Romans 9 must be read in its context. That is why, for example on pages 9-15 and 163-165, I discussed the limits of my focus and the structure of Romans 9-11. With regard to Pinnock's

two specific points: we are indeed included or excluded in salvation on the condition of faith. But that does not account for how one person comes to faith and not another. Nor does Paul's "heart's desire and prayer to God" for the salvation of the Jews in Romans 10:1 contradict the explicit statement that "a hardening has come [from God] upon part of Israel until [God lifts it after] the full number of the Gentiles [appointed by God for salvation] come in" (Romans 11:25).

*"May the glory of the Lord endure forever,
may the Lord rejoice in his works."*

Psalm 104:31

Chapter 3

The Pleasure of God in His Creation

The Cottage in Georgia Woods

Two nights ago I took a kitchen chair, put it in the grass beside the cottage and sat down to watch the moon. Ordinarily I live beside a busy freeway in downtown Minneapolis where the car lights and street lights hide the sky. But for these few weeks of vacation and study-leave I live with Noël and our sons on the outskirts of Barnesville, Georgia, on a piece of wooded property called "Brightwood." There are no street lights and no freeways. We sleep in a little cottage down the hill from where my wife's parents live. Just across the barbed wire fence there is a tiny "mobile study" about sixteen-by-eight-feet with windows on two sides. It sits in a clearing surrounded by two-hundred-year-old oak trees and eighty-foot arrow-straight Georgia pines mingled with maple and sweet gum trees. This is where I sit and write and, between paragraphs, stare out over the four-acre lake at the bottom of the hill.

This is a place made for eyes and ears and nose and skin, and a big heart. Almost every day I simply stop and stand still between the cottage and the study or between the lake and the woods or on the hill going up to "the house"—I feel so moved by the beauty of this amazing world of sight and sound and smell and touch that I want the moment to last long enough for all the beauty to soak in and to stay.

Coming down to the cottage from the house the other day I stopped at a rotting stump and broke off a piece of wood. It was surprisingly hard and snapped instead of crumbling. I looked and saw that the broken part was streaked and reddish and even moist. I put it to my nose and was jolted by the best cedar fragrance I have ever smelled. All the way to the cottage I kept inhaling this amazing aroma from a piece of wood that has probably been dead for ten years.

About fifty yards from the cottage toward the pecan orchard we are cultivating a worm bed. There's a pile of mulch with some old tires and cement bricks and a wooden door lying on the mulch to keep it moist underneath. We water it now and then with the hose. When we want some worms we lift up the door and turn over the tires and blocks and let the granddaddy longlegs scatter by the hundreds. Then I use the pitchfork to scrape off the top layer of mulch while my seven-year-old son spots the crawlers and wigglers, snatches them with his hand and puts them in a bucket. They are floppy and fast. But Barnabas is faster.

Three or four times a day I stoop down to go under the barbed wire fence between the study and the cottage. There is a big pink rope wrapped around the wire so that we won't get snagged. The metal post, holding the wire where we crawl through, is hollow. To our amazement we discovered that a little gray tree frog lives in the post. There is a little water in the hollow and he goes up or comes down in the post according to the heat and the light. He will let us walk right up to him as he sits on the edge of the post in the evening. It is clearly his place, because he has been there for several weeks now and nothing we do chases him away. This has made me wonder about all the other tree frogs that at night produce such an incredible whirring and buzzing and scratching in these peaceful woods (along with the crickets and cicadas). I have wondered if all the tree frogs are as possessive of their turf as he is. If so, there are thousands of little knotholes and crooks and branches all staked out and claimed by their own little tree frogs. It must be an amazing world of turf and territorialism up in those trees that completely escapes us humans.

Where we swim, at the north end of the lake, the fish eat

freckles and moles and chigger bites and other assorted blemishes on my back and legs. So I have to keep moving in the water, or go out in the deep part. The water is generally warm like a bath on the surface and wonderfully cool down under. But what I like best about the water is the way it looks from the window of my study. It is always moving peacefully. And early in the morning it catches the sun with ten thousand flashes and makes a constant display of crystal pieces moving on the surface. The leaves between me and the lake turn green-yellow-black-and-back-to-greenish-yellow as the breeze conspires with the reflections of the lake and the shadows to make the whole hillside burst with golden light and life.

To stay fit I run about three mornings a week—early enough to avoid the 95 degree heat we have been having most of this visit. I set my new stopwatch that I got for Father's Day and take off about 7:15. I run up Atlanta Street toward town, turn right on the two-block-long Main Street, run past the two banks, the First Methodist Church, and the library, and head out of town on the other side passing the old mansions with gigantic trees in their front yards that go back past the Civil War days to the times of the Revolution. I assume all the dogs in Barnesville have been attacked by humans because if they ever start barking at me all I have to do is stoop down like I am picking up a stick and they turn and run away. About twenty minutes out I make a U-turn and find a new way back for variety. It takes me past the cemetery. (How desolate is a cemetery without trees!) It takes me by First Baptist and then the pecan praline plant; then across the kudzu gully and the pasture where they keep Flash, the asthmatic horse. By now I am soaked in sweat. My legs are numb, so they don't hurt. But the enemy is the heat. Sweat pours off my head and down my face. (I always forget to wear the headband.) It is salty to the taste and burns my eyes. Some mornings my lungs and heart just can't get enough coolant and oxygen to the muscles to keep me going and I have to walk for a while. This morning it was cool enough to keep on going for about four-and-a-half miles without stopping. I even sprinted the last fifty yards to win an imaginary race. Ah, the glory of exhaustion and triumph!

Real Life Is Physical

The point of all this happy rambling is to say that real life is physical. It has to do with touch and smell and sight and sound and taste. It has to do with trees and stumps and fish and frogs and ants and birds and leaves and water and heat and slaw and iced tea and numb thighs and salty sweat and worms and granddaddy longlegs and ten thousand other creatures and sensations that come to us because God made a physical world.

As I said, two nights ago I took a kitchen chair and went outside at about 10:30 and sat down to watch the moon. It's been making a lower and lower arc over the southeastern hemisphere these last nights. This night it was just above the power lines that trespass with modern technology on this little Georgia paradise. The moon was almost full. The gray-orange face was pocked with beautiful gray blemishes. The constant caressing of the thin clouds could do nothing to cleanse the old man. His defects are too deep and too old.

I sat there and soaked again in the lavish beauty of the sky and the droning crickets and tree frogs, with the soft breeze on my face and the smell of pine; and I marveled that God, who is spirit and cannot be seen or touched, would make an ocean of physical reality that smells and shines and feels and tastes and sounds. As C. S. Lewis said,

> There is no use trying to be more spiritual than God. God never meant man to be a purely spiritual creature. That is why He uses material things like bread and wine to put the new life into us. We may think this rather crude and unspiritual. God does not: He invented eating. He likes matter. He invented it . . .
>
> I know some muddle-headed Christians have talked as if Christianity thought that sex, or the body, or pleasure, were bad in themselves. But they were wrong. Christianity is almost the only one of the great religions which thoroughly approves of the body—which believes that matter is good, that God Himself once took on a human body, and that some kind of body is going to be given to us even in Heaven and is going to be an essential part of our happiness, our beauty, and our energy.[1]

I admit that when I sit beneath the beauty of a Georgia moon or look out over an early morning lake or marvel at the age and strength of a great tree, I wrestle with doubts that this much joy should come from material things. I touched on this problem in *Desiring God* (pp. 136-137) and explained how I have resolved it in my own experience.[2] But I did not raise the problem for God himself.

So there are two questions that I want to raise in this chapter: 1) Does God take pleasure in his creation? And 2) if so, what becomes of the fullness of delight that he has in his Son? Why is God not an idolater to love the creation?

Does God Like the World?

The first question I would answer with a resounding, "Yes!" God *does* take pleasure in his creation. How do we know this? Genesis 1 describes for us not only the fact of a well-ordered creation by God, but also God's response to his creation. Six times God stands back, as it were, and takes stock of his creation. Each time the text says, "And God saw that it was *good*" (verses 4, 10, 12, 18, 21, 25). And when all was finished and man and woman were created in his own image, it says, "And God saw everything that he had made, and behold, it was *very* good."

I take this to mean at least that God was delighted with his work. He approved of it. He was glad that he had done it. When he looked at it, it gave him pleasure. It is as though he said, "Yes, that's it. That will do just fine. That's exactly right." And we get the clue early on in the story that the root of his delight in creation has to do with imaging forth his own glory, because only after he created man and woman *in his image* did God add the word "very" to the word "good."

We can see the joy of God in his creation best perhaps in Psalm 104. It is a song to express God's exuberance over what he has made. The key verse is verse 31:

> May the glory of the Lord endure for ever,
> may the Lord *rejoice* in his works.

This is not a prayer for something that might not happen, as though I were to say, "May Noël make spaghetti for supper tonight." The psalmist does not mean: "Oh, I hope God will rejoice in his works, but I am not sure he will." If that were the meaning then the first line of the verse would have to have the same sense: "Oh, I hope God's glory will endure for ever, but I am not sure it will." But that is surely not what he means. The rock solid confidence of the whole Bible is that the glory of the Lord will not only endure forever but that it will cover the whole earth like the waters cover the sea (Numbers 14:21; see also Habakkuk 2:14).

The psalmist is not praying that an uncertainty might come to pass. He is exulting in a certainty that *will* come to pass, and indeed has come to pass and is taking place right now. There is no doubt behind the shout, "May the glory of the Lord endure for ever!" And there is no doubt behind the shout: "May the Lord rejoice in his works!"

So the answer to the first question is *yes!* God does take pleasure in his creation, because this whole psalm shows (as we shall see) that the "works" in mind are the works of creation—things like water and clouds and wind and mountains and thunder and springs and wild asses and birds and grass and cattle and wine and bread and cedars and wild goats and badgers and rocks and young lions and sea monsters. God delights in all the work of his hands.

The Exultation of Heaven at Creation

I love the picture that God paints for Job when he is interrogating Job about creation. In Job 38:4-7, God queries,

> Where were you when I laid the foundation of the earth?
> Tell me, if you have understanding.
> Who determined its measurements — surely you know!
> Or who stretched the line upon it?
> On what were its bases sunk,
> or who laid its cornerstone,
> *when the morning stars sang together,*
> *and all the sons of God (angels) shouted for joy?*

Do you see the picture? No man was there. So Job should humble himself and realize there are a few things he (and we!) may not understand. But in making this point God cannot resist, it seems, mentioning what the mood of heaven was like at the moment of creation. "All the sons of God shouted for joy." All the angels had evidently been created before the universe. And it is not hard to see why. God meant there to be an audience when he created the world. I am sure he said, "Watch this!" when he spoke the galaxies into existence. Imagine the awe and wonder that exploded among the angels. They had never seen or even imagined matter. They are all "ministering *spirits*" (Hebrews 1:14) and have no material bodies as we do. When God brought material stuff into existence with all its incredible variety and utterly unheard of qualities of sight and sound and smell and touch and taste, this was totally unknown to the angels. God had made it all up. It was not like the unveiling of a new painting made of all the colors and paints we are all familiar with. It was absolutely, totally, unimaginably new! And the response of the sons of God was to shout for joy.

Now I admit that God does not say explicitly in this text that he himself shouted for joy. But do you suppose that God sat by with a blank face and no emotion, while millions of holy angels shouted for joy over his creation? Something would be very out of sync in heaven if that were true. I think God told Job about the joy of the "*sons* of God" because sons get their dispositions from their Father. If the finite sons were shouting for joy over the greatness and wonder of the Father's creation, you can be sure that the Father's delight both in the creation and in the sons' joy was immense.

Now the question is, *why*? Why does God have pleasure in his creation? There are two reasons why this question is important to me.

Should the Son Be Jealous?

One is that I feel compelled to explain why this pleasure God has in his creation is not an act of idolatry. Why is it not a dishonor to the Son of God? Why shouldn't the Son be jealous? Should the Father really share his affection with the world? Should he not be totally satisfied in the beauty of his own perfections reflected back to him in the person of his Son?

The other reason for asking why God delights in his creation is that we need to know this before the delight itself can tell us very much about God's character. Two people can desire the same thing for such different reasons that one is honorable and the other is perverse. (One man might want grain to make bread; another might want it to make booze.) Our aim is to see the true glory and worth of God. And our assumption is that "the worth and excellency of a soul is to be measured by the object of its love." So we want to see what God loves—what he has pleasure in. But this assumes that we understand why God loves a thing. Unless we know why God has pleasure in creation we will not be able to draw any clear conclusions about what this pleasure implies about God's worth and excellence.

I will try to sum up my answer to this second question in five statements based mainly on Psalm 104 as well as some other parts of Scripture. These five statements about why God delights in his creation are not really five separate reasons because they overlap so much. But they each express a little differently the basic reason. It helps to appreciate the true beauty of a precious stone when you turn it in the light and look at it from different angles. And we will see that the answer to this second question also answers the first, namely, why God's love for nature is not idolatry.

What Day and Night Proclaim

First, God rejoices in his works because his works express his glory. I see this first in Psalm 104:31.

> May the *glory* of the Lord endure for ever;
> May the Lord rejoice in his works.

What these two lines show is that God enjoys his works because they express his glory. In other words, the two halves of this verse are related something like this: "As long as the *glory* of the Lord endures in his works, God will indeed *rejoice* in his works." Or you could say, "May the glory of the Lord endure for ever, *so that* the Lord may rejoice in his works."

I find this idea confirmed in Psalm 19:1-2:

> The heavens are telling the *glory of God*;
> and the firmament proclaims his handiwork.
> Day to day pours forth speech,
> and night to night declares knowledge.

It is clear that there is one main message creation has to communicate to human beings, namely, the glory of God. Not primarily the glory of creation, but the glory of God. The glory of creation and the glory of God are as different as the love poem and the love, the painting and the landscape, the ring and the marriage. It would be a great folly and a great tragedy if a man loved his wedding band more than he loved his bride. But that is what Romans 1:19-23 says has happened. Human beings have fallen in love with the echo of God's excellency in creation and lost the ability to hear the incomparable original shout of love.

> What can be known about God is plain to them, because God has shown it to them. Ever since the creation of the world his invisible nature, namely, his eternal power and deity, has been clearly perceived in the things that have been made. So they are without excuse; for although they knew God *they did not glorify him as God* or give thanks to him, but they became futile in their thinking and their senseless minds were darkened. Claiming to be wise, they became fools, and *exchanged the glory of the immortal God* for images resembling mortal man or birds or animals or reptiles.

The message of creation is this: *there is a great God of glory and power and generosity behind all this awesome universe; you belong to him; he is patient with you in sustaining your rebellious life; turn and bank your hope on him and delight yourself in him, not his handiwork.* Day pours forth the "speech" of that message to all that will listen in the day, speaking with blindingly bright sun and blue sky and clouds and untold shapes and colors of all things visible. Night pours forth the "knowledge" of the same message to all who will listen at night, speaking with great dark voids and summer moons and countless stars and strange sounds and cool breezes and northern lights. Day and night are saying one thing: God is glorious! God is glorious! God is glorious!

This is the most basic reason that God delights in his creation. In creation he sees the reflection of his own glory. This is why he is not an idolater when he has pleasure in the work of his hands.

Creation and Christ

But what about the Son of God? Does this mean that the creation is in competition with the Son for the affection of the Father? Remember that the Son too is called the radiance of God's glory (Hebrews 1:3). Does God delight partly in the Son and partly in the creation? Does the creation rob the Son of any of the Father's delight? Should the Son be jealous of the creation?

No. Before creation the Father and the Son rejoiced in each other with overflowing satisfaction. That was the point of chapter 1. When the time came for creation, the Bible says that *both* the Father *and* the Son were active in the work of creation. The Father had not wearied of the Son and decided to create another enjoyment to make up for his disappointment with the Son. This is plain from Scripture:

> For us there is one God, the Father, from whom are all things and for whom we exist, and one Lord, Jesus Christ, through whom are all things and through whom we exist. (1 Corinthians 8:6)
>
> By [Christ] all things were created. (Colossians 1:16)
>
> In these last days [God] has spoken to us by a Son, whom he appointed the heir of all things, through whom also he created the world. (Hebrews 1:2)
>
> In the beginning was the Word and the Word was with God and the Word was God. All things were made through him and without him was not anything made that was made. (John 1:1,3)

In other words, the work of creation is not merely the work of the Father as though he had to satisfy a need that the Son couldn't meet. Nor was creation merely the work of the Son as though he had to satisfy some need that the Father couldn't meet. Instead it was the work of both of them together. And the impulse was not deficiency of delight but a spilling over of mutual joy. Jonathan Edwards expresses it like this: "Surely it is no argument of the emptiness or deficiency of a fountain, that it is inclined to overflow."[3] If someone should ask whether God was less happy before the Father and the Son released their joyful creative energy, Edwards answers, "Though these communications of God [in creation]—these exercises, operations, and expressions of his glorious perfections, which God rejoices in—are in time; yet his joy in them is without beginning or change. They were always equally present in the divine mind."[4]

So when the Bible teaches that creation expresses the glory of God, we must not think merely of the glory of the Father or the glory of the Son, but rather the glory that they have together. And the glory that they have together is that overflowing mutual joy in each other's perfections. So creation is an expression of the overflow of that life and joy that the Father and the Son have in each other.[5] There is no competition or jealousy in the Godhead. The Son and Father are equally glorified in creation, because creation is the overflow of gladness that they have in each other.

So the first and most basic statement we can make about why God rejoices in his work of creation is that creation is an expression of his glory.

No Humans Hear the Praise of the Deeps

Second, God rejoices in the works of creation because they praise him. In Psalm 148 the psalmist calls on creation itself to praise the Lord:

> Praise him, sun and moon,
>   praise him, all you shining stars!
> Praise him, you highest heavens,
>   and you waters above the heavens!
> Let them praise the name of the Lord!
>   For he commanded and they were created . . .
> Praise the Lord from the earth,
>   you sea monsters and all deeps (verses 3-5,7).

Again in Psalm 103:22 David cries out,

> Bless the Lord, all his works,
> In all places of his dominion.

What does this mean? We might say that sun and moon and stars praise God by testifying to us about God. That would be true, as we have just seen (Romans 1:19-23). But what about Psalm 148:7? "Praise the Lord you sea monsters *and all deeps!*" What human is in the deeps to hear this praise?

One of my favorite poems is "Elegy Written in a Country Churchyard," written by Thomas Gray in 1751. One of the stanzas says,

> Full many a gem of purest ray serene,
>   The dark unfathomed caves of ocean bear:
> Full many a flower is born to blush unseen,
>   And waste its sweetness on the desert air.

Gray had been moved by the thought that on the bottom of the ocean there were beautiful gems that no human eye would ever see, and that in distant deserts millions of flowers would bloom, blush with vivid colors, give off a sweet fragrance and never be touched or seen or smelled by anybody but God!

God, it seems, wanted Job to think about this very thing. He asked him, "Have you entered into the springs of the sea, or walked in the recesses of the deep? . . . Who has cleft a channel for the torrents of rain, and a way for the thunderbolt, to bring rain on a land where no man is, on the desert in which there is no man . . . Do you know when the mountain goats bring forth? Do you observe the calving of the hinds?" (Job 38:16,25-26; 39:1) In other words God was claiming that he alone sees the deeps of the ocean and brings rain in the desert where no man is and watches, like a midwife, at the birth of every mountain goat and wild deer.

This is what moves the psalmist in Psalm 148:7, "Praise the Lord you sea monsters and all deeps!" He doesn't even know what is in all the deeps of the sea! So the praise of the deeps is not merely what they can testify to man. Creation praises God by simply being what it was created to be in all its incredible variety. And since most of the creation is beyond the awareness of mankind (in the reaches of space, and in the heights of mountains and at the bottom of the sea) it wasn't created merely to serve purposes that have to do with us. It was created for the enjoyment of God.

Ranger Rick *Is a Theological Journal*

I have a confession to make. *Ranger Rick* is one of my favorite magazines. When it arrives in our house with the address, "Piper Boys," I am one of the first Piper boys to take it to the couch. The reason is simple: in spite of its utterly unwarranted and unnecessary evolutionary bias, it inspires more praise in me than most other journals. It is a monthly record of man's discovery of incredible phenomena in nature that up till recently have only been enjoyed by God for thousands of years.

For example, I read about the European water spider that lives at the bottom of a lake, but breathes air.[6] It comes to the top of the water, does a somersault on the surface and catches a bubble of air. Then it holds the bubble over the breathing holes in the middle of its body while it swims to the bottom of the lake and spins a silk web among the seaweed. It goes up and brings down bubble after bubble until a little balloon of air is formed under its silk web where it can live and eat and mate. When I read that, there was a moment of worship on our living room couch. Doesn't that make you want to shout, "O Lord, how manifold are your works! In wisdom you have made them all; the earth is full of your creatures" (Psalm 104:24)?

I sit there with my mouth open and I think God smiles and says, "Yes, John, and I have been enjoying that little piece of art since before the days of Abraham. And if you only knew how many millions of other wonders there are beyond your sight that I behold with gladness every day!"

Consider sea monsters that we virtually never see. Psalm 104:25-26 says,

> Yonder is the sea, great and wide,
>> which teems with things innumerable, living things
>>> both small and great.
> There go the ships,
>> and Leviathan which you formed to sport in it.

Why did God create great sea monsters? Just to play, to frolic in the ocean where no man can see, but only God. The teeming ocean declares the glory of God, and praises him a thousand miles from any human eye. That's the second reason God rejoices in his works.

Wisdom Beyond Comprehension

Third, God rejoices in the works of creation because they reveal his incomparable wisdom. This is the point of Psalm 104:24.

> O Lord, how manifold are your works!
> *In wisdom* you have made them all;
> the earth is full of your creatures.

"*In wisdom* you have made them all!" In other words the Lord delights in the expressions of his wisdom. This universe is a masterpiece of wisdom and order. Or if you just take a part of it, like the human body—what an amazing work of knowledge and wisdom! Who can fathom the human brain and the mystery of how mind and body work together? Whether you look near or far, whether you look for bigness or smallness, the wonders of nature stagger the mind with the wisdom woven through it all.

Did you know that there are ten thousand known species of diatoms? In a teaspoon of ordinary lake water there may be a million of these tiny invisible plants. And what are they doing while entertaining God with their microscopic beauty? (I know they are beautiful because Ranger Rick had magnified color photographs!) What are they doing? They are making tons and tons of oxygen so that the animals in the water can breathe! The world is full of the wisdom of God!

> O Lord, how manifold are your works!
> In wisdom you have made them all.

The psalmist marveled at how everything works together so wisely.

> You cause the grass to grow for the cattle,
> and plants for man to cultivate,
> that he may bring forth food from the earth. (Psalm 104:14)

What a wonderful experience it is when God grants us a moment in which we don't take anything for granted, but see the world as though it was invented yesterday. How we would marvel at the wisdom of God. We should pray for the eyes of children again, when they saw everything for the first time. William Quayle reminded me of this recently in his lively book, *The Pastor-Preacher*. He said, "A cow has pretty eyes, as quiet as a pool of quiet water, but uneventful eyes. There is no touch of wonder in their dreamless depths. The eyes are therefore soulless. A child's eyes are fairly lightning. They are to see things: they are the windows of the brain, and bewilder like a play of swords of fire."[7] These are the eyes we need to the see the unending wisdom of God running through all the world. There will be no exhausting the understanding of God. We will be making new discoveries for all eternity.

> The Lord is the everlasting God,
> the Creator of the ends of the earth,
> He does not faint or grow weary,
> *his understanding is unsearchable* (Isaiah 40:28).

Power without Equal

Fourth, God rejoices in the works of creation because they reveal his incomparable power. In Isaiah 40:26 Isaiah looks up at the star-filled sky—perhaps on a night like I remember on a mountain in Utah in September 1968, when the sky was literally a sheet of light, and star could not be distinguished from star — he looks up and says,

> Lift up your eyes on high and see:
>   who created these?
> He who brings out their host by number,
>   calling them all by name;
> by the greatness of his might,
>   and because he is strong in power
>   not one is missing.

If Isaiah was stunned at the power of God to create and name and sustain every star in the heaven that he could see, what would be his worship today if he were shown that the nearest of those stars in his sky, Alpha Centauri and Proxima Centauri are twenty-five million million miles away? And what would be his worship if he knew that what he was seeing in his night sky was a tiny patch of our galaxy which has in it a hundred billion stars, and that beyond our galaxy there are millions of galaxies?

It seems in these days that God is enjoying keeping the astronomers on the edge of their seats with new glimpses of his power. In the fall of 1989, newspapers reported the discovery by two Harvard astronomers of a "Great Wall" of galaxies stretching hundreds of millions of light years across the known universe. The wall is supposedly some five hundred million light years long, two hundred million light years wide and fifteen million light years thick. In case your high school astronomy has grown fuzzy, a light year is a little less than six trillion (6,000,000,000,000) miles. This Great Wall consists of more than fifteen thousand galaxies, each with millions of stars, and was described as the "largest single coherent structure seen so far in nature."[8]

I say "was described" because three months later in February 1990, God opened another little window for tiny man to marvel again, and the newspapers reported that astronomers have discovered more than a dozen evenly distributed clumps of galaxies stretching across vast expanses of the heavens, suggesting a structure to the universe that is so regular and immense that it defies current theories of cosmic origins. The newly found pattern of galactic matter dwarfs the extremely long sheet of galaxies, dubbed the "great wall" (now written without caps!), that was reported in November 1989 to be the largest structure in the universe. They now say the great wall is, in fact, merely one of the closest of these clumps, or regions, that contain very high concentrations of galaxies.[9]

What is this universe but the lavish demonstration of the incredible, incomparable, unimaginable exuberance and wisdom and power and greatness of God! What a God he must be!

God and God Alone

Fifth, God rejoices in the works of creation because they point us beyond themselves to God himself. God means for us to be stunned and awed by his work of creation. But not for its own sake. He means for us to look at his creation and say: If the mere work of his fingers (just his fingers! Psalm 8:3) is so full of wisdom and power and grandeur and majesty and beauty, what must this God be like in himself!

These are but the backside of his glory, as it were, darkly seen through a glass. What will it be to see the Creator himself! Not his works! A billion galaxies will not satisfy the human soul. God and God alone is the soul's end. Jonathan Edwards expressed it like this:

> The enjoyment of God is the only happiness with which our souls can be satisfied. To go to heaven, fully to enjoy God, is infinitely better than the most pleasant accommodations here. . . . [These] are but shadows; but God is the substance. These are but scattered beams; but God is the sun. These are but streams; but God is the ocean."[10]

This is why Psalm 104 comes to a close like this with a focus on God himself:

> May the glory of the Lord endure for ever,
>   may the Lord rejoice in his works,
> who looks on the earth and it trembles,
>   who touches the mountains and they smoke!
> I will sing to the Lord as long as I live;
>   I will sing praise to my God while I have being.
> May my meditation be pleasing to him,
>   for I rejoice *in the Lord* (vv. 31-34).

In the end it will not be the seas or the mountains or the canyons or the water spiders or the clouds or the great galaxies that fill our hearts to breaking with wonder and fill our mouths with eternal praise. It will be God himself. This is why God has pleasure in his creation. It is the overflow of the satisfaction that God the Father and God the Son have in each other and therefore the revelation and proclamation of God's glory day and night.

Clyde Kilby's Resolutions

As I close this chapter I recall a lecture given by Clyde Kilby in Minneapolis on October 22, 1976, at the First Covenant Church. I attended mainly to see him because he had been one of my favorite teachers at Wheaton College where I was a literature major in his department. I recall the evening because what he said there is so relevant to what I am trying to do in this chapter. One of the things I would like to happen because of this chapter is that readers would open their eyes even wider to the glory of God in the world around them. Kilby had eyes. Oh, what eyes he had! He read to us eleven resolutions he had made for staying alive to God's glory. I will only mention one in closing.[11] He said, "I shall sometimes look back at the freshness of vision I had in childhood and try, at least for a little while, to be, in the words of Lewis Carroll, the 'child of the pure unclouded brow, and dreaming eyes of wonder.' "

One of the tragedies of growing up is that we get used to things. It has its good side of course, since irritations may cease to be irritations. But there is immense loss when we get used to the redness of the rising sun, and the roundness of the moon, and the whiteness of the snow, the wetness of rain, the blueness of the sky, the buzzing of bumble bees, the stitching of crickets, the invisibility of wind, the unconscious constancy of heart and diaphragm, the weirdness of noses and ears, the number of the grains of sand on a thousand beaches, the never-ceasing crash crash crash of countless waves, and ten million kingly-clad flowers flourishing and withering in woods and mountain valleys where no one sees but God. I invite you, with Clyde Kilby, to seek a "freshness of vision," to look, as though it were the first time, not at the empty product of accumulated millennia of aimless evolutionary accidents (which no child ever dreamed of), but at the personal handiwork of an infinitely strong, creative, and exuberant Artist who made the earth and the sea and everything in them. I invite you to believe (like the children believe) "that today, this very day, some stroke is being added to the cosmic canvas that in due course you shall understand with joy as a stroke made by the Architect who calls Himself Alpha and Omega" (note 11, resolution 10).

Notes

1. Quoted from *Mere Christianity*, in *A Mind Awake: An Anthology of C. S. Lewis*, ed. Clyde Kilby (New York Harcourt, Brace and World, 1968), 210-211.
2. The problem was raised there especially by the Psalms. For example Psalm 73:25-26 says,

> Whom have I in heaven but you?
> And there is nothing upon earth
> that I desire besides you.
> My flesh and my heart may fail,
> but God is the strength of my heart
> and my portion for ever.

And Psalm 27:4 says,

> One thing have I asked of the Lord,
> that will I seek after;
> that I may dwell in the house of the Lord
> all the days of my life,
> to behold the beauty of the Lord,
> and to inquire in his temple.

These Psalms seem to say that a true saint will be so filled with joy in God that the joys of material things, like moonlit nights, will not be able to add anything. They seem to say that the only joy we should have is joy in God, not in the creation. But St. Augustine said something that was very helpful in putting it all together. He prayed like this: "He loves Thee too little who loves anything together with Thee which he loves not for thy sake." Quoted from "Confessions," in *Documents of the Christian Church*, ed. Henry Bettenson (London: Oxford University Press, 1967), 54. What Augustine showed me was that there is a way to delight in God's creation that is not for its sake but for God's sake. Discovering how to do that is the secret of not committing idolatry on moonlit nights and beside sparkling morning lakes and over bi-yearly catfish feasts.
3. Jonathan Edwards, *Dissertation Concerning the End for Which God Created*

the World, in *The Works of Jonathan Edwards*, 1 (Edinburgh: Banner of Truth Trust, 1974), 102.

4. Ibid.

5. It would not be wrong, I think, to say that this is why the Bible says, "The Spirit of God was moving over the face of the waters" (Genesis 1:2). The Spirit is the life and joy of the Father and the Son, standing forth with so much of the perfection and fullness of each of them that he too is a divine Person. See chapter 1, note 23.

6. Ellen Holtzen, "Home is a Bubble," *Ranger Rick*, January 1987, 14-15.

7. William A. Quayle, *The Pastor-Preacher*, ed. Warren W. Wiersbe (Grand Rapids: Baker Book House, 1979), 76-77.

8. *Minneapolis Star Tribune*, 18 November 1989, 13A.

9. *Minneapolis Star Tribune*, 23 February 1990, 2A.

10. "The Christian Pilgrim," in *The Works of Jonathan Edwards*, 2 (Banner), 244.

11. The other ten of Kilby's resolutions are worthy of serious reflection:

(1) At least once every day I shall look steadily up at the sky and remember that I, a consciousness with a conscience, am on a planet traveling in space with wonderfully mysterious things above and about me.

(2) Instead of the accustomed idea of a mindless and endless evolutionary change to which we can neither add nor subtract, I shall suppose the universe guided by an Intelligence which, as Aristotle said of Greek drama, requires a beginning, a middle, and an end. I think this will save me from the cynicism expressed by Bertrand Russell before his death, when he said: "There is darkness without, and when I die there will be darkness within. There is no splendour, no vastness anywhere, only triviality for a moment, and then nothing."

(3) I shall not fall into the falsehood that this day, or any day, is merely another ambiguous and plodding twenty-four hours, but rather a unique event, filled, if I so wish, with worthy potentialities. I shall not be fool enough to suppose that trouble and pain are wholly evil parentheses in my existence but just as likely ladders to be climbed toward moral and spiritual manhood.

(4) I shall not turn my life into a thin straight line which prefers abstractions to reality. I shall know what I am doing when I abstract, which of course I shall often have to do.

(5) I shall not demean my own uniqueness by envy of others. I shall stop boring into myself to discover what psychological or social categories I might belong to. Mostly I shall simply forget about myself and do my work.

(6) I shall open my eyes and ears. Once every day I shall simply stare at a tree, a flower, a cloud, or a person. I shall not then be concerned at all to ask what they are but simply be glad that they are. I shall joyfully allow them the mystery of what Lewis calls their "divine, magical, terrifying, and ecstatic" existence.

(7) I shall follow Darwin's advice and turn frequently to imaginative things such as good literature and good music, preferably, as Lewis suggests, an old book and timeless music.

(8) I shall not allow the devilish onrush of this century to usurp all my energies but will instead, as Charles Williams suggested, "fulfill the moment as the moment." I shall try to live well just now because the only time that exists is now.

(9) If for nothing more than the sake of a change of view, I shall assume my ancestry to be from the heavens rather than from the caves.

(10) Even if I turn out to be wrong, I shall bet my life on the assumption that this world is not idiotic, neither run by an absentee landlord, but that today, this very day, some stroke is being added to the cosmic canvas that in due course I shall understand with joy as a stroke made by the Architect who calls himself Alpha and Omega.

"For the Lord will not cast away his people,
for his great name's sake,
because it has pleased the Lord
to make you a people for himself."

1 Samuel 12:22

Chapter 4

The Pleasure of God
in His Fame

A few months before his death at age twenty-nine in 1747, David Brainerd, the missionary to the Indians in New England, wrote to a young ministerial candidate, "Give yourself to prayer, to reading and meditation on divine truths: strive to penetrate to the bottom of them and never be content with a superficial knowledge."[1] It was good advice. And not just for pastors, because at the bottom of things you find a granite foundation of hope for victory in the global mission of the church. You find a God whose commitment to the cause of his people is grounded not in his people but in himself. His passion to save and to purify feeds itself not from the shallow soil of our value but from the infinite depth of his own. What we will see as this chapter moves forward is that the time it takes to dig deep into the heart of God is often repaid by striking a vein of gold or an oil gusher. The effort is repaid with joy and power beyond all expectation.

Did You Mean to Say "Name" or "Fame"?

Over the first draft of this chapter I put the title, "The Pleasure of God in His Name." I still think that would be a thoroughly biblical title. Dozens of times Scripture says that God does things "for his name's sake." But if you ask what is really moving the heart of God in that statement (and many like it), the answer is that God delights in having his name known. The first and most important prayer that can be prayed is, "Hallowed be thy name." This is a request to God that he would work to cause people to hallow his name. God loves to have more and more people "hallow" his name, and so his Son teaches Christians to put their prayers in line with this great passion of the Father. "Lord, cause more and more people to hallow your name," that is, esteem, admire, respect, cherish, honor, and praise his name. It is basically a missionary prayer. So the more I thought about it the more it seemed right to put the stress on fame and not just name. Fame means well-known name. His name is who he really is, especially, who he is for us.[2] The point of the present chapter is that he delights in being known for who he really is. He loves a worldwide reputation. That's why I will talk much about the name of God in this chapter, but have chosen the title, "The Pleasure of God in His Fame."

A Story of God-centered Hope for Sinners

We begin with a story about human sin and divine mercy. It is a story I love because it is so full of God-centered hope. It puts on the table immediately the great news that God's love for his fame is the foundation of his mercy to desperate sinners. The key sentence in this story is 1 Samuel 12:22, "The Lord will not cast away his people, for his great name's sake." Here everyone can see immediately that God's mercy ("The Lord will not cast away his people") is grounded in his allegiance to his name ("for his great name's sake"). But to feel the full force of this God-centered gospel truth, we need to get the story before us.

The period of the Old Testament judges (Gideon, Deborah, Samson, and the rest) is past. Samuel is now on the scene as a kind of bridge between the judges and the kings and the prophets. Until now Israel had no king. But now the chaos of the land, with everyone doing what was right in his own eyes (Judges 21:25), drove Israel to demand that Samuel give them a king.

You can see this in 1 Samuel 8. Samuel is old. His sons Joel and Abijah have become judges in his place and are corrupt. So the elders of Israel say to Samuel (in verse 5): "Behold, you are old and your sons do not walk in your ways; now appoint for us a king to govern us like all the nations." Samuel is displeased and goes to God for counsel. But surprisingly God says to Samuel, "Hearken to the voice of the people in all that they say to you; for they have not rejected you, but they have rejected me from being king over them" (8:7). But it is not that simple. God also says to Samuel, "Only, you shall solemnly warn them, and show them the ways of the king who shall reign over them" (8:9).

So Samuel tells the people how their king will take their sons and daughters into his service and demand a tenth of all they have for his purposes. But he can't talk the people out of their desire for a king. They give their final response in verses 19 and 20: "No! But we will have a king over us, that we also may be like all the nations, and that our king may govern us and go out before us and fight our battles." So Samuel anoints Saul king over Israel (chapter 10). Then in chapter 11 Saul defeats Nahash and the Ammonites, and Samuel calls all the people together at Gilgal to renew the kingdom—to give Saul an official installation.

Samuel gives an inauguration speech in chapter 12, but it turned out to be a very unusual inauguration speech—not what the people wanted to hear! Samuel does have some astonishingly good news for them. But before he tells them the good news he wants to make sure that they know and feel the magnitude of the evil they have done in wanting to be like the other nations and not being satisfied with God as their king (1 Samuel 8:5). So in 12:17 he says, "Is it not wheat harvest today? I will call upon the Lord, that he may send thunder and rain; and *you shall know and see that your wickedness is great*, which you have done in the sight of the Lord, in asking for yourselves a king." When God sends thunder and rain, the people fear and confess their sins: "Pray for your servants to the Lord your God, that we may not die; for we have added to all our sins this evil, to ask for ourselves a king" (12:19).

When the people have been brought to fear and repent of their sin, then comes the good news: "Fear not; you have done all this evil, yet do not turn aside from following the Lord, but serve the Lord with all your heart; and do not turn aside after vain things which cannot profit or save, for they are vain" (12:20-21). This is the gospel—even though you have sinned greatly, and terribly dishonored the Lord, even though you now have a king which it was a sin to get, even though there is no undoing that sin or its painful consequences that are yet to come, nevertheless there is a future and a hope. Fear not! Fear not! Then comes the great ground of the gospel in verse 22: "For the Lord will not cast away his people, *for his great name's sake*, because it has pleased the Lord to make you a people *for himself*."

Why Won't He Cast Them Away?

What is the basis of the fearlessness they should have according to this verse? First of all it is the promise that God will not cast them away. In spite of their sin in wanting a king, the verse says, "The Lord will not cast away his people." But that is not the deepest foundation of hope and fearlessness. *Why* will God not cast away his people? The answer Samuel gives is that God will not cast away his people "for his great name's sake." The deepest reason given for God's commitment to his people is his prior commitment to his own name. The rock bottom foundation of our forgiveness and our fearlessness and our joy is the commitment of God to his own great name. First, he is committed to act for his own name's sake. And then, *for that reason*, he is committed to act for his people.

How does Samuel make that connection for us in 1 Samuel 12:22? Why is it that God's commitment to his own name results in not casting away his people? How does his commitment to his name produce a commitment to this people?

The last part of verse 22 gives the answer: "Because it has pleased the Lord to make you a people *for himself*." Or to put it another way, it was God's good pleasure to join you to himself in such a way that his name is at stake in your destiny. Or again: it was God's good pleasure to possess you in such a way that what becomes of you reflects upon his name. Therefore, *for his name's sake*, he will not cast you away.

What starts to become clear is that 1 Samuel 12:22 is not just the basis for God's pleasure in his fame (this chapter), but also for his pleasure in election (chapter 5). These two pleasures are very closely related. So let me just point ahead to the next chapter on

God's pleasure in election and then focus on his pleasure in his fame. Samuel said, "It has pleased the Lord to make you a people for himself." In other words, it was God's pleasure to choose you, to elect you from all the peoples on the earth, and make you his own special possession. We will see that this election of Israel was free and unconditional, and that it was God's delight to exercise his freedom in this way.

But 1 Samuel 12:22 shows that God's election of Israel is not God's main goal, but is a *means* to the main goal of his name being honored and his fame being spread. It says he chose Israel *for himself*: "It pleased the Lord to make you a people *for himself.*" He chose them as a means of *making a name for himself.* Thus Samuel says that God will not cast them away *"for his great name's sake."* Therefore, beneath and behind God's delight in choosing a people (which we will deal with in chapter 5), there is a more basic delight, namely, the pleasure God has in his own name (which is what we are dealing with now).

The Glory of God Gone Public

What does that mean—that God has pleasure in his name? We have seen that, even though it might not mean anything different than God's pleasure in his own intrinsic glory, it often means something slightly different, namely, the glory of God gone public. In other words, the name of God often refers to his reputation, his fame, his renown. This is the way we use the word "name" when we say someone is making a name for himself. Or we sometimes say, that's a "name" brand. We mean a brand with a big reputation.

This is what I think Samuel means in 1 Samuel 12:22 when he says that God made Israel a people "for himself" and that he would not cast Israel off "for his great name's sake." This way of thinking about God's zeal for his name is confirmed in many other passages. For example, in Jeremiah 13:11 God describes Israel as a waistcloth, or belt, God chose to highlight his glory, but which turned out to be temporarily unusable.

> For as the waistcloth clings to the loins of a man, so I made the whole house of Israel and the whole house of Judah cling to me,

says the Lord, that they might be for me a people, *a name, a praise, and a glory*, but they would not listen.

Why was Israel chosen and made the garment of God? That it might be a "name, a praise, and a glory." The words "praise" and "glory" in this context tell us that "name" means "fame" or "renown" or "reputation." God chose Israel so that the people would make a reputation for him. God says in Isaiah 43:21 that Israel is "the people whom I formed for myself *that they might declare my praise.*" And when the church came to see itself in the New Testament as the true Israel, Peter described God's purpose for us like this: "You are a chosen race . . . *that you may declare the wonderful deeds of him who called you out of darkness into his marvelous light*" (1 Peter 2:9). In other words, Israel and the church are chosen by God to make a name for him in the world.

David teaches the same thing in one of his prayers in 2 Samuel 7:23. He says that what sets Israel apart from all the other peoples is that God has dealt with them in such a way as to make a name for himself.

> What other nation on earth is like your people Israel, whom God went to redeem to be his people, *making himself a name*, and doing for them great and terrible things, by driving out before his people a nation and its gods?

In other words, when God went to redeem his people in Egypt and then bring them through the wilderness and into the promised land he was not just favoring the people; he was acting, as Samuel says, for his own great name's sake (1 Sam. 12:22); or, as David says, he was making himself a name—a reputation. He was revealing the pleasure that he has in his fame.

At the end of this chapter we will see that knowing this truth about God is immensely practical and has to do with the way we live and serve Christ every day. It is fitting then that we not hurry over this pleasure of God. It is such a crucial part of the foundation of our hope and our joy and our obedience. So we turn to trace the pleasure of God in his fame.[3]

Why Didn't God Make Short Work of Pharaoh?

Remain with me for a moment at the exodus. This is where God began to shape the corporate life of his chosen people. For the rest of her existence Israel looked back to the exodus as the key event in her history. So in the exodus we can see what God is up to in choosing a people for himself. In Exodus 9:16 God speaks to Pharaoh a word that lets him (and us) know why God is multiplying his mighty acts into ten plagues, instead of making short work of Egypt's stubbornness in one swift catastrophe. This text is so crucial that the apostle Paul quotes it in Romans 9:17 to sum up God's purpose in the exodus. God says to Pharaoh,

"But for this purpose I have caused you to stand (or "appointed you"), to show you my power, *so that my name may be declared throughout all the earth.*" Romans 9:17 says, "For the Scripture says to Pharaoh, 'I have raised you up for the very purpose of showing my power in you, *so that my name may be proclaimed in all the earth.*'"

So the point of the exodus was to make a worldwide reputation for God. The point of the ten plagues and miraculous Red Sea crossing was to demonstrate the incredible power of God on behalf of his freely chosen people, with the aim that this reputation, this name, would be declared throughout the whole world. Is it not clear then that God has great pleasure in his fame?

One of the great implications of God's pleasure in his fame is found in the story of Rahab, the harlot in Jericho. She was converted to the true God and spared from death, because of the fame of God from the exodus that had run before the Israelites and reached her city. "We have heard how the Lord dried up the water of the Red Sea before you when you came out of Egypt . . . the Lord your God is he who is God in heaven above and on earth beneath" (Joshua 2:10-11). Thus God's love for his fame became the means of Rahab's conversion. We will see this wonderful connection again and again.

Gospel Logic: God-centeredness is the Ground of Mercy

Isaiah too says that God's aim in the exodus was to make for himself an everlasting name. He described God as the one

. . . who caused his glorious arm to go at the right hand of Moses, who divided the waters before them *to make for himself an everlasting name,* who led them through the depths. Like a horse in the desert, they did not stumble. Like cattle that go down into the valley, the Spirit of the Lord gave them rest. So you led your people, *to make for yourself a glorious name.* (Isaiah 63:12-14)

So when God showed his power to deliver his people from Egypt through the Red Sea, he had his sights on eternity and the everlasting reputation that he would win for himself in those days.

Psalm 106:7-8 teaches the same thing:

Our fathers, when they were in Egypt, did not consider your wonderful works; they did not remember the abundance of your steadfast love, but rebelled against the Most High at the Red Sea. Yet he saved them *for his name's sake, that he might make known his mighty power.* (See also Nehemiah 9:10; Ezekiel 20:9; Daniel 9:15.)

Do you see the same gospel logic at work here? It's the same precious logic that we saw in 1 Samuel 12:22. There the sinful people had chosen a king and angered God. But God does not cast them off. Why? Because his great name was at stake. Here it says that the sinful people had rebelled against God at the Red Sea and failed to consider his love. Yet he saved them with tremendous power. Why? Same answer: for his name's sake, to make known his mighty power.

So God's first love is rooted in the value of his holy name, not the value of a sinful people. And because it is, there is hope for the sinful people—since they are not the ground of their salvation, God's name is. Do you see why the God-centeredness of God is the ground of the gospel?

Take Joshua as another example of someone who understood this God-centered gospel logic and put it to use like Moses did to plead for God's sinful people.[4] In Joshua 7 Israel has crossed the Jordan and entered the promised land and defeated Jericho. But now, to everyone's dismay, they have been defeated at the city of Ai. Joshua is stunned. He goes to the Lord in one of the most desperate prayers in all the Bible.

O Lord, what can I say, when Israel has turned their backs before their enemies! For the Canaanites and all the inhabitants of the land will hear of it, and will surround us, and cut off our name from the earth; and *what will you do for your great name?* (Joshua 7:8-9)

The great ground of hope in all the God-centered servants of the Lord has always been the impossibility that God would let his great name be dishonored for long among the nations. It was inconceivable. This was bedrock confidence. Other things change, but not this—not the commitment of God to his "great name."

Profaned and Vindicated in Babylon

But what then are we to make of the fact that eventually Israel proved to be so rebellious that she was indeed given into the hands of her enemies during the Babylonian captivity in the time of Ezekiel? How does a God-centered prophet like Ezekiel handle this terrible setback for the reputation of God?

Listen to the word of the Lord that came to him in Ezekiel 36:20-23. This is God's answer to the captivity of his people which he himself had brought about.

> But when they came to the nations [during captivity], wherever they came, they profaned my holy name, in that men said of them, "These are the people of the Lord, and yet they had to go out of his land." But *I had concern for my holy name*, which the house of Israel caused to be profaned among the nations to which they came. Therefore say to the house of Israel, "Thus says the Lord God: it is not for your sake, O house of Israel, that I am about to act, but *for the sake of my holy name*, which you have profaned among the nations to which you came. And I *will vindicate the holiness of my great name*, which has been profaned among the nations, which you have profaned among them; and the nations will know that I am the Lord, says the Lord God, when through you I vindicate my holiness before their eyes."

Similarly in Ezekiel 39:25 God says,

> Now I will restore the fortunes of Jacob, and have mercy upon the whole house of Israel; and *I will be jealous for my holy name*.

When every other hope was gone and the people lay under the judgment of God himself because of their own sin, one hope remained—and it will always remain—that God has an indomitable delight in the worth of his own reputation and will not suffer it to be trodden down for long.

Isaiah, writing much earlier, but dealing with the same problem—the dishonoring of God in the captivity of his people—made the motive of God unmistakably clear in saving his people from Babylon:

For my name's sake I defer my anger,
for the sake of my praise I restrain it for you,
that I may not cut you off.
Behold, I have refined you, but not like silver;
I have tried you in the furnace of affliction.
For my own sake, for my own sake, I do it,
for how should my name be profaned?
My glory I will not give to another. (Isaiah 48:9-11)

Daniel, who was caught in the captivity himself, prayed with the same view of God in mind, "O Lord, hear; O Lord, forgive; O Lord, give heed and act; delay not, *for your own sake,* O my God, because your city and your people are *called by your name*" (Daniel 9:19).

Pardon Flows from the Pleasure of His Fame

The great ground of hope, the great motive to pray, the great well-spring of mercy is God's awesome commitment to his name. The pleasure that he has in his fame is the pledge and passion of his readiness to forgive and save those who lift his banner and cast themselves on his promise and mercy. The saints of the Old Testament stake their hope for forgiveness not on their merit or their external rituals. They plead mercy on the basis of God's love for his great name: "*For your name's sake,* O Lord, pardon my guilt, for it is great" (Psalm 25:11). "Help us, O God of our salvation, *for the glory of your name;* deliver us, and forgive our sins, *for your name's sake!*" (Psalm 79:9). "Though our iniquities testify against us, act, O Lord, *for your name's sake;* for our backslidings are many, we have sinned against you. . . . You, O Lord, are in the midst of us, and *we are called by your name;* leave us not" (Jeremiah 14:7,9).

I recall hearing one of my professors in seminary say that one of the best tests of a person's theology was the effect it has on one's prayers. This struck me as true because of what was happening in my own life. Noël and I had just been married and we were making it our practice to pray together each evening. I noticed that during the biblical courses which were shaping my theology most profoundly, my prayers were changing dramatically. Probably the most significant change in those days was learning to make my

case before God on the ground of his glory. Beginning with
"Hallowed be Thy name," and ending with "In Jesus' name"
meant that the glory of God's name was the goal and the ground
of everything I prayed. And what a strength came into my life
when I learned that praying for forgiveness should be based not
only on an appeal to God's mercy, but also on an appeal to his
justice in crediting the worth of his Son's obedience. "God is
faithful and *just* and will forgive your sins" (1 John 1:9).

In the New Testament the basis of all forgiveness of sins is
revealed more clearly than it was in the Old Testament, but the
basis in God's commitment to his name does not change. Paul
teaches that the death of Christ demonstrated the righteousness
of God in passing over sins and vindicated God's justice in
justifying the ungodly who bank on Jesus and not themselves
(Romans 3:25-26).[5] In other words Christ died once for all *to
clear the name of God* in what looks like a gross miscarriage of
justice—the acquittal of sinners simply for Jesus' sake. But Jesus
died in such a way that forgiveness "for Jesus' sake" is the same as
forgiveness "for the sake of God's name."

We can see this not only in Romans 3:25-26 but also in the
Gospel of John. According to this Gospel, *Jesus came in his
Father's name* (5:43) and does his works *in his Father's name*
(10:25). At the end of his life he said that he had *manifested the
Father's name* to those whom the Father had given him (17:6)
and that he would yet *make that name known* to them (17:26). So
all of Jesus' life and work seems to be aimed at revealing and
honoring the Father's name. This is especially true of Jesus'
death, as he shows us in John 12:27-28. Here Jesus is praying just
before his death: "Now is my soul troubled. And what shall I say?
'Father, save me from this hour'? No, for this purpose I have
come to this hour. *Father, glorify your name.*" Then a voice came
from heaven, "I have glorified it, and I will glorify it again." The
hour of Jesus' death was at hand and the purpose for coming to
that hour was *to glorify the name of the Father.* Therefore we
should think of the death of Jesus as the way the Father
vindicated his name—his reputation—from all accusations of
unrighteousness in the forgiveness of sinners.

On this side of the cross we should pray just like David did in Psalm 25:11, "*For your name's sake*, O Lord, pardon my guilt, for it is great." But when we Christians pray this, we should mean, "Forgive me, O Lord, because your great and holy name has been vindicated by the death of your Son and I am banking all my hope on him and not myself." This is what John meant when he said in 1 John 2:12, "I am writing to you, little children, because your sins are forgiven *for the sake of his name*." So, whether we are reading in the Old Testament or the New, the great ground of our forgiveness is God's allegiance to his holy name and the unswerving pleasure that he takes in making the worth and righteousness of that name known, especially in the gospel message that Christ died both to justify the ungodly and vindicate the Father's justice. If God were ever to lose his delight in the fame of his glorious name, the foundation of our pardon would be imperiled.

The pleasure of God in his fame is not only the basis of our pardon but also our obedience and service and mission. David teaches us to believe that God "leads [us] in paths of righteousness *for his name's sake*" (Psalm 23:3). And Jesus commends the persevering saints at Ephesus, "I know that you are bearing up *for my name's sake*" (Revelation 2:3). Paul tells the Christian slaves at Ephesus to regard their masters as worthy of all honor, *so that the name of God and the teaching may not be defamed*" (1 Timothy 6:1). This is probably what Paul means in Colossians 3:17 when he sums up the whole Christian life with the words, "Whatever you do, in word or deed, *do everything in the name of the Lord Jesus*." That is, live your whole life to honor the name of Jesus—to give him a good reputation and spread his fame.

The Fame of God as the Goal of Missions

God's zeal for his fame to be spread bursts out in the Scriptures again and again. He wants his fame to be spread to all the peoples of the world that have not yet known his name. So there seem to be two kinds of missionaries needed in the world. There is the Timothy-type missionary and the Paul-type missionary. I call Timothy a missionary because he left home (Lystra, Acts 16:1), joined a traveling team of missionaries, crossed cultures, and ended up overseeing the church in Ephesus (1 Timothy 1:3). But I distinguish this Timothy-type missionary from the Paul-type missionary because Timothy stayed and ministered on the "mission field" long after there was a church planted there with its own elders (Acts 20:17) and outreach (Acts 19:10).

Paul, on the other hand, was driven by a passion to make God's name known in all the unreached peoples of the world. He never stayed in a place long once the church was established. He said that he made it his ambition "to preach the gospel, not where Christ has already been *named*" (Romans 15:20). The real significance of the word "named" comes out when we go back to the beginning of Paul's letter to the Romans and hear him say that Christ had given him "apostleship to bring about the obedience of faith *for the sake of his name* among all the nations" (Romans 1:5). The aim of missions is to bring about the obedience of faith among all the unreached peoples of the world. But that is not the ultimate goal. The ultimate goal—even of faith and obedience—is *"for the sake of his name."* The fame of Christ, the reputation of Christ is what burned in the heart of the apostle Paul. The faith of the nations was not an end in itself. It was the way that the name of Christ would be honored. This is what filled him with such a passion for the Great Commission. Jesus had told Ananias "how much [Paul] must suffer *for the sake of my name*" (Acts 9:16). And he had never turned back from his willingness to suffer if only the fame of Christ would result. Near the end of his life he could still say, "I am ready not only to be imprisoned but even to die at Jerusalem *for the name of the Lord Jesus*" (Acts 21:13).

Of course Paul wasn't the only one who went out for the glory of the name of Christ. Third John is a beautiful little letter that describes how to minister to missionaries. For example, it says,

> Beloved, it is a loyal thing you do when you render any service to the brothers, especially to strangers, who have testified to your love before the church. You will do well to send them on their journey as befits God's service. For they have set out *for the sake of the name* and have accepted nothing from the heathen. So we ought to support such ones, that we may be fellow workers in the truth (3 John 5-8).

Too Few Paul-Type Missionaries

Today there seems to be a great imbalance with too few Paul-type missionaries. Notice how many more missionaries are listed below in the column titled "reached" than there are in the column called "unreached." About 90 percent of the missionary force today are Timothy-type missionaries.[6] The point is not at all to criticize the Timothy-type missionaries. These people are doing a tremendously important work, and we must keep in mind that they too are advancing the cause of reaching unreached peoples by mobilizing the churches where they are for frontier, pioneering missionary work.[7] Nevertheless, a resounding call should go out to every church in all the world that there is a great tradition stemming from the apostle Paul to spread the fame of Christ's name to unreached peoples and the job is not yet done. The following table (from 1989) makes this clear.

Distribution of North American Missionary Force Among the Reached and Unreached Peoples of the World[8]

	Reached	Unreached[9]
Europe, Latin America, N. Zealand, Australia	700 groups 1.1 billion people 26,600 missionaries	150 groups 143 million people 400 missionaries
USA, Canada	500 groups 270 million people 5,000 missionaries	50 groups 7 million people 600 missionaries
Buddhists	20 groups 50 million people 1,000 missionaries	1,000 groups 274 million people 400 missionaries
Han Chinese	2,200 groups 900 million people 3,000 missionaries	1,000 groups 150 million people 300 missionaries
Hindus	1,300 groups 150 million people 3,000 missionaries	2,000 groups 550 million people 200 missionaries
Muslims	30 groups 70 million people 600 missionaries	4,000 groups 860 million people 400 missionaries

Tribals	3,000 groups	3,000 groups
	80 million people	140 million people
	13,000 missionaries	4,500 missionaries
Other Africans	2,950 groups	500 groups
	250 million people	25 million people
	15,000 missionaries	200 missionaries
Other Asians	1,300 groups	300 groups
	173 million people	50 million people
	10,000 missionaries	800 missionaries
Totals:	12,000 groups	12,000 groups
	50%	50%
	3.05 billion people	2.2 billion people
	58%	42%
	77,200 missionaries	7,800 missionaries
	90%	10%

A Finishable Task

To make sure that this chart does not communicate an unwarranted pessimism, we should also take note of the following table which is truly amazing. It shows that the number of unreached peoples is decreasing dramatically in proportion to the number of evangelical congregations available to evangelize them.

The Proportion of Unreached Peoples to Congregations of Christians[10]

Year A.D.	Non-Christians[11] per Believer[12]	Unreached People Groups[13]	Congregations per Unreached People Group[14]
100	360 to 1	60,000	1 to 12
1000	220 to 1	50,000	1 to 5
1500	69 to 1	44,000	1 to 1
1900	27 to 1	40,000	10 to 1
1950	21 to 1	24,000	33 to 1
1980	11 to 1	17,000	162 to 1
1989	7 to 1	12,000	416 to 1
2000	?	0?	?

Ralph Winter observes that the drop from 11 to 7 (62 percent) between 1980 and 1989 (in the second column) is equivalent to the drop from 360 to 220 (62 percent) in the first 900 years of church history! Then he gives his own estimate of this chart's significance: "I have to confess that the two measurements [in the second and fourth columns], and the trends that they reveal, are two of the most hopeful insights I know of. And their significance is virtually irrefutable, in my opinion."[15] In other words, even though the call for more Paul-type missionaries is urgent, and the task remaining is great, it is, as many are saying, "a finishable task!"

Indomitable Delight

The main reason for this confidence, however, is not any statistics but the indomitable delight God has in his fame among the nations. His promises make plain that he will see his fame extend to all the peoples and his name praised by every nation.

> I will send survivors to the nations . . . to the coastlands afar off, *that have not heard my fame* or seen my glory; and they shall *declare my glory among the nations* (Isaiah 66:19).
> All the earth shall worship you,
> and shall sing unto you;
> *they shall sing to your name* (Psalm 66:4).
> All nations whom you have made
> shall come and worship before you, O Lord;
> and *shall glorify your name* (Psalm 86:9).
> So the nations *shall fear the name of the Lord,*
> and all the kings of the earth your glory (Psalm 102:15).

All these promises lead inevitably to the earnest prayer for such mission triumph to come:

> O that you would rend the heavens and come down,
> that the mountains might quake at your presence
> . . . *to make your name known to your adversaries,*
> and that the nations might tremble at your presence!
> (Isaiah 64:1-2)

And the prayers of God's people inevitably lead to the call for the church to move out with courage and confidence:

> Give thanks to the Lord,
> call upon his name;
> make known his deeds among the peoples,
> *proclaim that his name is exalted.* (Isaiah 12:4)

In the east give glory to the Lord;
in the coastlands of the sea,
to the name of the Lord, the God of Israel.
From the ends of the earth we hear songs of praise,
of glory to the Righteous One. (Isaiah 24:15-16)

Peter's Unforgettable Lesson

It is scarcely possible to overemphasize the centrality of the fame of God in motivating the mission of the church. When Peter had his world turned upside down by the vision of unclean animals in Acts 10, and by the lesson from God that he should evangelize gentiles as well as Jews, he came back to Jerusalem and told the apostles that it was all owing to God's zeal for his name. We know this because James summed up Peter's speech like this: "Brothers, listen to me. Simeon has related how God first visited the Gentiles, *to take out of them a people for his name*" (Acts 15:14). It's not surprising that Peter would say that God's purpose was to gather a people *for his name*; because the Lord Jesus had stung Peter some years earlier with an unforgettable lesson.

You recall that, after a rich young man turned away from Jesus and refused to follow him, Peter said to Jesus, "Look, we have left everything and followed you (unlike this rich fellow). What then shall we have?" Jesus responded with a mild rebuke, which in effect said that there is no ultimate sacrifice when you live for the *name* of the Son of Man. "Every one who has left houses or brothers or sisters or father or mother or children or lands, *for my name's sake*, will receive a hundredfold, and inherit eternal life" (Matthew 19:29).

The truth is plain: God is pursuing with omnipotent delight a worldwide purpose of gathering a people *for his name* from every tribe and language and nation (Revelation 5:9; 7:9). He has an inexhaustible enthusiasm for the fame of his name among the nations. Therefore when we bring our affections in line with his, and, for the sake of his name, renounce the quest for worldly comforts and join his global purpose, God's omnipotent commitment to his name is over us and we cannot lose, in spite of many tribulations (Acts 9:16; Romans 8:35-39).

David Brainerd's Final Written Words

David Brainerd was right. It is good to strive to penetrate to the bottom of divine truths. At the bottom of all our hope, when everything else has given way, we stand on this great reality: the everlasting, all-sufficient God is infinitely, unwaveringly and eternally committed to his great and holy name. For the sake of his fame among the nations he will act. His name will not be profaned for ever. The mission of the church will be victorious. He will vindicate his people and his cause in all the earth. David Brainerd was sustained by this confidence to his death. Seven days before he died he gave expression to the kind of affections this chapter of *The Pleasures of God* is meant to kindle. These are the last words he had the strength to write with his own hand:

> Friday, October 2. My soul was this day, at turns, sweetly set on God: I longed to be "with him" that I might "behold his glory;" I felt sweetly disposed to commit all to him, even my dearest friends, my dearest flock, and my absent brother, and all my concerns for time and eternity. Oh, that his kingdom might come in the world; that they might all love and glorify him for what he is in himself; and that the blessed Redeemer might "see of the travail of his soul, and be satisfied." Oh, "come, Lord Jesus, come quickly! Amen."[16]

Notes

1. Jonathan Edwards, *The Life of David Brainerd*, ed. Norman Pettit, *The Works of Jonathan Edwards*, 7 (New Haven: Yale University Press, 1985), 496.

2. Gustav F. Oehler, *Theology of the Old Testament* (Minneapolis: Klock and Klock Christian Publishers, 1978, orig. 1873), 125. "In short God names Himself, not according to what He is for Himself, but to *what He is for man*. . . . But the biblical notion of the divine name is not exhausted by this. It is not merely the title which God bears in virtue of the relation in which He places Himself to man; but the expression 'name of God' designates at the same time the whole divine self-presentation by which God in personal presence testifies of Himself—the whole side of the divine nature which is turned toward man." Thus it is fully in accord with the meaning of "the name of God" to draw the implication "fame of God."

3. We won't go all the way back to creation here, because in chapter 3 we saw God's delight in creation. It was implicit in that chapter that the reason God enjoys creation is that it proclaims his glory (Psalm 19:1) and spreads his fame. It makes his name majestic for all who will stop suppressing the truth (Romans 1:18). That's the point of Psalm 8 which begins and ends

with the exclamation, "O Lord, our Lord, how majestic is *your name* in all the earth!" The creation of the world is part of God's advance answer to the prayer, "Hallowed be your name!"

4. When God was angry at the disobedience of the people of Israel and threatened to destroy them, Moses interceded for them with arguments based squarely on the premise that God loves his reputation, and shrinks back from acts which may bring disrepute on his power and holiness (Exodus 32:11-12; Deuteronomy 9:27-29; Numbers 14:13-16).

5. For a detailed exegetical explanation and defense of this interpretation of Romans 3:25-26 see John Piper, *The Justification of God* (Grand Rapids: Baker Book House, 1983), 115-131. Also see chapter 6 of this book, pp. 165-166.

6. There are many ways to make the present state of imbalance shockingly obvious. One is to say, "Although Hindus, Muslims, and Chinese make up about 75 percent of the non-Christian world, only 5 percent of today's expatriate missionaries live among them." This is taken from a special news letter of the Lausanne Committee for World Evangelization, June 1988.

7. In *Mission Frontiers*, 9, No. 12 (December 1987), Larry Pate estimated that at the current rate of growth, the size of the non-Western missionary force will increase to 100,000 by the year 2000. This is in part owing to the faithfulness and strategic wisdom of many Timothy-type missionaries. For a full description of the state of third world mission agencies see Larry Pate, *From Every Nation* (co-published by OC Ministries and MARC Publications, 1989).

8. These statistics are taken from the 1989 unreached peoples chart of the U.S. Center for World Mission, which can be ordered from the USCWM, 1605 Elizabeth St. Pasadena, CA 91104. For the meaning of "unreached people" see note 9.

9. An "unreached people" is a group of people whose maximum size is still unified enough culturally so that the gospel could spread without cultural barriers, and in which there is not yet an indigenous, evangelizing church movement. For those interested in a more detailed statement about the meaning of "unreached peoples" I will quote from Ralph Winter's report on the most recent missiological thinking available as I write this book. The quote is taken from an essay entitled "Crucial Issues in Missions: Working Towards the Year 2000," in *Missions Frontiers*, 1990 Special Edition (Pasadena, Calif.: U.S. Center for World Missions), 13.

> For many missiologists, the most strategic goal is that there might be a viable, indigenous, evangelizing church movement within every human culture—that is, within every community sufficiently homogeneous to enable all to hear and understand in their own milieu. If such an internal witness is lacking, such groups are defined (by a widely representative Lausanne-sponsored meeting in March of 1982), as "unreached peoples". . . .
>
> This is so crucial a goal, and is so foundational to mission, that I have thought it justified to coin a term for the basic concept behind this March 1982 definition. I have suggested the term *unimax* peoples, since, as defined, the concept involves the

*max*imum sized groups still sufficiently *uni*fied to allow "the spread of a church planting movement without encountering barriers of understanding or acceptance."

It is fascinating to note that when we think in terms of the necessity of a separate missionary penetration . . . for every unimax group, the significance of political boundaries and even great geographical distances may often be ruled out. This is perhaps more obviously true of Bible translation. Once the Bible is in the language of the people in one place, it does not need to be translated all over again for the same group on the other side of a national border or across the ocean, unless there has been sufficient time and isolation to allow divergent language and cultural development. Similarly, whenever a viable, indigenous, evangelizing church movement exists in one portion of a unimax group, it would be inefficient to initiate pioneer missionary work all over again in another part of the same group, even thousands of miles away. In that case, instead of undertaking brand new missionary efforts, the existing church within the same unimax group is the best source upon which to draw. And in that case it is ordinary evangelism, not *pioneer mission strategy*, that is in order.

Careful compilations of two or three thousand groups already exist. These compilations, according to the 1982 definition 1) list some unreached peoples (unimax peoples) more than once if their people are found in more than one country, and 2) often list as a single group what are actually clusters of unreached unimax groups, but at least 3) include virtually all remaining unreached unimax groups within these clusters. Nevertheless, it is fairly safe to say that once church planting efforts take place in these clusters, these lists of two thousand to three thousand groups [which have already been identified] will turn out not to include many more than twelve thousand total unreached peoples—by the March 1982 definition. The Lausanne Statistics Task Force has agreed on twelve thousand as a reasonable estimate of the number of these relatively small people groups. Even as we enter the nineties, the task of making new missionary penetrations into twelve thousand new cultures is being parceled out to the various sectors of the mission sending base all over the world—continent by continent, country by country, and even denomination by denomination.

Thus, all of this lays down one of the most concrete and significant mandates for the nineties: reach all such (unimax) groups by the year 2000. Or, to use more precise language: by 2000, establish a viable, indigenous evangelizing church movement within every people which is the largest group within which the gospel can spread by a church planting movement without encountering barriers of understanding or acceptance.

10. This table appeared as part of an article by Ralph Winter, "The Momentum is Building in Global Missions: Basic Concepts in Frontier Missiology,"

Mission Frontiers, 1990 Special Edition, 17-26. Winter said the numbers are provided by David Barrett and the Statistics Task Force of Lausanne Committee for World Evangelization.

11. "Non-Christian" refers to those who make no claim to be Christian.

12. "Believer" in this chart means "Great Commission Christian" (a term suggested by David Barrett), that is, someone "born again into a personal relationship with the Lord Jesus Christ."

13. See note 9 for a definition of "unreached people group." The estimate for the total number of people groups in the world is about twenty-four thousand, half of which are unreached. The reason for the decrease from sixty thousand to twenty-four thousand is the dying out or the amalgamation of some groups over the centuries.

14. The numbers in this column are based on an estimated one hundred persons per congregation worldwide.

15. Winter, *Mission Frontiers*, 23.

16. Edwards, *The Life of David Brainerd*, 474.

Behold, to the Lord your God belong heaven and the heaven of heavens, the earth with all that is in it; yet the Lord delighted in your fathers to love them and chose their descendants after them, you above all the peoples, as at this day.

Deuteronomy 10:14-15

Chapter 5

The Pleasure of God
in Election

Can controversial teachings nurture Christlikeness? Before you answer this question, ask another one: Are there any significant biblical teachings that have not been controversial? I cannot think of even one, let alone the number we all need for the daily nurture of faith. If this is true, then we have no choice but to seek our food in the markets of controversy. We need not stay there. We can go home and feast if the day has been well spent. But we must buy there. As much as we would like it, we do not have the luxury of living in a world where the most nourishing truths are unopposed. If we think we can suspend judgment on all that is controversial and feed our souls only on what is left, we are living in a dreamworld. There is nothing left. The reason any of us thinks that we can stand alone on truths that are non-controversial is because we do not know our history or the diversity of the professing church. Besides that, would we really want to give to the devil the right to determine our spiritual menu by refusing to eat any teaching over which he can cause controversy?

The teaching of Scripture on election has been controversial. But I believe with all my heart that it is precious beyond words and a great nourishment for the Christlikeness of faith. If I understand the teaching of the Bible, God has pleasure in election. To know that this is true, and to know why it is, is to see another facet of the glory of God. And that sight is the power to make us holy and happy people.

George Mueller's Life-changing Discovery

George Mueller found this to be so. Mueller is famous for the orphanages he founded and for the amazing faith he had to pray for God's provision. Not many people know the theology that undergirded that great ministry. In 1829 when he was twenty-four years old, he had an experience which he later recorded in his autobiography. He describes the period when he "came to prize the Bible alone as [his] standard of judgment."

> Before this period I had been much opposed to the doctrines of election, particular redemption and final persevering grace. But now I was brought to examine these precious truths by the Word of God. Being made willing to have no glory of my own in the conversion of sinners, but to consider myself merely an instrument; and being made willing to receive what the Scriptures said, I went to the Word, reading the New Testament from the beginning, with a particular reference to these truths.
>
> To my great astonishment I found that the passages which speak decidedly for election and persevering grace, were about four times as many as those which speak apparently against these truths; and even those few, shortly after, when I had examined and understood them, served to confirm me in the above doctrines.
>
> As to the effect which my belief in these doctrines had on me, I am constrained to state for God's glory, that though I am still exceedingly weak, and by no means so dead to the lusts of the flesh, and the lust of the eyes, and the pride of life, as I might be, and as I ought to be, yet, *by the grace of God, I have walked more closely with Him since that period. My life has not been so variable, and I may say that I have lived much more for God than before.*[1]

George Mueller began with controversy and ended with a long life of faith and holiness and stable Christlikeness. It can happen. It has happened for thousands.

And it does not have to happen in school. Christians are sometimes cowed into thinking, "If the scholars can't agree, surely there's no hope for me." But that is not true. God means for the Bible to be read and understood by all his people. He does not mean for the church to be limited in its nourishment by what a priesthood of scholars can agree on. There are no significant biblical truths on which all scholars agree. Ordinary Christians simply must not yield to an elitist academic mentality that puts all confident insight into the hands of a few scholars. Scholarship has its utterly crucial place in the life of the church. We would have no English Bible without it. Nor would the church long withstand the force of secular ideas without faithful scholars devoted to the life of the mind and dedicated to the intellectual credibility of Christianity. But the task of scholarship is not to rob ordinary Christians of their confidence in understanding the Bible and feeding their souls with great biblical truth.

How Spurgeon Grew from a Babe to a Man

The experience of Charles Spurgeon is not beyond the ability of any ordinary Christian. Spurgeon (1834-1892) was a contemporary of George Mueller. He served the Metropolitan Tabernacle in London for over thirty years as the most famous pastor of his day. His preaching was so powerful that people were converted to Christ every week. His sermons are still in print today and he is held up by many as a model soul-winner. He recalls an experience when he was sixteen that shaped his life and ministry for the rest of his days.

> When I was coming to Christ, I thought I was doing it all myself, and though I sought the Lord earnestly, I had no idea the Lord was seeking me. I do not think the young convert is at first aware of this. I can recall the very day and hour when first I received those truths [the doctrine of election] in my own soul—when they were, as John Bunyan says, burnt into my heart as with a hot iron, and I can recollect how I felt that I had grown on a sudden from a babe into a man—that I had made progress in Scriptural knowledge, through having found, once for all, that clue to the truth of God.
>
> One week-night, when I was sitting in the house of God, I was not thinking much about the preacher's sermon, for I did not believe it. The thought struck me, *"How did you come to be a Christian?"* I sought the Lord. *"But how did you come to seek the Lord?"* The truth flashed across my mind in a moment—I should not have sought Him unless there had been some previous influence in my mind to make me seek Him. I prayed, thought I, but then I asked myself, *How came I to pray?* I was induced to pray by reading the Scriptures. *How came I to read the Scriptures?* I did read them, but what led me to do so? Then, in a moment, I saw that God was at the bottom of it all, and that He was the Author of my faith, and

so the whole doctrine of grace opened up to me, and from that doctrine I have not departed to this day, and I desire to make this my constant confession, "I ascribe my change wholly to God."[2]

This is not a sequence of thought beyond anyone's ability. If it happened this way to Spurgeon it can happen to anyone. There had been influences in Spurgeon's life to prepare him for this discovery. But the main ones were not scholars—one was the cook, at the school in Newmarket where Spurgeon attended when he was fifteen.

> The first lessons I ever had in theology were from an old cook in the school at Newmarket. . . . She was a good old soul, and used to read *The Gospel Standard*. She liked something very sweet indeed, good strong Calvinistic doctrine, but she lived strongly as well as fed strongly. Many a time we have gone over the covenant of grace together, and talked of the personal election of the saints, their union to Christ, their final perseverance, and what vital godliness meant; and I do believe that I learnt more from her than I should have learned from any six doctors of divinity of the sort we have nowadays.[3]

She liked something very sweet—the truth of God's personal election. It is sweet to the saints because it is sweet to God. It is his pleasure to magnify the glory of his free and sovereign grace in choosing a people that they might be for him "a name, a praise and a glory" (Jeremiah 13:11). In other words, to extend the pleasure that God has in his own name, he calls out a people to enjoy and praise and proclaim that name. The Bible calls these people "the elect," "the chosen." That is what we want to look at in this chapter: the pleasure of God in election.

Israel Elect from All the Peoples (and for All the Peoples)

We take our starting point from the election of Israel in the Old Testament and then turn to the New Testament and see whether the church is thought of in a similar way. The Old Testament teaches repeatedly that Israel became God's people because he chose her freely from all the peoples of the world. Israel did not compete with others and win. God chose her unconditionally and made her his special possession. Abraham was the original patriarch of the people of Israel, and God says in

Joshua 24:2-3 that he was part of an idolatrous family when God called him: "Thus says the Lord, the God of Israel, 'Your fathers lived of old beyond the Euphrates, Terah, the father of Abraham and of Nahor; and *they served other gods*. Then *I took your father Abraham* from beyond the river and led him through all the land of Canaan, and made his offspring many.' "

This "taking" of Abraham (or Abram at that time) out of idolatry is called in Nehemiah 9:7 "choosing" or "election." Ezra prays, "You are the Lord, the God who chose Abram and brought him forth out of Ur of the Chaldeans, and gave him the name Abraham." Another way of talking about this "choosing" is to say that God "knew" Abraham in the sense of setting his special attention on Abraham and ac*know*ledging him as his own possession. This is what God said about Abraham just before he destroyed Sodom and Gomorrah. He pondered, "Shall I hide from Abraham what I am about to do?" Then he answered himself, "No, for *I have known him*, that he may charge his children and his household after him to keep the way of the Lord by doing righteousness and justice; so that the Lord may bring to Abraham what he has promised him" (Genesis 18:17-19). This special way of "knowing" is used again in Amos when God declares his unique relation to the people of Israel: "You only have I *known* of all the families of the earth" (Amos 3:2). This does not mean that God is ignorant about all the families of the earth. It means that he has set his special attention on Israel and ac*know*ledged them to be his unique possession out of all the other peoples of the earth.[4]

On the basis of this initial election of Abraham from all the people of the earth, the Old Testament most often speaks of the *entire people* of Israel as God's elect or chosen. For example Moses says in Deuteronomy 14:2, "You are a people holy to the Lord your God, and the Lord has *chosen you* to be a people for his own possession, out of all the peoples that are on the face of the earth." The reaffirmation of God's possession of Israel at the deliverance from Egypt is sometimes spoken of as Israel's election, as in Ezekiel 20:5, "Thus says the Lord God: on the day when *I chose Israel*, I swore to the seed of the house of Jacob, *making myself known to them in the land of Egypt*, I swore to them, saying

I am the Lord your God." Moses connects the Exodus with God's taking possession of Israel in these words from Deuteronomy 4:20: "The Lord has taken you, and brought you forth out of the iron furnace, out of Egypt, *to be a people of his own possession*, as at this day." "You have seen what I did to the Egyptians and how I bore you on eagles' wings and brought you to myself" (Exodus 19:4). God's work in choosing Israel for himself was free like the flight of an eagle carrying helpless little eaglets to safety where God could help them become what he wanted them to be.

Sometimes the "choosing" of the people at the time of the Exodus is shown to be an extension of the electing love that had been shown to Abraham, the patriarch. For example, in Deuteronomy 4:37-39 Moses says, "Because *he loved your fathers and chose their descendants after them, and brought you out of Egypt* with his own presence, by his great power . . . know therefore this day, and lay it to your heart, that the Lord is God in heaven above and on the earth beneath; there is no other." Thus the Scripture can speak of God's electing the people of Israel by freely loving and choosing Abraham at the beginning, or by freely choosing to take the entire people from Egypt in fulfillment of the promises made to elect Abraham. In either case the people should "lay it to heart" and stand in awe that the Lord alone is God.

The Freedom of God in Choosing Israel

The sovereign freedom of God in election is suggested by the way Isaiah compares God's choosing to God's creating or begetting: "But now hear, O Jacob, my servant, Israel whom I have chosen! Thus says the Lord *who made you, who formed you from the womb* and will help you . . ." (Isaiah 44:1-2). God "chose" Israel and he "made" Israel. These are both true because the choosing was such a unique, sovereign work of God that it was in a real sense a creating or making of Israel. Again Isaiah writes: "Thus says the Lord, he who created you, O Jacob, he who *formed you*, O Israel: Fear not" (Isaiah 43:1). "I am the Lord, your Holy One, the *Creator of Israel*, your King" (Isaiah 43:15). " Thus says the Lord, the Holy One of Israel, and *his Maker*: Will you question me about *my children,* or command me concerning *the work of my hands?*" (Isaiah 45:11). In other words, God's electing Israel is virtually the same as his fathering her or creating her.

Moses says essentially the same thing: "Do you thus requite the Lord, you foolish and senseless people? *Is not he your father, who has gotten you,*[5] *who made you* and established you?" (Deuteronomy 32:6). Thus God says to Pharaoh at the Exodus, "Israel is my first-born son, and I say to you, 'Let *my son* go that he may serve me' " (Exodus 4:22-23; see also Hosea 11:1). Similarly the prophet Malachi describes God's choosing Israel as what a Father or a Creator does: "*Have we not all one Father? Has not one God created us?* Why then are we faithless to one another?" (Malachi 2:10; see also 1:6). And Isaiah again makes the strongest statement of all in saying that Israel's relation to God is like the relationship between a pot and a potter: "Yet, O Lord, You are our Father; *we are the clay, and you are our Potter,* we are all the work of your hand" (Isaiah 64:7-8). This shows how free God was in election. He was not influenced by the moral fitness of Abraham or of the people of Israel,[6] any more than a father is moved by the moral fitness of the non-existent child to beget him, or a potter is influenced by the beauty of his non-existent pot to make it. This is what we mean by unconditional election.

God's Delight in Electing Love

If God's choice of Israel from all the peoples on the earth was not motivated by some distinctive in Abraham and his posterity, by what was it motivated? The answer is that it came from God's good pleasure. God's electing love is absolutely free. It is the gracious overflow of his boundless happiness guided by his infinite wisdom. Deuteronomy 10:14-15 describes the delight God had in choosing Israel from all the peoples of the earth.

14) Behold, to the Lord your God belong heaven and the heaven of heavens, the earth with all that is in it; 15) yet the Lord set his heart in love upon your fathers (literally: the Lord *delighted in*[7] your fathers to love them) and chose their descendants after them, you above all peoples, as at this day.

Notice two things. First, notice the contrast between verses 14 and 15. Why does Moses describe the election of Israel against the backdrop of God's ownership of the whole universe? Why does he say in verse 14, "To God belongs everything in heaven and on earth" and then say in verse 15, "Yet he chose you for his people"? The reason seems to be to get rid of any notion that God was somehow hedged in to choose this people. The point is to explode the myth that each people has its own god and *this* god has a right to his own people but no more. The truth is that this is the only true God. He owns everything in the universe and can take any people he wants for his own special possession.

Thus the unspeakably wonderful truth for Israel is that he chose them. He did not have to. He had rights and privileges to choose absolutely any people on the face of the earth for his redeeming purposes. Therefore, when he calls himself "their God" he does not mean that he is on a par with the gods of Egypt or the gods of Canaan. He owns those gods and their peoples. If it had pleased him, he could have chosen a totally different people to accomplish his purposes. The point of putting verses 14 and 15 together in this way is to stress the freedom and the universal rights and authority of God.

The second thing to notice (in verse 15) is the way God exercises his sovereign freedom to "set his love upon the fathers." "He *delighted in* your fathers to love them." He freely chose to take pleasure in loving the fathers. God's love for the fathers of Israel was free and merciful and wasn't constrained by anything that the fathers were in their Jewishness or in their virtue.

Free and Unconditional

One of the ways God makes this clear is that when Abraham fathered two sons, God chose only one of them—Isaac, not Ishmael—to be the son of promise. And when Isaac had two sons, even before they were born God chose only Jacob, not Esau, to continue the line of his chosen people. In each case God acts in a way that highlights his sovereign freedom in election. In Isaac's case the child is born by miraculous, divine intervention when Abraham and Sarah are too old to have children. The point is to show that God's purposes in election are not limited by human abilities or inabilities. He is free to choose whomever he pleases, even if he has to create a child by a miraculous birth.

This is the truth that John the Baptist had in mind when he warned the Pharisees and Sadducees, "Do not presume to say to yourselves, 'We have Abraham as our father'; for I tell you, God is able from these stones to raise up children to Abraham" (Matthew 3:9). In other words, don't ever think that God is obliged to choose you because of some human distinctive like your physical descent from Abraham. If God needs descendants from Abraham to fulfill the promises of election, he can create them out of stones. He is not boxed in. He is not limited to you. Beware of presuming on his electing grace. It is absolutely free.

God makes the same point in the way he chooses Jacob and not Esau. In their case God chooses the son who, according to all ordinary custom and human expectation, should not have been chosen, namely, the younger one. Thus he shows that God aims to undermine any attempt to limit his freedom in election. He is not bound or constrained by any human distinctives. The apostle Paul stresses in Romans 9:10-13 that the reason for the election of Jacob, not Esau, and Isaac, not Ishmael, was to show that God's election is free and unconditional. It is not based on Jewishness or primogeniture or virtue or faith; it is free, and therefore completely merciful and gracious.

> 10) When Rebecca had conceived children by one man, our forefather Isaac, 11) though they were not yet born and had done nothing either good or bad, in order that *God's purpose of election* might continue, not because of works but because of his call, 12) she was told, "The elder will serve the younger."

What this text says is that God chooses the "children of promise" (Romans 9:8) in a way that will free his choosing from human works and make it totally dependent on his own call. This is why election is called unconditional. Paul brings it out in three ways: 1) Jacob and Esau had the same parents (verse 10), unlike Isaac and Ishmael, so that parentage would not seem like the "work" that made Jacob a better candidate for election. 2) The choice was made before they were born (verse 11) so that the choice was not based on birth order. In fact God turned the tables and chose the younger. 3) The choice for Jacob was made before they had done anything good or evil. The point seems clear: election is not based on what someone does after birth. It is free and unconditional.

He Loved Them Because He Loved Them

Another place in the Old Testament where this is stressed is Deuteronomy 7:6-8.[8] Moses describes the election of Israel like this:

> 6) For you are a people holy to the Lord your God; *the Lord your God has chosen you* to be a people for his own possession, out of all the peoples that are on the face of the earth. 7) It was not because you were more in number than any other people that the Lord set his love[9] upon you and chose you, for you were the fewest of all peoples; 8) but it was because the Lord loves you and is keeping the oath which he swore to your fathers, that the Lord has brought you out with a mighty hand, and redeemed you from the house of bondage, from the hand of Pharaoh king of Egypt.

This passage teaches again the freedom of God's grace in loving and choosing Israel. Notice the question that verse 7 raises: Why did God "set his love upon you and choose you"? Moses answers that it was not because of their greatness. They were very small, unlikely candidates for being chosen by God. Why then *did* God delight in them and choose them?

Verse 8 gives two answers. First: "It is *because the Lord loves you.*" Now remember what the question was from verse 7. The question was: Why did God set his *love* upon you? So the first answer Moses gives is: "Because he loves you." *He loves you because he loves you.* That is what I mean by the freedom of God and the freedom of electing love. He doesn't set his love upon them because they qualify for his love. He loves them because he loves them.

But what about the second reason Moses gives in Deuteronomy 7:8 for why God loved Israel and chose them and brought them out of Egypt? He says that it is because God was "keeping the oath which he swore to their fathers." Does this mean that God's choice to love and save wasn't free after all? Was he bound to save them? I don't think so.

The oath of blessing (referred to in verse 8) had been given to Abraham *in divine freedom.* It was confirmed *in freedom* to Isaac, not Ishmael; and it was confirmed *in freedom* to Jacob, not Esau. And in the same way God was free at the Red Sea to save that rebellious generation (Psalm 106:7-8) or to let them justly be destroyed by Pharaoh and then raise up children to Abraham from stones if necessary. God's choice to rescue Israel at the Red Sea and make them into an earthly people for his name was free and merciful and gracious! It was simply an extension and partial fulfillment of that first free oath that God made to Abraham, then to Isaac and Jacob.

So I conclude from Deuteronomy 10:14-15 and 7:6-8 that the way God decided to make a name for his glorious grace in the Old Testament was to choose a people for himself from all the peoples of the earth and to make that people the showcase of his redeeming work. And so you read in Isaiah that God created Israel "for his glory" (43:7), and that he formed them "that they might declare [his] praise" (43:21). In other words, in order to extend the pleasure that God has in his own name he chooses a people to enjoy and praise and proclaim that name to all the peoples. And so God has pleasure in election.

The Times of the Gentiles

Now what happens in the New Testament with the coming of Christ? God continues to rejoice in election, but now we move into a period when Israel as a people is no longer the focus of God's dealings. He turns for now to the Gentiles and begins to assemble a people for himself called the church. This is what Jesus meant in Matthew 21:43 when he said, "Therefore I tell you, the kingdom of God will be taken away from you (Israel) and given to a nation producing the fruits of it (the church)." Jesus called these days, when the focus of his saving work is on the nations, "the times of the Gentiles." "Jerusalem will be trodden down by the Gentiles until *the times of the Gentiles* are fulfilled" (Luke 21:24). During this time Paul says that "a hardening has come upon part of Israel *until the full number of the Gentiles comes in*" (Romans 11:25). Thus God is now at work gathering this "full number of Gentiles" (the elect) from all the peoples of the world.

Prior to the coming of Jesus the focus of God's saving reign was on Israel. "In past generations [God] allowed all the nations to walk in their own ways; yet he did not leave himself without witness, for he did good and gave you from heaven rains and fruitful seasons, satisfying your hearts with food and gladness" (Acts 14:16-17). These past centuries were "times of ignorance" among the nations (Acts 17:30). But now the Great Commission is pressing the gospel outwards to every people, tribe, language, and nation. Nevertheless, God is not finished with Israel. He will move again on that nation to draw it to himself and banish ungodliness from Jacob (Romans 11:12, 15, 24, 32; Zechariah 12:10).

Since the church is not an ethnic group like Israel was, God does not elect a whole nation for earthly purposes like he did Israel. Instead, the New Testament speaks of election as God's choice of individuals to believe and become part of the redeemed people of God.[10]

Revealed to Babes—with Joy

With a view to God's pleasure in election, consider first Luke 10:21. The reason I choose this verse is because it is one of the only two places in the Gospels where Jesus is said to rejoice.[11] The seventy disciples have just returned from their preaching tours and reported their success to Jesus. Luke writes in verse 21:

> In that same hour [*Jesus*] *rejoiced in the Holy Spirit* and said, "I thank you, Father, Lord of heaven and earth, that you have hidden these things from the wise and understanding and revealed them to babes: yes, Father, for thus it *was well-pleasing before you.*"[12]

Notice that all three members of the Trinity are rejoicing here: Jesus is rejoicing; but it says he is rejoicing *in the Holy Spirit.* I take that to mean that the Holy Spirit is filling him and moving him to rejoice. Then at the end of the verse it describes the pleasure of God the Father. The NIV translates it: "Yes, Father, for this was your good pleasure."

Now what is it that has the whole Trinity rejoicing together in this place? It is the free electing love of God to hide things from the intellectual elite and to reveal them to babes. "I thank you, Father, Lord of heaven and earth, that you have hidden these things from the wise and understanding and revealed them to babes." And what is it that the Father hides from some and reveals to others? Luke 10:22 gives the answer: "No one knows who the Son is except the Father." So what God the Father must reveal is the true spiritual identity of the Son. So when the seventy disciples return from their evangelistic mission and give their report to Jesus, he and the Holy Spirit rejoice that God the Father has chosen, according to his own good pleasure, to reveal the Son to babes and to hide him from the wise. The point of this is not that there are only certain classes of people who are chosen by God. The point is that God is free to choose the least likely candidates for his grace. Just as with the election of Abraham (the unlikely idolater from Ur) and Isaac (the miracle-born son of old age) and Jacob (the younger of twins), God contradicts what human merit might dictate. He hides from the wise and reveals to the most helpless and unaccomplished. When Jesus sees the Father freely enlightening and saving people whose only hope is free grace, he exults in the Holy Spirit and takes pleasure in his Father's election.

Confounding Man-centered Expectations

God the Son and God the Holy Spirit are so devoted to exalting God the Father that they rejoice when he exerts his wisdom and power and grace to choose a people for himself in a way that will confound all the man-centered expectations of the world. The wise are passed over in their pride and the babes, the unlikely, the helpless, are surprised with the sovereign freedom of divine favor. The tables are turned from what the world expects. The wisdom of man is put down. And the freedom of God's grace is exalted when the prime candidates of the world are passed over and God surprises everyone with his choice of the babes. This is what make Jesus and the Holy Spirit rejoice—the humbling of human pride and the exaltation of God's freedom and grace.

This is exactly what Paul focuses on when he describes God's election in forming the church in 1 Corinthians 1:26-31. As you read, look for what is being opposed and what is being promoted in the election described in these verses.

26) Consider your call, brethren; not many of you were wise according to worldly standards [recall whom Jesus passed over!],

not many were powerful, not many were of noble birth; 27) but
God *chose* [election!] what is foolish in the world to shame the
wise, God *chose* what is weak in the world to shame the strong, 28)
God *chose* what is low and despised in the world, even things that
are not, to bring to nothing things that are, 29) *so that no human
being might boast in the presence of God.* 30) From him [that is,
from the working of his election and call] you are in Christ Jesus,
whom God made our wisdom, our righteousness and sanctification
and redemption; 31) in order that, as it is written, "*Let him who
boasts, boast of the Lord.*"

The thought here is similar to that in Luke 10:21. God chooses
freely who will belong to his people. God does not simply elect
Christ and then wait on human self-determination, to govern who
will be "in Christ." Paul says very explicitly, "*From God* are you in
Christ" (v. 30). Your union with Christ is the choice and work of
God. Election is not God's choice of an unknown group of people
who come to Christ by virtue of their self-determining power.[13]
Election is the act of God by which he determines who will be in
Christ. "From him are you in Christ." The main point of this
passage would be undermined if election were not the election of
individuals to belong to Christ. For the point of the passage is:
"Look at what sort of individuals are in Christ: the foolish, the
weak, the despised. How is it that such unimpressive kinds of
people are 'in Christ'? It's because God *chose* them. '*God chose* what
is foolish . . . *God chose* what is weak . . . *God chose* what is low and
despised . . . *From God* are you in Christ.'" This is not the election
of Christ. This is the election of who belongs to Christ.[14]

And there is a reason for this kind of election. An utterly crucial
reason. God is not acting willy-nilly. He has a very definite goal in
mind to accomplish in election. And this goal is accomplished by
choosing who will be in Christ, not just by choosing Christ. His
goal has two parts, one positive and one negative. Negatively, his
goal is "that no human being might boast in the presence of God"
(verse 29). The goal of God in election is the elimination of all
human pride, all self-reliance, all boasting in man. Positively, his
goal is that boasting would be in the Lord: "Let him who boasts
boast in the Lord" (verse 31). In other words, the goal of election
is to take all boasting off of man and focus all boasting on God.
Humble man and exalt Christ. Make man see his utter dependence

on God's mercy and magnify the glory of God's free grace. That's why God has pleasure in election—it magnifies his name!

To the Glory of His Grace

Three times in the first chapter of Ephesians Paul trumpets this great purpose of God in his electing work. It is all "to the praise of the glory of his grace." First, in verses 4-6 he says God chose us in Christ[15] before the foundation of the world, that "we might be holy and blameless before him, in love having predestined us unto sonship through Jesus Christ for himself, according to the good pleasure of his will, *to the praise of the glory of his grace.*" Second, in verses 11-12 he says, "In Christ we were appointed, having been predestined according to the purpose of the one who works all things according to the counsel of his will, *unto the praise of his glory.*" Third, in verse 14 he says, "The Holy Spirit is the guarantee of our inheritance securing the redemption of [God's purchased] possession *unto the praise of his glory.*" In each of these instances what is being expressed is *God's* goal. God elects, predestines, and secures for one great ultimate purpose—that the glory of his grace might be praised forever and ever with white-hot affection. This is why God delights in election. It is the great first work of free grace that takes away the final refuge of human self-reliance and casts man on the unshakable Rock of covenant love.

For many people today it is astonishing that Jesus puts such a value on the sovereign rights of God's electing freedom that he would speak the way he does to those who refuse him. He speaks in such a way as to prevent them from boasting that they can overrule the ultimate purposes of God.[16] For example, in John 10:25-26 Jesus responded to the skeptics who demanded more and more proof: "I told you, and you do not believe. The works that I do in my Father's name they bear witness to me; but *you do not believe, because you do not belong to my sheep.*" Think about this for a moment. Think about what it *means*, and think about the fact that Jesus would dare to say it to unbelievers.

Jesus does *not* say, "You do not belong to my sheep because you do not believe." Belonging to the sheep, in this text, is not dependent on believing. It's the other way around. Believing is dependent on being a sheep. Belonging to the sheep enables a person to believe. So Jesus says, "The reason you don't believe is that you don't belong to my sheep." What Jesus means by "*my sheep*" is that the Father has given the sheep to him. That is what makes them his. We see this in John 10:27-29, "*My sheep* hear my voice, and I know them, and they follow me; and I give them eternal life, and they shall never perish, and no one shall snatch them out of my hand. My Father, who *has given them to me*, is greater than all, and no one is able to snatch them out of the Father's hand." The Father has given the sheep to the Son. So they are "his."

This is Jesus' way of talking about *election* in the Gospel of John. God has chosen a people for his own. These are his elect sheep. He then gives them to his Son so that they can be saved by faith in him. You can see this clearly in John 17:6 where Jesus says to his Father, "I have manifested your name to the people whom *you gave me* out of the world; *yours they were, and you gave them to me*, and they have kept your word." So Jesus can speak with confidence about some sheep among the flock of Israel that are definitely *his*, because they first belonged to the Father by election ("yours they were") and then were given to the Son by the Father ("and you gave them to me"). Belonging to the Father, precedes coming to Jesus. That's what Jesus says in John 6:37-39, "*All that the Father gives me will come to me*; and him who comes to me I will not cast out . . . and this is the will of him who sent me, that I should lose nothing of all that he has given me*, but raise it up at the last day."[17]

Picture yourself as a Pharisee hearing the message of Jesus and saying to yourself, "If he thinks I am going to be sucked into this movement along with the tax collectors and sinners, he's crazy. I have a will of my own and the power to determine my own destiny." And then picture Jesus, knowing what is in your heart, and saying, "You boast in your heart that you are in control of your life. You think that you can frustrate the ultimate plans of my ministry. You think that the great purposes of God in salvation are dependent on your wavering will. Truly, truly I say to you, the ultimate reason you do not believe is because the Father has not chosen you to be among my sheep." In other words, Jesus is saying, "The final boast of unbelief is destroyed by the doctrine of election." Those whom God chose, he also gave to the Son; and those whom he gave to the Son, the Son also called; and for those whom he called, he laid down his life; and to them he gave eternal joy in the presence of his glory. This is the Father's pleasure.

Infallible Salvation

We can sum up this great salvation from John's Gospel with the following steps: all that the Father has chosen to be his, he has given to the Son (17:6); and all whom he has given to the Son, the Son knows (10:14) and calls (10:3); and all whom he calls, know him (10:14) and recognize his voice (10:4-5) and come to him (6:37) and follow him (10:27); and the Son lays down his life for the sheep (10:11, 15); and to all for whom he dies he gives eternal life (10:28) and keeps them in the Father's word (17:6), so that none is lost (6:39) or snatched out of his hand (10:28), but is raised up at the last day (6:39) to glorify the Son forever (17:10). This is why the Father has pleasure in election. It is the indestructible foundation for an infallible salvation that redounds in the end to the glory of the Father and the Son.

It is no accident that this teaching from John's Gospel sounds just like the great teaching on election in Romans 8:28-32. One great reality lies behind both texts.

> 28) We know that all things work together for good for those who love God, who are called according to his purpose. 29) For whom he foreknew, he also predestined to be conformed to the image of his Son, in order that he might be the firstborn among many brothers. 30) And whom he predestined, these he also called; and whom he called, these he also justified; and whom he justified, these he also glorified.

Is Election Based on Foreknown Faith?

The plain point of this passage is that God is working infallibly to save his people, from foreknowing in eternity past to glorifying in eternity future. None is lost at any stage of redemption along the way. Nevertheless this text is often used to argue against unconditional election on the basis of verse 29 which says, "Those whom he *foreknew* he also predestined." Some say that people are not chosen unconditionally; rather they are chosen on the basis of their faith which they produce by their own powers of self-determination. God sees this self-determining choice by his divine foreknowledge and responds by choosing and predestining the believer to Christlikeness and glory.

But this will not square with the context. Notice that Romans 8:30 says, "And whom he predestined, these he also called; and whom he called, these he also justified; and whom he justified, these he also glorified." Focus for a moment on the fact that all whom God calls he also justifies. This calling in verse 30 is not given to all people. The reason we know it is not is that all those who are called are also justified—but all people are not justified. So this calling in verse 30 is not the general call to repentance that preachers give or that God gives through the glory of nature (Psalm 19:1-2). Everybody receives that call.[18] The call here is given only to those whom God predestined to be conformed to the image of his son, as verse 30 says, "Those whom he predestined, *these* he also called." And this call leads necessarily to justification, as verse 30 says, "Those whom he called, *these* he also justified." All the called are justified, not just some of them.

But we know that justification is by *faith* (Romans 5:1). So if all the called are infallibly justified, then the call itself must effect or guarantee the faith, since none can be justified without faith. Between God's act of predestination and justification there is a divine act of calling. Since justification is only *by faith*, the calling in view must be the act of God whereby he calls faith into being.[19] And since it necessarily results in justification, it must be effectual or irresistible. None is called (in this sense) who is not justified. All the called are justified. So the calling of verse 30 is the sovereign work of God which brings people to faith by which they are justified.

There Is No Self-engendered Faith to Foreknow

Now notice the implication this has for the meaning of "foreknowledge" in verse 29. When Paul says in verse 29, "Those whom he *foreknew* he also predestined," he can't mean (as so many try to make him mean) that God knows in advance who will use their power of self-determination to come to faith, so that he can predestine them to sonship on that basis. It can't mean that, because we have seen from verse 30 that people do not come to faith on their own. They are *called* effectually. That is why Paul can say that everyone who is called is infallibly justified—justification is by faith, and so the divine call guarantees the faith. It is not the product of self-determination that God responds to. It is the product of God's grace which God initiates.

So the *foreknowledge* of Romans 8:29 is not the mere awareness of something that will happen in the future apart from God's effective grace. Rather it is the kind of knowledge referred to in Old Testament texts like Genesis 18:19 ("I have chosen [literally: *known*] Abraham so that he may charge his children . . . to keep the way of the Lord"), and Jeremiah 1:5 ("Before I formed you in the womb, I *knew* you, and before you were born I consecrated you; I appointed you a prophet to the nations"), and Amos 3:2 ("You only [Israel] have I *known* from all the families of the earth"). As C.E.B. Cranfield says, the foreknowledge of Romans 8:29 is "that special taking knowledge of a person which is God's electing grace."[20] Such foreknowledge is virtually the same as election: "Those whom he foreknew (that is, chose) he predestined to be conformed to the image of his Son."

From Start to Finish, God

Therefore what this magnificent text (Romans 8:28-30) teaches is that God really accomplishes the complete redemption of his people from start to finish. He foreknows (elects) a people for himself before the foundation of the world, he predestines this people to be conformed to the image of his Son, he calls them to himself in faith, he justifies them through that faith, and he finally glorifies them. And nothing can separate them from the love of God in Christ forever and ever (Romans 8:39). This great work of salvation is rooted and grounded in the electing love of God. If that foundation stone crumbles, biblical salvation crumbles. But it cannot and will not crumble, because God has pleasure in election, the unshakable ground of the glory of his grace.

I am often asked by people, "Does it really matter what we

believe about election? Is it really relevant to how we live and minister?" My answer is, obviously, yes. And I think it will be helpful if I close this chapter with seven reasons why this teaching is precious to me and why I believe God has pleasure in it. In each of the following points "this truth" refers to the truth of God's free, sovereign, unconditional, individual election by grace of who will be saved.

First, this truth is biblical. It is biblical not only in being found once in Scripture, but in being found throughout Scripture. Recall the experience of George Mueller described at the beginning of this chapter: "To my great astonishment I found that the passages which speak decidedly for election and persevering grace, were about four times as many as those which speak apparently against these truths; and even those few, shortly after, when I had examined and understood them, served to confirm me in the above doctrines." George Whitefield, the great eighteenth century evangelist spoke for many saints when he wrote to John Wesley to explain why he believed in the truth of election: "Alas, I never read anything that Calvin wrote; my doctrines I had from Christ and His apostles; I was taught them of God."[21] God has pleasure in election because he exalts his word (Psalm 138:2) and his word teaches that these things are so.

Second, this truth humbles sinners and exalts the glory of God. This was the point of 1 Corinthians 1:26-31 that we saw above: "God *chose* . . . so that no human being might boast in the presence of God . . . [but] let him who boasts boast in the Lord." The great design of God's way of salvation is to magnify his glory and bring down human pride. George Whitefield wrote to John Wesley urging that they seek the truth that

> shall most debase man and exalt the Lord Jesus. Nothing but the doctrines of the Reformation can do this. All others leave free will in man and make him, in part, at least, a savior to himself. My soul, come not thou near the secret of those who teach such things. . . . I know Christ is all in all. Man is nothing: he hath a free will to go to hell, but none to go to heaven, till God worketh in him to will and to do his good pleasure.
>
> Oh, the excellency of the doctrine of election and of the saints' final perseverance! I am persuaded, till a man comes to believe and feel these important truths, he cannot come out of himself, but

when convinced of these and assured of their application to his own heart, he then walks by faith indeed.[22]

Third, this truth tends to preserve the church from slipping toward false philosophies of life. History seems to show that this is so. For example, toward the end of the eighteenth century "Calvinistic convictions waned in North America. In the progress of a decline which [Jonathan] Edwards had rightly anticipated, those Congregational churches of New England which had embraced Arminianism after the Great Awakening gradually moved into Unitarianism and universalism, led by Charles Chauncy."[23] It seems that there is something about the truth of God's free and sovereign election that stands guard over the mind and heart of the church and keeps her alert to tendencies and shifts that swing wide from the plumb line of God's Word.

Fourth, this truth is the good news of a salvation that is not just offered but effected. Election is the guarantee that God not only invites people to be delivered, but also actually delivers them. "You shall call his name Jesus because *he shall save his people* from their sins" (Matthew 1:21). God undertakes with omnipotence to save his people. He plans it in election, and he achieves it through the work of his Son, and he applies it infallibly by his Holy Spirit through faith. The predestined are called, the called are justified, the justified are glorified (Romans 8:30). The destiny of God's people, rooted in election, is unshakably sure. And that is good news.[24]

God's Compassion on All People

It is perfectly legitimate to ask whether this teaching means that the gospel is a sincere expression of compassion to those whom God has not chosen to convict and call and draw to the Son with effectual grace. Many people stumble over the straightforward biblical teaching on election because they are more controlled by the kind of logic that says John 3:16 ("For God so loved the world . . .") cannot be true if God only elects some people for salvation. They say that the weeping of Jesus over Jerusalem cannot be sincere if he is only going to give life to the elect (Luke 19:41-42—"Would that even today you knew the things that made for peace!"). They say that passages like Ezekiel 18:32 and 33:11, which we looked at in chapter 2 (pp. 61-62), can have no natural meaning if God elects some to salvation and not others ("I do not have pleasure in the death of the wicked"). Similarly 1 Timothy 2:4 and 2 Peter 3:9 are often brought in as problem passages for the teaching on election ("God desires all men to be saved and come to a knowledge of the truth . . . God is not willing that any should perish").

My aim is to let Scripture stand—to let it teach what it will and not to tell it what it cannot say. Sometimes I hear people say that we who believe in unconditional election are controlled more by the demands of logic than by the demands of Scripture. As much as I know my heart, I believe this is not so. On the contrary, it seems to me that more often philosophical assumptions cause the *rejection* of election. For example, the statement, "God cannot choose individuals unconditionally and yet have compassion on all men," is based on a certain kind of philosophical assumption, not on Scripture. Scripture leads us precisely to this paradoxical position. I am willing to let the paradox stand even if I can't explain it.[25] It seems to me that those who teach against unconditional election are often controlled by non-biblical logic. They take the texts just mentioned and say (because of a certain philosophical assumptions) that these texts can't coexist with the teaching on election that I have developed here. So they deny that the Bible teaches unconditional election because it teaches things they can't fit together with election. This, however, is not the method I follow. I do not deny that Jesus wept over Jerusalem. I do not deny that he felt genuine compassion for perishing people. I do not deny that God loves the world of lost men—elect and non-elect. On the contrary, all I want to do is try to give an account for how both of these biblical teachings can be so—the plain teaching of the Bible on election *and* the plain teaching that God has sincere compassion for the non-elect which he expresses in various ways in the Bible. I do not allow some alien logic to force me to choose between these two teachings of Scripture.

The way I would give an account of this is explained by Robert L. Dabney in an essay written over a hundred years ago.[26] His treatment is very detailed and answers many objections that go beyond the scope of this book. I will simply give the essence of his solution which seems to me to be on the right track, though he, as well as I, would admit we do not "furnish an exhaustive explanation of this mystery of the divine will."[27]

How Is God Like George Washington?

Dabney uses an analogy from the life of George Washington taken from Chief-Justice Marshall's *Life of Washington*. A certain Major André had jeopardized the safety of the young nation through "rash and unfortunate" treasonous acts. Marshall says of the death warrant, signed by Washington, "Perhaps on no occasion of his life did the commander-in-chief obey with more reluctance the stern mandates of duty and of policy." Dabney observes that Washington's compassion for André was "real and profound." He also had "plenary power to kill or to save alive." Why then did he sign the death warrant? Dabney explains, "Washington's volition to sign the death-warrant of André did not arise from the fact that his compassion was slight or feigned, but from the fact that it was rationally counterpoised by a complex of superior judgments . . . of wisdom, duty, patriotism, and moral indignation."

Dabney imagines a defender of André, hearing Washington say, "I do this with the deepest reluctance and pity." Then the defender says, "Since you are supreme in this matter, and have full bodily ability to throw down that pen, we shall know by your signing this warrant that your pity is hypocritical." Dabney responds to this by saying, "The petulance of this charge would have been equal to its folly. The pity was real, but was restrained by superior elements of motive. Washington had official and bodily power to discharge the criminal, but he had not the sanctions of his own wisdom and justice."[28] The corresponding point in the case of divine election is that "the absence of a volition in God to save does not necessarily imply the absence of compassion."[29] God has "a true compassion, which is yet restrained, in the case of the . . . non-elect, by consistent and holy reasons, from taking the form of a volition to regenerate."[30]God's infinite wisdom regulates his whole will and guides and harmonizes (not suppresses) all its active principles."[31]

In other words, God has a real and deep compassion for perishing sinners. His expression of pity and his entreaties have heart in them. There is a genuine inclination in God's heart to spare those who have committed treason against his kingdom. But his motivation is complex and not every true element in it rises to the level of effective choice. In his great and mysterious heart there are kinds of longings and desires that are real—they tell us something true about his character. Yet not all of these longings govern God's actions. He is governed by the depth of his wisdom through a plan that no ordinary human deliberation would ever conceive (Romans 11:33-36; 1 Corinthians 2:9). There are holy and just reasons for why the affections of God's heart have the nature and intensity and proportion that they do.

Dabney is aware that several kinds of objections can be raised against the analogy of George Washington as it is applied to God.[32] He admits that "no analogy can be perfect between the actions of a finite and the infinite intelligence and will."[33] Yet I think he is right to say that the objections do not overthrow the essential truth that there can be, in a noble and great heart (even a divine heart), sincere compassion for a criminal that is nevertheless not set free. Therefore I affirm that God loves the world with a deep compassion that desires their salvation; yet I also affirm that he has chosen from before the foundation of the world whom he will save from sin. Election is the good news that salvation is not only a sincere offer made to all, but a sure effect in the life of the elect and a transformation of faith produced by the power of God's grace.

Fifth, this truth enables us to own up to the demands for holiness in the Scripture and yet have assurance of salvation. The Bible teaches that there is a holiness without which we will not see the Lord (Hebrews 12:14). Dozens of passages in the Bible speak of our final salvation (though not our election) as conditional upon a changed heart and life.[34] The question arises then, how can I have the assurance I will persevere in faith and in the holiness necessary for inheriting eternal life?

The answer is that assurance is rooted in our election (2 Peter 1:10). Divine election is the guarantee that God will undertake to complete by sanctifying grace what his electing grace has begun. This is the meaning of the new covenant: God does not merely command obedience, he gives it. "The Lord your God will circumcise your heart and the heart of your offspring, so that you will love the Lord your God with all your heart and with all your soul, that you may live" (Deuteronomy 30:6). "I will put my Spirit within you and cause you to walk in my statutes" (Ezekiel 36:27; 11:20; see also Hebrews 13:20; Philippians 2:13). Election is the final ground of assurance because, since it is God's commitment to save, it is also God's commitment to enable all that is necessary for salvation.[35]

St. Augustine put it like this:

> I have no hope at all but in thy great mercy. Grant what thou commandest and command what thou wilt. Thou dost enjoin on us continence . . . Truly by continence are we bound together and brought back into that unity from which we were dissipated into a plurality. For he loves thee too little who loves anything together with thee, which he loves not for thy sake. O love that ever burnest and art never quenched! O Charity, my God, enkindle me! Thou commandest continence. Grant what thou commandest and command what thou wilt.[36]

The assurance that God will answer this prayer in accordance with the oath of the new covenant is that election secures that "those who are justified will be glorified" (Romans 8:30), so that all the conditions laid down for glorification will be met by the power of God's grace. "God chose you from the beginning to be saved *through sanctification by the Spirit*" (2 Thessalonians 2:13).[37]

Election guards us from falling off the horse on either of two sides. It guards against the error of thinking that we can earn our way into God's favor through "works of the law," since God's favor toward us is rooted in the free act of love before the foundation of the world. We cannot earn what God has chosen to bestow freely "before we had done anything good or evil" (Romans 9:11). It also guards us from the error of thinking that in order for us to be loved freely and to be eternally secure, obedience must be optional, not necessary. Thus the incentive for holiness retains its urgency, since holiness is necessary (Hebrews 12:14); but it does not become a legalistic burden, because we serve in the strength which God supplies (1 Peter 4:11; see also 1 Corinthians 15:10; Romans 15:18). It is true *both* that "the gate is narrow and the way is hard that leads to life" (Matthew 7:14), *and* that "my yoke is easy and my burden is light" (Matthew 11:30). The truth of election preserves both the urgency and freedom of biblical obedience. (For more on this see chapter 9.)

Sixth, this truth opens us to the overwhelming experience of being loved personally with the unbreakable electing love of God. Many people have no personal experience of knowing that they were loved by God eternally and will be cared for by him with omnipotent, all-supplying love for ever and ever. Many people think of God's love only in terms of a love that offers and waits, but does not take us for himself and work with infinite enthusiasm to keep us and glorify us forever. Yet this is the experience available for any who will come and drink the water of life freely (Revelation 22:17).

The Comfort and Strength of Christian Hearts

There is a general love of God that he bestows on all his creatures. This is plain from Matthew 5:44-45, "Love your enemies and pray for those who persecute you, so that you may be sons of your Father who is in heaven; for he makes his sun rise on the evil and on the good, and sends rain on the just and on the unjust." (See also Acts 14:17; I Timothy 4:10.) But this love, which is extended to all people, is not the comfort and strength of the Christian heart. Our comfort and strength is the assurance that we belong to God's covenant community and are loved with an electing love that not only *offers* good things but *accomplishes* all things necessary to our individual salvation.

One beautiful expression (among many[38]) of this love in the Old Testament is found in Jeremiah 31:2-3, "The people who survived the sword found grace in the wilderness; when Israel sought for rest, the Lord appeared to him from afar. *I have loved you with an everlasting love*; therefore I have continued my faithfulness to you." Here is the preciousness of an everlasting (electing) love that secures not just the offer of help, but the commitment of covenant faithfulness. To know this kind of love is God's will for his people. But it is not likely to be known where the truth of election is neither taught nor known.

The expressions of this love in the New Testament are too many to quote, but too precious not to mention in part. "For we know, brothers, *loved by God*, that *he has chosen you*" (1 Thessalonians 1:4). "We are bound to give thanks to God always for you, brethren, *loved by the Lord*, because God chose you from the beginning to be saved" (2 Thessalonians 2:13). Election is the first gift, and continuing channel, of covenant love to God's people. "Put on then as *God's chosen ones*, holy and *loved*, compassion, kindness . . ." (Colossians 3:12). To be a "chosen one" is to be uniquely "loved", as one of Christ's "own." "Now before the feast of the passover, when Jesus knew that his hour had come to depart out of this world to the Father, *having loved his own who were in the world, he loved them to the end*" (John 13:1; see also 15:13-14; 17:22-23). "But God, who is rich in mercy, *out of the great love with which he loved us*, even when we were dead through our trespasses, *made us alive* together with Christ (by grace you have been saved)" (Ephesians 2:4-5). The covenant love of God is not only a response to our faith, but a resurrecting power of grace that made us alive when we were dead and could not yet exert faith (see also Romans 8:7; 1 Corinthians 2:14; John 10:27).

There is a desperate need in the world for a sense of being loved that only this truth about election can satisfy. God means for us to enjoy this experience. And seeing his people strengthened and emboldened by it is another reason why he has pleasure in election.

Seventh, this truth gives hope for effective evangelism and guarantees the triumph of Christ's mission in the end. Nothing I have said should be taken to imply that the urgency of evangelism is lessened. Evangelism and missions are not imperiled by the biblical truth of election, but empowered by it, and their triumph is secured by it. Jesus said, "I have other sheep that are not of this fold; I must bring them also, and they will heed my voice" (John 10:16). This means that there are elect sheep scattered throughout the world (John 11:52). They will be there among "every people, language, tribe and nation" when the missionary arrives to issue God's absolutely essential call through the gospel (Revelation 5:9). Therefore Jesus says he *must* bring them in. And he says they *will* heed his voice. In other words, the triumph of the ingathering of world missions is a certainty because of the truth of election: he does have other sheep.

What Paul Dreamed in Corinth

Paul was tremendously heartened by this truth. The Lord came to him one night in a dream while he was evangelizing in Corinth. To encourage him the Lord said, "Do not be afraid, but speak and do not be silent; for I am with you, and no man shall attack you to harm you; *for I have many people in this city*" (Acts 18:9-10). The ground of Paul's encouragement was the assurance from the Lord that there were "other sheep" in Corinth—many of them. God had chosen them, and he would call them—but it must be through the preaching of the gospel (see Acts 13:48; 16:14). The truth of election embraces the necessity of evangelism and missions and guarantees their success in God's time and God's way. This has been the strength and courage of thousands of faithful missionaries.

The Power of Livingstone's Tomb

David Livingstone's explorations were not mere secular adventures. "Viewed in relation to my calling," he wrote, "the end of the geographical feat is only the beginning of the enterprise." The great object was to "bring unknown nations into the sympathies of the Christian world" and thus introduce them to the gospel. "O Jesus, fill me with Thy love now," he wrote in his diary in 1852, "and I beseech Thee, accept me, and use me a little for Thy glory."[39] To his wife he wrote, "I will go no matter who opposes: I know you wish as ardently as I can that all the world may be filled with the glory of the Lord."[40] He died so far from civilization that eleven months passed before his body was buried in Westminster Abbey. The text chosen to be inscribed on his grave was not only a driving power in his own life but later would prove to be the same in the life of another young man as well.

Peter Cameron Scott was born in Glasgow, Scotland, in 1867 and founded the African Inland Mission. His efforts to take the gospel to Africa met with tragedy and discouragement. His brother John had joined him in the mission, but within months John fell victim to the fever. Alone in the jungle, Scott buried him, and at the grave rededicated himself to preach the gospel. But, to compound his heartache, his health broke and, utterly discouraged, he had to return to England.

In London something wonderful happened. Scott needed a fresh source of inspiration and he found it at a tomb in Westminster Abbey that held the remains of a man who had inspired so many others in their missionary service to Africa. The spirit of David Livingstone seemed to be prodding Scott onward as he knelt reverently and read the inscription:

OTHER SHEEP I HAVE WHICH ARE NOT OF THIS FOLD;
THEM ALSO I MUST BRING.

He would return to Africa and lay down his life, if need be, for the cause for which this great man had lived and died.[41] It is the truth of election ("I have other sheep")—the sovereign freedom of God in saving a people for himself—that guarantees the triumph of the gospel and the universal fame of God's grace. This triumph and this fame bring overflowing pleasure to the heart of God.

Notes

1. George Mueller, *Autobiography of George Mueller*, compiled by G. Fred. Bergin (London: J. Nisbet and Co., 1906), 33-34, italics added.

2. Charles Spurgeon, *Autobiography*, 1 (Edinburgh: Banner of Truth Trust, 1962, orig. in 4 vols. 1897-1900), 164-165.

3. Ibid., 38-39. We learn on page 40, note 2, that the cook's name was Mary King.

4. Gustav Oehler points out that this use of "know" is also found in Psalm 1:6 and 37:18. It is similar to Exodus 33:12 where God says to Moses, "I know you by name." And it stands behind the New Testament use of electing foreknowledge as in Romans 8:29. Thus Oehler says, "As *yd'* (know) is said of God not simply in reference to the relation in which He already stands to man, but also in reference to His placing man in a relation to Him in virtue of which he acknowledges himself as His property, *yd'* (know) becomes another name for the divine election (synonymous with *bahar*)." Gustav

Oehler, *Theology of the Old Testament* (Minneapolis: Klock and Klock Christian Publishers, 1978, orig. 1873), 177.

5. The Hebrew word for "has gotten" you is used in Genesis 4:1 in the sense of making a child. Eve says, "I *have gotten* a man with the help of the Lord."

6. When the possibility is raised that Israel's power or righteousness might have won for them the blessings of God's electing grace, Moses shoots this down with no uncertain words. "Beware lest you say in your heart, 'My power and the might of my hand have gotten me this wealth.' You shall remember the Lord your God, for it is he who gives you power to get wealth. . . ." (Deuteronomy 8:17-18). Concerning the driving out of the pagan nations from Canaan, as part of the covenant promise, Moses warns, "Do not say in your heart, after the Lord your God has thrust them out before you, 'It is because of my righteousness that the Lord has brought me in to possess this land;' whereas it is because of the wickedness of these nations that the Lord is driving them out before you. Not because of your righteousness or the uprightness of your heart are you going in to possess their land; but because of the wickedness of these nations the Lord your God is driving them out from before you, and that he may confirm the word which the Lord swore to your fathers, to Abraham, to Isaac, and to Jacob" (Deuteronomy 9:4-5).

7. The Hebrew word *hashaq* ordinarily means "to love" or "be attached to." F. Brown, S.R. Driver, C. Briggs, *Hebrew and English Lexicon of the Old Testament* (Oxford: Clarendon Press, 1962), 365f. It is full of feeling and desire as love for a woman. It is not a word denoting dispassionate and benevolent commitment. It's other uses are Genesis 34:8; Exodus 27:17; 38:17, 28; Deuteronomy 7:7; 21:11; 1 Kings 9:19; 2 Chronicles 8:6; Psalm 91:14; and Isaiah 38:17. The unusual thing about its use in Deuteronomy 10:15 is that it is used with the infinitive "to love" (*le'ahabah*). Literally it would be, "The Lord *loved* your fathers *to love them*." Or, "The Lord *was attached* to your Fathers to love them." It seems that the double word for love (*hashaq* and *'ahabah*) is a way of strongly emphasizing that the motive here was love rooted only in love and nothing else. The love was deep and passionate and full of desire. Hence it seems right to suggest the translation: "The Lord delighted in your fathers to love them." (See below on the use of the word in Deuteronomy 7:7.)

8. This is not the only other place. For example, see Malachi 1:1-5.

9. This is the same Hebrew word for love (*hashaq*) discussed in note 7.

10. On the view that election refers not to God's choice of specific individuals but to God's choice of Christ and an unspecified body of people who will be in Christ not because of God's determination but their own self-determination, see below, especially note 13. Note also that God's "election" of the nation of Israel as a whole in the Old Testament does not imply that each individual was "elect" in the sense of eternally saved. This confusion is what Paul was correcting in Romans 9:6-8.

11. The other place is John 11:15. I am not saying that these are the only times in his ministry that Jesus expressed joy or gladness. Far from it. However these are the only explicit references in the Gospels (that I have found) to

instances when Jesus rejoiced.

12. See chapter 1, note 10, for a discussion of the verb *eudokeō*. Here the noun form is used, *eudokia*. It is used eight other times in the New Testament: Matthew 11:26 (parallel with Luke 10:21); Luke 2:14 ("On earth peace to men of [God's] good pleasure"); Romans 10:1 ("My heart's *desire* is that they may be saved"); Ephesians 1:5, 9 (the good pleasure of God's will); Philippians 1:15 ("Some preach Christ on account of envy and strife, and some on account of *good pleasure*"); Philippians 2:13 ("God is the one at work to will and to work for his *good pleasure*"); 2 Thessalonians 1:11 ("that [God] might fulfill every *good intention* of goodness").

13. This whole text would make no sense if God only elected Christ, but left the individual make-up of the church to the self-determination of man. Yet this is a popular view that is taught today over against the view I am unfolding here. For example, R.T. Forster and V.P. Marston, *God's Strategy in Human History* (Wheaton: Tyndale House, 1973) say, "The prime point is that the election of the church is a corporate rather than an individual thing. It is not that individuals are in the church because they are elect, it is rather that they are elect because they are in the church which is the body of the elect One" (p. 136). More recently Clark Pinnock, "From Augustine to Arminius: A Pilgrimage in Theology," in: *A Case for Arminianism: The Grace of God and the Will of Man* (Grand Rapids: Zondervan Publishing House, 1990) said, "Election is a corporate category and not oriented to the choice of individuals for salvation." Election speaks "of a class of people rather than specific individuals" (p. 20). Similarly, in the same volume William G. MacDonald ("The Biblical Doctrine of Election") says, "Christ is the chosen one in and through whom in corporate solidarity with him the church is selected to be God's own" (p. 228).

The text most often referred to in defending this "corporate" view of election is Ephesians 1:3-5, "Blessed be the God and Father of our Lord Jesus Christ, who blessed us with every spiritual blessing in the heavenly places in Christ Jesus, just as *he chose us in him* before the foundation of the world that we might be holy and blameless before him; in love having predestined us unto sonship through Jesus Christ for himself, according to the good pleasure of his will." The key question is what does "*he chose us in him*" mean? Is this Paul's way of saying that God did not choose specific individuals? Or is it his way of saying that the individuals who were chosen were chosen in relation to Christ? The wording of the text is fully honored in the second view because all elect individuals are elect with a view to their relation to Christ. Christ was not an afterthought to election. As God contemplated electing people for salvation, he contemplated them as coming to salvation in relation to Christ.

There is nothing about the phrase "chose us in Christ · that demands a non-individual interpretation. On the contrary, there are numerous passages that demand an individual view of election, e.g. Matthew 22:14; 1 Corinthians 1:27-28; James 2:5; John 6:37, 39; 10:16, 26; 13:18; 17:6, 9, 24; Romans 8:28-33; 11:4-7; etc. Moreover the non-individual interpretation of Ephesians 1:4 does not square well with Ephesians 1:11 where Paul says that in this matter of election and predestination God "*works all things according to the counsel of his will.*" This "working all things" suggests that God is not leaving to the mere self-determining power of man the incredibly crucial reality of how many and who constitute the body of Christ. Not only that, but neither does the literal wording of Ephesians 1:4 fit the corporate interpretation: "[God] chose us in him before the foundation of the world." The ordinary meaning of the word for "choose" in verse 4 is to "select" or "pick out" of a group (see Luke 6:13; 14:7; John 13:18; 15:16,19). The object of this "selection" is said to be "us." So the natural meaning of the verse is that God selects his people from all humanity, before the foundation of the world; and he does this "in Christ," that is, by viewing them in relationship to Christ their redeemer.

14. James argues in much the same way Paul does here, emphasizing the implications of God's choice of who belongs to the church. He criticizes the favoritism shown to the rich and the discrimination against the poor by saying, "Listen, my beloved brethren. *Has not God chosen those who are poor in the world to be rich in faith and heirs of the kingdom* which he has promised to those who love him?" (James 2:5).

15. See note 13 above on the "corporate sense" of "in Christ."

16. In spite of strong statements of God's unstoppable counsel (like Isaiah 46:10 and Ephesians 1:11), R.T. Forster and V.P. Marston argue from Luke 7:30 that people do in fact frustrate God's specific purpose for them. Luke 7:30 says, "The Pharisees and the lawyers rejected the purpose of God for themselves, not having been baptized by John" (RSV). From texts like this (Matthew 23:37; 12:50; 7:21; John 7:17; 1 John 2:17; 1 Thessalonians 4:3; 5:17-19; Acts 7:51) Forster and Marston say, "Nothing in Scripture suggests that there is some kind of will or plan of God which is inviolable." *God's Strategy in Human History* (Wheaton: Tyndale House, 1973), 32. But in fact there are many texts in Scripture that suggest precisely that God's plans will stand and that his counsel cannot fail (Genesis 50:20; Deuteronomy 29:2-4; Proverbs 16:4, 9, 33; 19:21; 21:1; Isaiah 46:10; 63:17; Jeremiah 10:23; 32:40; Lamentations 3:37-38; Acts 2:23; 4:27-28; 13:48; 16:14; Romans 8:28; 9:14-23; 11:24-36; Philippians 2:12-13; 2 Timothy 2:24-26; Hebrews 13:20-21; Revelation 17:17, and many more). With regard to Luke 7:30 the phrase "for themselves" very likely, because of its location in the word order, does not modify "the purpose of God" (as the RSV quoted above might suggest). Rather it probably modifies "rejected." Thus Luke would be saying that the plan of salvation preached by John the Baptist was accepted by some and rejected by others "for themselves." The text cannot prove one way or the other whether God has a specific plan for each life that can be successfully frustrated. To answer that, one would have to reflect on the possibility that God wills different things in different ways allowing his will in one sense to be resisted while overruling all such resistance according to his ultimate will to accomplish his purpose which none can frustrate (Daniel 4:35; Job 42:2). See a discussion of this in *Desiring God*, pp. 28-30, 38-39; and in *The Justification of God* (Grand Rapids: Baker Book House, 1983), 172.

17. See also John 6:44-45, 65; 10:16; 17:9, 24; 18:9.

18. This is the kind of call mentioned in Matthew 22:14, "Many are called but few are chosen."

19. This understanding of God's call is seen most clearly in 1 Corinthians 1:23-24, "We preach Christ crucified, a stumbling block to Jews and folly to Gentiles, but to those who are *called*, both Jew and Greeks, Christ the power of God and the wisdom of God." Notice the two kinds of "calls" implied in this text.

    First, the preaching of Paul goes out to all, both Jews and Greeks. This is the general call of the Gospel. It offers salvation to all who will believe on the crucified Christ. But by and large it falls on unreceptive ears and is considered foolishness. This is the kind of call referred to in Matthew 22:14, "Many are called, but few are chosen."

    But then, secondly, Paul refers to another kind of call. He says that among those who hear, there are some who are "called" in such a way that they no longer regard the cross as foolishness but as the wisdom and power of God. What else can this call be but the effectual call of God out of darkness into the light of God? "Effectual" means that the call itself effects what it demands, namely, faith. If *all* who are called in this sense regard the cross as the power of God, then something in the call must effect the faith. This is what is sometimes called irresistible grace—not that grace cannot be resisted (Acts 7:51), rather that this grace can, when God pleases overcome all resistance and make the heart happily willing to believe.

    It is further explained in 2 Corinthians 4:4-6, "The god of this world has blinded the minds of unbelievers, to keep them from seeing the light of the gospel of the glory of Christ, who is the likeness of God. . . . It is the God who said, 'Let light shine out of darkness,' who has shone in our hearts to give the light of the knowledge of the glory of God in the face of Christ." Since men are blinded to the worth of Christ, a miracle is needed in order for them to come to see and believe. Paul compares this miracle with the first day of creation when God said, "Let there be light." It is in fact a new creation, or a new birth. This is what is meant by the effectual call in 1 Corinthians 1:24.

    Those who are called have their eyes opened by the sovereign, creative power of God so that they no longer see the cross as foolishness, but as the power and the wisdom of God. The effectual call is the miracle of having our blindness removed.

    Another example of it is in Acts 16:14, where Lydia is listening to the preaching of Paul. Luke says, "The Lord opened her heart to give heed to what was said by Paul." Unless God opens our hearts, we will not heed the message of the gospel. This heart-opening is what happens when God "calls" those whom he predestined to be conformed to the image of his Son (Romans 8:29-30). This is why all the called are justified and glorified. The call is not merely an opportunity for man to choose, but also an infallible work of God to create a new heart of willing faith.

20. C.E.B. Cranfield, *The Epistle to the Romans*, 1, ICC. (Edinburgh: T. & T. Clark Ltd, 1975), 431. See above note 4.

21. Arnold Dallimore, *George Whitefield*, 1 (Edinburgh: Banner of Truth Trust, 1970), 574.

22. Ibid., 407.

23. Iain H. Murray, *Jonathan Edwards: A New Biography* (Edinburgh: Banner of Truth, 1987), 454. Remarkably, C. H. Spurgeon chronicles the same doctrinal moves a hundred years later in England. He notes the abandonment of the confessions and the catechisms of the seventeenth century during the eighteenth century and says, "There followed an age of drivelling, in which our Nonconformity existed, but gradually dwindled down, first into Arminianism, and then into Unitarianism, until it almost ceased to be. Men know that it was so and yet they would act it all over again. They read history, and yet demand that the old doctrine should again be given up. . . . Oh, fools and slow of heart! Will not history teach them? No, it will not if the Bible does not. . . . Surely evil days are near, unless the church shall again clasp the truth to her heart." Quoted in Iain Murray, *The Forgotten Spurgeon* (Edinburgh: Banner of Truth Trust, 1973), 189. I see the same kind of theological shifting (if not to the same extent) in Clark Pinnock's pilgrimage as he revises more and more of historic theism (see note 13 above and chapter 2, notes 5 and 6).

24. Spurgeon said, "I have my own private opinion that there is no such thing as preaching Christ and Him crucified, unless we preach what is nowadays called Calvinism. It is a nickname to call it Calvinism; Calvinism is the gospel, and nothing else. I do not believe we can preach the gospel . . . unless we preach the sovereignty of God in His dispensation of grace; nor unless we exalt the electing, unchangeable, eternal, immutable, conquering love of Jehovah; nor do I think we can preach the gospel unless we base it upon the special and particular redemption of His elect and chosen people which Christ wrought out upon the Cross; nor can I comprehend a gospel which lets saints fall away after they are called" (Spurgeon, *Autobiography*, 168).

25. I do not believe the Scriptures contradict themselves. By paradox I mean what *appears* to be a contradiction, but in fact does have coherency. For an example of how Arminians are sometimes controlled by non-biblical logic, see chapter 2, note 6.

26. Robert L. Dabney, "God's Indiscriminate Proposals of Mercy, as Related to his Power, Wisdom, and Sincerity," *Discussions: Evangelical and Theological,* 1 (Edinburgh: Banner of Truth Trust, 1967, orig., 1890), 282-313.

27. Ibid., 309.

28. Ibid., 285.

29. Ibid., 299.

30. Ibid., 307.

31. Ibid., 309.

32. Ibid., 287-299. He cites three kinds of objections to the analogy:

1) "While it applies to a human ruler, who is not omnipotent, it does not apply to God, who is almighty." A human ruler foresees negative effects of his pardoning and cannot overcome them and therefore is constrained to condemn. God is omnipotent and therefore is not constrained by such inability. Dabney answers, "We know that [God's] ultimate end is his own glory. But we do not know all the ways in which God may deem his glory is promoted. . . . God may see in his own omniscience, a rational ground

other than inability for restraining his actual [inclination] of pity towards a given sinner" (pp. 288-289).

2) The second objection comes from advanced theological speculation: "Such a theory of motive and free agency may not be applied to the divine will, because of God's absolute simplicity of being, and the unity of his attributes with his essence, the unity and eternity of his whole will as to all events. It is feared that the parallel would misrepresent God's activities of will by a vicious anthropomorphism" (p. 287). The real issue here is whether God's unchangeableness is jeopardized and whether he is put at the mercy of creatures who bring about fluctuations in his heart that make him dependent on them and divided in his will. This is the concern when the historic confessions say that God is "without passions." Dabney responds by saying, "While God has no . . . mere susceptibility such that his creature can cause an effect upon it irrespective to God's own will and freedom, yet he has active principles. These are not passions, in the sense of fluctuations or agitations, but none the less are they affections of his will, actively distinguished from the cognitions in his intelligence" (p. 291). Moreover the actions of his creatures "are real occasions, though not efficient causes, of the action both of the divine affections and will" (p. 291). In other words, God is not at the mercy of his creatures, because, even though he genuinely responds to their actions with affections and choices, this response is always according to God's prior willing in complete freedom. Thus he is not forced to respond by others, nor is he, as it were, cornered into a frustrated compassion that he did not anticipate.

God's simplicity and unity should not be taken to mean what the Bible forbids that it mean: "The Bible always speaks of God's attributes as distinct, and yet not dividing his unity; of his intelligence and will as different; of his wrath, love, pity, wisdom, as not the same activities of the Infinite Spirit" (p. 290). The unity of God's Spirit lies not in his having no affections, nor in all his affections being one simple act; rather his unity lies in the glorious harmony and proportion of all that he is—each affection and propensity revealing something of the unified, harmonious complexity of the infinite Mind.

3) The third kind of objection to applying the analogy of George Washington to God is that "No such balancing of subjective motives takes place without inward strivings, which would be inconsistent with God's immutability and blessedness" (p. 287). Dabney agrees that this is difficult to imagine—that God is moved by all the energy of affections and yet shows all the equanimity of deity. But it is not impossible. He observes wisely that the more pure and steady a person's affections and thoughts are, the less struggle is involved in adjusting them into a rational and righteous decision. He imagines a man of more unstable condition than the "majestic calmness" of Washington facing the same choice: "He would have shown far more agitation; he would perhaps have thrown down the pen and snatched it again, and trembled and wept. But this would not have proved a deeper compassion than Washington's. His shallow nature was not capable of such depths of sentiment in any virtuous direction as filled the profounder soul. The cause of the difference would have been in this, that Washington's was a grander and wiser as well as a more feeling soul" (p. 298).

Dabney cites an analogy of how the deepening of mixed affections does not have to result in internal strife and agitation: "Dying saints have sometimes declared that their love for their families was never before so profound and tender; and yet were enabled by dying grace to bid them a final farewell with joyful calmness. If, then, the ennobling of the affections enables the will to adjust the balance between them with less agitation, what will the result be when the wisdom is that of omniscience, the virtue is that of infinite holiness, and the self-command that of omnipotence?" (p. 299).

33. Ibid., 287.

34. See the Appendix, "Letter to a Friend," for an extended discussion of the so-called "lordship salvation" and for a long list of Bible passages on the necessity of obedience.

35. See the Appendix, "Letter to a Friend," (pp. 292-305) for a list of Bible passages that show God's promise of preservation in holiness for his people.

36. St. Augustine, *Confessions, X*, 40, quoted in Henry Bettenson, *Documents of the Christian Church* (London: Oxford University Press, 1967), 54.

37. Gustav Oehler (see note 4) poses the problem this way: how can God's end in election be assured when the covenant with his people is conditional on obedience? "If Israel by breaking the covenant is exposed to God's judgment and rejected, this seems to nullify God's decree of election and the realization of the aim of His kingdom, which, though secured by God's covenant oath, is again dependent on man's action" (*Theology of the Old Testament*, p. 197). The answer of the Old Testament, he says (and it is the same answer given in the New Testament), is that God will so convert his people that the ethical prerequisites for eternal blessing will be secured by God himself: "The end of this conversion is attained when, by the operation of divine grace, that renovation of heart is accomplished in virtue of which the law is no longer to the people an external command, but, through the power of God, the cheerful expression of their own will and purpose" (p. 198).

38. See Deuteronomy 10:14-15; 23:5; Psalm 60:5; 127:2; Proverbs 3:12; Isaiah 43:4; 48:14; Hosea 14:4; Malachi 1:2-3.

39. Quoted in Iain Murray, *The Puritan Hope* (Edinburgh: Banner of Truth Trust, 1971), 172.

40. Ibid., 179.

41. Quoted in Ruth Tucker, *From Jerusalem to Irian Jaya* (Grand Rapids: Zondervan Publishing House, 1983), 301.

The Lord was pleased to bruise him;
he has put him to grief;
when he makes himself an offering for sin,
he shall see his offspring,
he shall prolong his days;
the pleasure of the Lord shall prosper in his hand.

Isaiah 53:10

Chapter 6

The Pleasure of God in Bruising the Son

Something troubling has emerged in these chapters.

We have seen that God has pleasure in his Son: he delights in the glory of his own perfections reflected back to him in the countenance of Christ. We have seen that God delights in his sovereign freedom: the Lord is in heaven and does all that he pleases. We have seen that he rejoices over the work of his hands: day by day they declare his glory. We have seen that God has pleasure in his fame: he aims to make a name for himself in all the world and win a reputation for the glory of his grace from every people and tribe and language and nation. And we have seen that, as a means to that end, God has had pleasure in election from before creation: he delights to reveal the glory of his Son to babes and to call out for himself an unlikely people who will make their boast only in the Lord.

Clearly God has a great passion to promote his glory. But the troubling thing that emerges is that God has chosen sinners. He is honoring and blessing and exalting a people who are sinners. And the essence of sin is the belittling of God's glory. Something is askew here. A God infinitely committed to promote the worth of his name and the greatness of his glory is engaging all his powers to bring the enemies of his name into everlasting joy and honor!

Make no mistake, sin is diametrically opposed to the glory of

God. Romans 3:23 says that sin is a "falling short" of God's glory. "All have sinned and fall short of the glory of God." Paul means that sinners have fallen short of *prizing* the glory of God. We have exchanged[1] the glory of God for something else: for images of glory, like a new home or car or VCR or computers or vacation days or impressive resumés or whatever makes our ticker tick more than the wonder of God's glory.

Schizophrenia in Heaven?

That's what sin is. And that is what all the people are like that God has chosen to save. Even after he makes them his own they often bring disgrace upon his name by their inconsistency and half-hearted response to Jesus' command to love God with their whole heart. So the troubling thing is that God is so enthusiastic about adopting and exalting people whose sinfulness is a blight on his name. It seems schizophrenic. The Bible makes God out to love his name and his glory with omnipotent energy and unbounded joy. And then it pictures him choosing God-belittling sinners for his court, and rejoicing over the very people who have despised his glory and cheapened his name.

I really don't believe it is possible to grasp the central drama of the Bible until we begin to feel this tension. Until the coming of Jesus Christ, the Bible is like a piece of music whose dissonance begs for some final resolution into harmony. Redemptive history is like a symphony with two great themes: the theme of God's passion to promote his glory; and the theme of God's inscrutable electing love for sinners who have scorned that very glory. Again and again all through the Bible these two great themes carry along the symphony of history. They interweave and interpenetrate, and we know that some awesome Composer is at work here. But for centuries we don't hear the resolution. The harmony always escapes us, and we have to wait.

The death and resurrection of Jesus Christ is the resolution of the symphony of history. In the death of Jesus the two themes of God's love for his glory and his love for sinners are resolved. As in all good symphonies there had been hints and suggestions of the final resolution. That is what we have in Isaiah 53 seven hundred years before Jesus came.

God's pleasure in his name and his pleasure in doing good to sinners meet and marry in his pleasure in bruising the Son of God. Before I quote Isaiah 53:10, I want to show you two texts that affect the way I translate this verse.

First, consider Isaiah 1:11.

What to me is the multitude of your sacrifices? says the Lord; I have had enough of burnt offerings of rams and the fat of fed beasts; I do not *delight in* (or: *I have no pleasure in*) the blood of bulls, or of lambs, or of he-goats.

The word for "delighting in" or "having pleasure in" is the same Hebrew word used in the first line of Isaiah 53:10, "The Lord was *pleased* to bruise him." Or, "The Lord had pleasure in bruising him." Or, "The Lord delighted to bruise him."

Then consider Isaiah 62:4. The Lord says to his people,

You shall no more be termed Forsaken, and your land shall no more be termed Desolate; but you shall be called My *delight* is in her, and your land Married; for the Lord delights in you and your land shall be married.

When God says, "My *delight* is in her," the noun used for "delight" is the same Hebrew word used in the last line of Isaiah 53:10, "The *delight* (or *pleasure*) of the Lord shall prosper in his hand." The same Hebrew word is used in the first line of Isaiah 53:10 and in the last line, only the *verb* form is used in the first line and the *noun* form is used in the last line.

So here is my translation of Isaiah 53:10:

The Lord was *pleased* to bruise him; he has put him to grief (or: caused his pain); when he makes himself an offering for sin, he shall see his offspring, he shall prolong his days; the *pleasure* of the Lord shall prosper in his hand.

This is a prophecy and picture of Jesus Christ crucified and raised from the dead hundreds of years before it happens. The *bruising* is the crucifixion and death of Jesus, making himself an offering for sin. It is a bruising unto death. This is confirmed in Isaiah 53:8, "He was cut off out of the land of the living . . . they made his grave with the wicked." And again in verse 12: "He poured out his soul to death." The reference to *prolonging his days*, on the other hand, is a reference to Christ's resurrection to eternal life after death. This is confirmed in verse 12 by the prophecy that God will "divide him a portion with the great" even though he had already died. And when it says he will see his *offspring* it means that the fruit of his suffering will be many people saved from sin and death. This is confirmed in verse 11: "He shall see the fruit of the travail of his soul and be satisfied; by his knowledge shall the righteous one, my servant, make many to be accounted righteous; and he shall bear their iniquities."

Who Killed Jesus?

The crucial thing to notice in solving the dissonance of redemptive history is that this is all the work of God the Father. "*The Lord* was pleased to bruise him; *he* has put him to grief." I have a friend in ministry who told me of a very powerful moment in preaching. He was speaking the Thursday night of Holy Week in a prison in Illinois. During his message on the death of Christ, he stopped and asked the inmates, "Who do you think killed Jesus?" One said, "The Jews." Another said, "The soldiers." Another said, "Pilate." Another said, "Judas." My friend said, "No, I don't think you're right." They said, "Who then?" He said, "His Father killed him."

There was a silence. Then he read from the Bible, "The *Lord* was pleased to bruise him; *he* has put him to grief." Jesus was not swept away by the wrath of uncontrolled men. He was bruised by his Father. Or, as the apostle Peter said, "[Jesus was] delivered up according to the definite plan and foreknowledge of God" (Acts 2:23). This terrible truth held the attention of the inmates—some of whom knew what it was like to be rejected and "bruised" by an angry, unjust father. They were eager to hear why *God* would do such a thing.

Why did God bruise his Son and bring him to grief? He did it to resolve the dissonance between his love for his glory and his love for sinners. We get a glimpse of this in Isaiah 53:6: "All we like sheep have gone astray; we have turned every one to his own way; and *the Lord has laid on him the iniquity of us all.*" Notice two things. Again (as in verse 10) it is the Lord who is at work:

"The Lord—God the Father—has laid on him the iniquity of us all." And then notice that the issue is *iniquity*, which is just another word for sin. "The Lord has laid on him the *iniquity* of us all." The Son was bruised because God-dishonoring sin could not be ignored. And why couldn't it be ignored? Why couldn't God just let bygones be bygones? Because God loves the honor of his name. He will not act as though sin, which belittles his glory, didn't matter. It cannot simply be swept under the rug of the universe, as though nothing awesome were at stake. The judge of all the earth will do right (Genesis 18:25). He will judge the world in righteousness (Psalm 9:8).

So God the Father makes an agreement with his Son that he will demonstrate to all the world the infinite worth of the Father's glory. How? By taking the punishment and suffering that our sin deserved. Isaiah 53:5 makes the substitution even more explicit: "He was wounded for *our* transgressions, he was bruised for *our* iniquities." Similarly verse 12 says, "He bore the sins *of many*, and made intercession *for transgressors.*" And verse 8 says he "was stricken *for the transgression of my people.*" Verse 9 makes plain that the bruising was not because of the Son's own sin: "And they made his grave with the wicked and with a rich man in his death, although *he had done no violence, and there was no deceit in his mouth.*"

It was not for his own sin that the Father bruised the Son. It was because he wanted to show us mercy. He wanted to forgive and heal and save and rejoice over us with loud singing. But he is righteous. That means his heart was filled with a love for the infinite worth of his own glory.[2] But we were sinners. And that means that our hearts were filled with God-belittling affections. So to save sinners, and at the same time magnify the worth of his glory, God lays our sin on Jesus and abandons him to the shame and slaughter of the cross.

The Most Important Paragraph in the Bible

The clearest and most important biblical statement of this truth is found in Romans 3:23-26. If I were asked, "What is the most important paragraph in the Bible?" I think this is the paragraph I would name. It goes to the very root of the Christian gospel and lays bare the heart of God like few other texts. If there is a moment in the symphony of biblical revelation when the contrasting themes of justice and mercy come together into a magnificent orchestral statement of unity and harmony and peace, it is here in Romans 3:23-26.

> 23) All have sinned and fall short of the glory of God; 24) they are justified by his grace as a gift, through the redemption which is in Christ Jesus, 25) whom God put forward as a propitiation by his blood, to be received by faith. This was to show God's righteousness, because in his divine forbearance he had passed over former sins; 26) it was to prove at the present time that he himself is righteous and that he justifies him who has faith in Jesus.

Should God Be Impeached?

This awesome text gives account for the apparent miscarriage of justice in the gospel. Justice proceeds on the principle laid down in Proverbs 17:15, "He who justifies the wicked and he who condemns the righteous are both alike—an abomination to the Lord." We impeach judges who acquit the guilty. Our moral sensibility is outraged when wrong is given legal sanction. Yet at the heart of the Christian gospel stands the sentence: God justifies the ungodly (Romans 4:5). He acquits the guilty. That *is* the gospel. But how can it be right for God to do that?

Romans 3:24 gives part of the answer. It says that the ungodly are acquitted (justified) on the basis of a divine transaction that happens in the experience of Jesus Christ. This transaction is called "redemption." "They are justified by his grace as a gift, *through the redemption which is in Christ Jesus.*" Redemption refers to a kind of purchase or ransom that was paid in the death of Jesus. Something happened in the death of Jesus that is so stupendous that it now serves as the basis for the acquittal of millions and millions of sinners who trust Christ. What happened in this redemption? What was the divine transaction that took place when Jesus died? Paul gives the answer in verses 25-26.

First, we see (as in Isaiah 53:10) that it is God the Father who puts Christ forward to die. "*God* put Christ forward as a propitiation by his blood" (verse 25). It pleased *the Lord* to bruise him. Next, we see that the reason he gave his Son up to death was to make a "propitiation" (NASB). This old word is important because other words like "expiation" (RSV) and "sacrifice of atonement" (NIV) do not press forward the idea of appeasing wrath which is in this word. The point of the word is that God's wrath is against the ungodly because of the way they have desecrated his glory, and a way must be found for this wrath to be averted. This is what happened in the death of Jesus. That is what propitiation means: God averted his own wrath through the death of his Son.[3]

Paul's Unmodern Problem with God

How this happened, and why it had to happen, is explained further in the last part of verse 25: "This was to show God's righteousness, because in his divine forbearance he had passed over former sins." Here we see most clearly the problem that the justification of the ungodly caused for Paul. God's righteousness is called into question when God passes over sins. This very moment God is passing over the sins of those who trust in Jesus (as verse 26 and 4:5 show). But not only that; he has been doing this same thing for generations of those who trust him. This is clear from Romans 4:6-8, "So also David pronounces a blessing on the one to whom God reckons righteousness apart from works: Blessed are those whose iniquities are forgiven, and whose sins are covered; blessed is the one against whom the Lord will not reckon his sin." God passed over "former sins" when he acquitted sinners like Abraham (Genesis 15:6) and David (Psalm 32:1-2) and many others (Hebrews 11:4,7). And Romans 3:25 says that *because of this*, God's righteousness is called into question.

The reason God's righteousness is impugned when he passes over sin and does not judge it, is that sin is an attack on the worth of his glory. And God's righteousness is his unswerving commitment to uphold the worth of his glory and promote its fame in all the world. When sin is treated as though it is inconsequential, then the glory of God is treated as inconsequential. When God passes over sin, it looks as though he is agreeing that his glory is of little value. But if God acts in such a way as to deny the infinite value of his own glory, then he commits the ultimate outrage; he desecrates what is infinitely holy and he blasphemes what is infinitely sacred. He joins the sinners of Romans 1:23 and exchanges the glory of the immortal God for the creature. This prospect is so terrible that if it came to pass there could be no gospel and no hope, for there would be no righteous God.

Nevertheless God has chosen sinners for himself. He means to pass over their sins and bring them into his presence and give them everlasting joy. He has done this even though their sin desecrates his glory. How then does he uphold the worth of his glory and yet save sinners? The answer is given very clearly in Romans 3:25-26. "God put Christ forward as a propitiation by his blood (that is, by his death on the cross) and this was to demonstrate God's righteousness (his unswerving commitment to the worth of his glory) . . . it was to prove at the present time that he himself is righteous and that he justifies him who has faith in Jesus." In other words, God would not just sweep the sins of his chosen people under the rug of the universe. If God was simply going to acquit guilty, God-belittling sinners by faith, then something terrible and awesome had to happen to vindicate his allegiance to the worth of his glory. And that something was the death of his Son. This death demonstrated the inexpressible passion God has for the worth of his glory and for the vindication of his righteousness.

How Christ Vindicates God and Justifies Sinners

How did the death of Christ do that? Paul doesn't spell this out for us in detail, but there are clear pointers in other parts of Scripture. We know that everything Jesus did in life and death he did for the glory of his Father. For example, as Jesus approaches the hour of his death, he says, "Now is my soul troubled, and what shall I say, 'Father, save me from this hour'? No! For this purpose I have come to this hour: *Father glorify your name*" (John 12:27-28). The very purpose for which Jesus came to the hour of his death was to glorify the Father. Jesus wants us to see that his willingness to lose his life is because of his love for the glory of the Father. This is how the worth of God's glory is magnified in the death of Jesus.

Again, when Judas had left the Last Supper and Jesus' death was imminent, he said, "Now is the Son of Man glorified and in him God is glorified" (John 13:31). This is the basic transaction happening in the last hours of Jesus' suffering. In Jesus' great prayer in John 17 he views his death as virtually accomplished and says, "I have glorified you (Father) upon the earth, having accomplished the work you gave me to do" (John 17:4). All of Jesus' work was designed to honor the worth of his Father's glory. Everything Jesus suffered, he suffered for the sake of God's glory. Therefore, all his pain and shame and humiliation and dishonor served to magnify the Father's glory, because they showed how infinitely valuable God's glory is, that such a loss should be suffered to demonstrate its worth. When we look at the wracking pain and death of the perfectly innocent and infinitely worthy Son of God on the cross, and hear that He endured it all so that the glory of his Father, desecrated by sinners, might be restored, then we know that God has *not* denied the value of his own glory; he has *not* been untrue to himself; he has *not* ceased to uphold his honor and display his glory; he *is* just—*and* the justifier of the ungodly.

This is an unspeakably wonderful truth. The foundation of our justification—our acquittal, our forgiveness—is not a flimsy sentimentality in God, nor is it a shallow claim of human worth. It is the massive rock of God's unswerving commitment to uphold the worth of his own glory, to promote the praise of his holy name and to vindicate his righteousness. The God-centeredness of God is the foundation of his grace to the ungodly. If God were not committed first to vindicate the worth of his own glory, there would be no gospel and no hope, for there would be no glorious God.

Tragic Rejection

Tragically this vision of God's atoning work in the death of his Son is rejected and even scorned by many people in the Christian church. I think our understanding will be deeper and our convictions stronger and our passion for God's glory warmer if we take note of this rejection and know why it is wrong. I take

George MacDonald as one example of a man who was repelled by
the vision of God's righteousness and the meaning of Christ's
death that I am portraying in this chapter. Even though he died in
1905 he is not irrelevant because his influence continues
significantly through his popular writings. And some Christian
philosophers and writers today seem to follow him very closely.[4]

George MacDonald is best known today for his popular novels
that are being reprinted in Americanized form from their original
Scottish coloring. His credibility has been catapulted into the
heights of evangelical affection by the amazing quotes of C. S.
Lewis in the anthology he put together of MacDonald's
quotations. He said, for example, "I know hardly any other writer
who seems to be closer, or more continually close, to the Spirit of
Christ Himself. . . . I have never concealed the fact that I
regarded him as my master; indeed I fancy I have never written a
book in which I did not quote from him."[5] Indeed it is hard not
to admire MacDonald's radical commitment to following Jesus
Christ. His novels are popular not only because he tells a good
story, but because he tells stories about the good. People come
away from the novels often with a new zeal to be pure. This was
the result of my first contact with MacDonald in the novels,
Phantastes and *Lilith* and *Sir Gibbie*. It would be much easier to
criticize his view of the atonement if he were a bad man. But he
was not a bad man.

MacDonald was born on December 10, 1824, the second son
of a Scottish tenant farmer at Huntly, in the Scottish Highlands.[6]
He was educated in King's College, Aberdeen, and Highbury
Theological College, London. In 1851 he married Louisa Powell.
He served as pastor of Trinity Congregational Church from 1851
to 1853 when he was forced to resign partly because he had come
to hold the view that all men would eventually be saved and that
hell, while real and terrible, would have a purifying effect on the
worst of sinners and bring them to repentance and eternal life.

MacDonald Loathed Edwards' Portrait of God (and mine)

For some years he preached from rented quarters to any who
would listen. In the early 1860s he began a literary career that

would last the rest of his life and that would result in fifty-two published volumes of poems and novels and sermons, many of which are being made available again today. There is much that is good in these writings—so much so that I was stunned some years ago when I read in one of MacDonald's sermons, "From all copies of Jonathan Edwards' portrait of God, however faded by time, however softened by the use of less glaring pigments, I turn with loathing."[7] This was a tremendous blow to me. For more than twenty years all my biblical studies and all my ministry and meditation have led me to love the God of Jonathan Edwards—whom I believe with all my heart to be the God and Father of Jesus Christ revealed in Scripture and ruling right now over all the universe, knowing the very hairs of my head and bearing my burdens. So I was stunned. I had to know why MacDonald said this. The result of my study was the sad discovery that MacDonald had thrown away the baby of much true biblical teaching with the bath water of a certain brand of gloomy, lifeless Calvinism. This was especially true of the biblical teaching on the justice of God and how it came to expression in the crucifixion of Christ.

Justice: Not the Punishment But the Destruction of Sin?

MacDonald taught that since God created a world in which sin happened, his justice demands that he destroy sin in everybody, not just punish it. "Primarily God is not bound to *punish* sin; He is bound to *destroy* sin. If He were not the Maker, He might not be bound to destroy sin—I do not know. But seeing He has created creatures who have sinned, and therefore sin has, by the creating act of God, come into the world, God is, in his own righteousness, bound to destroy sin" (p. 69).[8] "He is bound by His justice to destroy sin in His creation" (p. 72). "He is bound in Himself to make up for the wrong done by His children" (p. 73).

Thus MacDonald rejects the concept of justice or righteousness which demands appropriate punishment or deserved suffering for sin. He says that the punishment or suffering of a sinner does not settle accounts. "Punishment is *nowise* an *offset* to sin. . . . Punishment, or deserved suffering, is no equipoise to sin" (p. 69). Punishment may indeed be just, but only as a means to eventual holiness. "Where [punishment] can help the sinner to know what he has been guilty of, where it can soften his heart to see his pride and wrong and cruelty, justice requires that punishment shall not be spared" (p. 73). But as a just recompense of suffering, punishment has no part in justice. Vengeance, therefore, is no part of God's justice. "Vengeance on the sinner, the law of tooth for tooth, is not in the heart of God, neither in His hand" (p. 69). The reason for this is that the only justice MacDonald will allow is a justice that destroys sin rather than merely punishing the sinner. "The only vengeance worth having on sin is to make the sinner himself its executioner" (p. 70). In other words justice must bring about the execution of sin and the deliverance for the sinner. He asks, "What setting right would come from the sinner's suffering?" (p. 70). His answer is clearly, none. The only thing that can "make up" for sin is repentance, not suffering. "Sorrow and confession and self-abasing love will make up for the evil word; suffering will not" (70). He is emphatic and clear about his concept of God's justice: "I am saying that justice is not, never can be, satisfied by suffering—nay, cannot have any satisfaction in or from suffering" (p. 71).

No Eternal Hell and No Substitutionary Atonement?

Certain consequences follow inevitably from these convictions about God's justice. First, MacDonald is committed to universalism—everyone must eventually be saved. And second, he rejects a view of the atonement that says God's justice demanded the punishment of sin and that says Christ bore that punishment as our substitute. These two views go together. If God's justice means he is bound to destroy sin not punish it (p. 69), then there is no necessary condemnation for Christ to bear for us, and there is no hell of eternal retribution. Let's consider these two consequences one at a time.

MacDonald was a universalist (as are many of his followers[9]) because eventually "hell" would bring all men to repent and be saved. "I believe that no hell will be lacking which would help the just mercy of God to redeem His children" (p. 77). An eternal hell of terrible torments would be an injustice for man and a defeat for God. "I do not believe that any being, never good enough to see the essential ugliness of sin, could sin so as to deserve such punishment" (p. 71), thus hell would be an injustice to man. Moreover, "God is triumphantly defeated, I say, throughout the hell of His vengeance. Although against evil, it is but the vain and wasted cruelty of a tyrant" (p. 71), thus hell is a defeat for God. "God remains defeated, for He has created that which sinned, and which would not repent and make up for its sin" (p. 74). The problem with MacDonald here is that he is more committed to his own conceptions of what must be just than to what the Bible actually teaches. The biblical teaching on the eternity of hell is inescapable.[10] And I have tried to show earlier in this chapter and elsewhere[11] that the righteousness of God is his unswerving commitment to uphold the worth of his glory, and that the desecration of that glory can indeed be "made up" by a just punishment—a corresponding loss of glory. An eternal hell is not unjust, because the sin of man against an infinitely glorious God is deserving of an infinite punishment.[12]

Christ: Assistant in Our Self-atonement?

The other consequence of MacDonald's view of God's justice is the rejection of the kind of atonement I have unfolded in this chapter. This, in my judgment, is a more serious error even than universalism. It strikes right at the heart of our faith and attacks the ground of the gospel. MacDonald speaks of an atonement, but it is one that we make for ourselves. The death of Christ is not in our place, but for our inspiration. For MacDonald, atonement means making up for evil. "In the sense of the atonement being a making-up for the evil done by men toward God, I believe in the atonement" (p. 78). How is this "making up" of evil to happen? "Sorrow and confession and self-abasing love will make up for the evil word; suffering will not" (p. 70). Suffering or punishment has no necessary place in atonement. Atonement is necessary but it is the work of the sinner, not the work of Christ for him. "There must be an atonement, a making-up, a bringing together—an atonement which, I say, cannot be made except by the man who has sinned" (p. 70).

Why then did Christ die, if we make the only atonement that is necessary? The death of Christ is God's merciful way of bringing us to the point of recognizing the evil of sin and repenting of it. "Repentance, restitution, confession, prayer for forgiveness, righteous dealing thereafter, is the sole possible, the only true make-up for sin. For nothing less than this did Christ die" (p. 73). Christ died to inspire us to make atonement for our sin. "He could not do it without us, but He leads us up to the Father's knee: He makes us make atonement" (p. 79). MacDonald denies that there is "one word in the New Testament about reconciling God to us; it is we that have to be reconciled to God" (p. 78).[13] Thus there is no divine transaction on the cross to avert the wrath of God from sinners. All reconciliation happens in the heart of man, not God. "[God] can do nothing to make up for wrong done but by bringing about the repentance of the wrong-doer" (p. 73).

This is a massive reinterpretation of biblical teaching concerning the cross. It is right in affirming that the death of Christ is designed to overcome sin and not just forgive sin. But if what we have seen earlier in Romans 3:24-26 is correct, MacDonald is deeply wrong about the very essence of what happened when Jesus died. God is indeed a God of vengeance (Romans 12:19). He does indeed need to be reconciled to man—that is, his wrath against sinners needs to be averted (see note 13). Put the words of William Childs Robinson over against MacDonald's denial of this need:

> Man's rebellious enmity against God (Colossians 1:12; Romans 8:7f) has called forth his holy enmity against evil (1 Corinthians 15:25f; Romans 11:28; James 4:4); his wrath (Romans 1:18; 2:5, 8-9; Ephesians 2:3, 5; Colossians. 3:6); his judgments (Romans 1:24-32; 2:3, 16; 3:6, 19; 2 Corinthians 5:10); his vengeance (Romans 12:19; 2 Thessalonians 2:8); and the curse of the broken law (Galatians 3:10). The wrath of God in the final judgment stands in immediate connection with the enmity which is removed by the reconciliation (Romans 5:9-10). Thus God so acted in giving his Son to be made sin and a curse for us that his wrath was averted and his righteousness made manifest even in forgiving believers (Romans 3:25-26). The grace of the Lord Jesus Christ assures them that the sentence of condemnation is no longer against them.[14]

I Return to Edwards

It is a great tragedy that MacDonald and his followers construct a concept of divine justice that seems to bear good tidings in overthrowing hell, but backfires with the bad tidings that the death of Jesus accomplishes no more for me than what it inspires me to accomplish for myself. It is a high price to pay for the overthrow of something that is inescapably biblical. It is no act of love to deny the reality of a terrible future which men and women can escape if they know it is coming. And it is no act of love to Christ to reduce his awesome sin-bearing substitution to a model martyrdom. James Denney warned years ago that if we say God would still be to us what he is apart from any reconciling value which the death of Christ has *for God*, then "this is really to put Christ out of Christianity altogether."[15] Therefore, for the sake of love to Christ and love to man, I find myself returning from George MacDonald to the friend of my soul, Jonathan Edwards. Neither MacDonald nor his contemporary followers[16] have come close to shaking the biblical foundations of divine righteousness demonstrated so magnificently in Edwards' two works, *The End for Which God Created the World* and *Concerning the Necessity and Reasonableness of The Christian Doctrine of Satisfaction for Sin.*[17]

My prayer is that more and more people will come to see the utterly awesome and liberating truth that the Son of God "*bore the sin* of many. . . . He was *stricken for the transgression* of my people" (Isaiah 53:12,8). May the message of Isaiah spread to every people on the earth: "He has *borne our griefs* and *carried our sorrows . . . smitten by God* and afflicted. . . . The *Lord has laid on him the iniquity of us all.* . . . The Lord was *pleased* to bruise him."

How Could God Delight In the Death of His Son?

Thus we return now to the course of our meditation on the pleasure of God described in Isaiah 53:10. This verse says that the great transaction between God the Father and God the Son that took place in the death of Jesus was the Father's *pleasure*. It *pleased* the Lord to bruise him. Or as Paul said, the sacrifice of Christ was "a fragrant aroma to God" (Ephesians 5:2). So the question we may be better able to answer now is, How could the Father delight in the sacrifice of his own Son?

One part of the answer is stressed at the end of verse 10, namely, that God's pleasure is in what the Son *accomplishes* in dying. It says, "The *pleasure* of the Lord will prosper in his hand." God's pleasure is not so much in the suffering of the Son, considered in and of itself, but in the great success of what the Son would accomplish in his suffering. For example, it says, "When he makes himself an offering for sin, *he shall see his offspring, he shall prolong his days;* the pleasure of the Lord shall prosper in his hand." This means that by his death Jesus begets, as it were, spiritual offspring, and he goes before them into eternity, *prolonging his days* forever. He rises from the dead and says, to use the words of Hebrews 2:13, "Here I am and the *children* God has given me." The way God's pleasure prospers in the hand of the Son is by creating what we might call the "offspring of the cross." Who are these people?

Isaiah 53:11 describes who they are in terms virtually the same as those used by Paul in Romans 3:24. They are justified sinners—people who are reckoned righteous because of the death of Jesus. "He shall see the fruit of the travail of his soul and be satisfied; by his knowledge shall the righteous one, my servant, *make many to be accounted righteous.*" This is the pleasure of God that prospers in the hand of God's servant, Jesus—the justification of the ungodly. This is the first part of the answer why the Father was pleased to bruise the Son.

But I think another part of the answer must also be what we have seen in Romans 3:25-26—that the depth of the Son's suffering was the measure of his love for the Father's glory. It was the Father's righteous allegiance to his own name that made recompense for sin necessary. So when the Son willingly took the suffering of that recompense on himself, every footfall on the way to Calvary echoed through the universe with this message: *The glory of God is of infinite value! The glory of God is of infinite value!*

Forsaken But Loved

When the Father forsook the Son and handed him over to the curse of the cross and lifted not a finger to spare him pain, he had not ceased to love the Son. In that very moment when the Son was taking upon himself everything that God hates in us, and God was forsaking him to death, even then the Father knew that the measure of his Son's suffering was the depth of his Son's love for the Father's glory. And in that love the Father took deepest pleasure. The crucifixion of Jesus was a mysterious event. In that hour Jesus "became a curse for us" (Galatians 3:13). But in the very moment when God's curse rested most heavily on Jesus because of sin, the Father's love for his Son reached explosive proportions. This is why Jesus, with his dying breath, could say, "Father, into your hands I commit my spirit!" (Luke 23:46). Though he knew the wrath of his Father was being poured out on him, he also knew that he was bearing it for the Father's glory, and that the Father loved him for it. "For this reason the Father loves me," Jesus said, "*because* I lay down my life, that I may take it again" (John 10:17). And the Father rewarded his Son for the very suffering which was the Father's curse: "We see Jesus, who for a little while was made lower than the angels, crowned with glory and honor *because of* the suffering of death" (Hebrews 2:9; see also Philippians 2:9).

When Jesus died he glorified the Father's name and saved his Father's people. And since the Father has overflowing pleasure in the honor of his name, and since he delights with unbounded joy in the election of a sinful people for himself, how then shall he not delight in the bruising of his Son by which these two magnificent divine joys are reconciled and made one!

A Closing Parable

Once there was a land ruled by a wicked prince. He had come from a foreign country and enslaved all the people of the land and made them miserable with hard labor in his coal mines across the deep canyon. He had built a massive trestle for the trains that carried his slaves across the canyon to the mines each morning, and it was heavily guarded.

Two men were still free in this kingdom—one old and the other young. They lived on an inaccessible cliff overlooking the trestle. They hated the trestle. At last they resolved together to blow it up and destroy the slave labor of the enemy prince. They planned and they prayed and they reminded themselves of the reality of heaven.

The night came when the deed would be done. Their hearts were pounding with joy. It was a hard plan. It would be possible to time the trek of the trestle guard so that the explosive could be carried quickly to the vulnerable spot on the trestle. But there would be no time for the carrier of the explosives to return. It was certain that he would be seen and the plan foiled if he tried to return. To make sure the trestle blew up the two men agreed that the young man would detonate it by hand on the trestle. He would blow up with it.

But they believed in heaven, and they loved the people of the land. And so the honor of this sacrifice made their hearts leap with joy. The hour came. They folded up the map of their strategy, stood from the table and embraced each other. When the young man got to the door, he turned with the explosive strapped to his back, looked at the old man, and said, "I love you, Father." And the old man took a deep breath—with joy—and said, "I love you too, Son."

Notes

1. The literal rendering of Romans 3:23 is, "For all sinned and *are lacking* the glory of God." If we ask, In what sense do sinners lack the glory of God, it is not as though God meant for us to be as glorious as he is. Rather it is that he meant us to *reflect* his glory. We reflect his glory as we cherish it and keep it ever before us and make it the treasure and the goal of our lives. But Romans 1:23 describes us all as having "exchanged" the glory of the Lord for the glory of his creation. Thus we have traded treasures. We prefer other things in life to the delights of seeing and knowing the God of glory. This is the sense in which we "lack" the glory of God. We lack it as the treasure of our lives. We lack it as our passion and goal. We lack it as our all-satisfying vision. This is the essence of sin: preferring other things to the glory of God.

2. This understanding of the righteousness of God is given extensive exegetical defense in John Piper, *The Justification of God* (Grand Rapids: Baker Book House, 1983), 81-130. "The *righteousness of God* consists most basically in God's unswerving commitment to preserve the honor of his name and display his glory. Thus if God ever abandoned this commitment and no longer sought in all things the magnifying of his own glory, then there indeed would be unrighteousness with God" (p. 97).

3. For an extensive exegesis of Romans 3:25-26 see *The Justification of God*, chapter 8. There has been an extended debate over whether the Greek word

hilaskesthai has the idea of propitiation in it. See Roger Nicole, "C. H. Dodd and the Doctrine of Propitiation," *Westminster Journal of Theology*, 17 (1955), 117-157; and "Hilaskesthai Revisited," *Evangelical Quarterly*, 49 (1977), 173-177. C. K. Barrett gives a well-balanced assessment when he says, "'Propitiation' is not [entirely] adequate, for this means that the offender does something to appease the person he has offended, whereas Paul says that God himself put forward Christ. *Propitiation is truly there, however, for, through the sacrifice of Christ, God's wrath is turned away,* but behind the propitiation lies the fact that God actually wiped out (expiated) our sin, and made us right with himself," *Reading though Romans* (Philadelphia: Fortress Press, 1977), 16, italics added.

4. For example, Thomas Talbott, professor of philosophy at Willamette University puts forth MacDonald's ideas in periodic writings such as "What Jesus Did for Us," *Reformed Journal*, 40, Issue 3 (March 1990), 8-12; "On Predestination, Reprobation and the Love of God," *Reformed Journal*, 33, Issue 2 (February 1983), 11-14; and "God's Unconditional Mercy—A Reply to John Piper," *Reformed Journal*, 33, Issue 6 (June 1983), 9-12. I responded in writing to these last two articles: "How does a Sovereign God Love?" *Reformed Journal*, 33, Issue 4 (April 1983), 9-13; "Universalism in Romans 9-11? Testing the Exegesis of Thomas Talbott," *Reformed Journal*, 33, Issue 7 (July 1983), 11-14.

One popular Christian writer, Madeleine L'Engle, seems to share MacDonald's view of the cross and of hell, though I do not know if she would credit MacDonald as her primary guide. In her book, *The Irrational Season* (New York: Seabury Press, 1977), she refers to the substitutionary atonement and the necessity of Christ dying to appease the wrath of God and says, "Many of us have had at least part of that horror thrust on us at one time or other in our childhood. For many reasons I never went to Sunday School, so I was spared having a lot of peculiar teaching to unlearn. It's only lately that I've discovered that it was no less a person than St. Anselm who saw the atonement in terms of appeasement of an angry God, from which follows immediately the heresy that Jesus came to save us from God the Father" (p. 88). One could wish she had gone to a good Sunday School in order to learn the elementary truth that the Father sent the Son to rescue us from his own wrath as Romans 5:8-9 plainly says.

On the reality of hell and universalism she says, "I know a number of highly sensitive and intelligent people in my own communion who consider as a heresy my faith that God's loving concern for his creation will outlast all our willfulness and pride. No matter how many eons it takes, he will not rest until all of creation, including Satan, is reconciled to him, until there is no creature who cannot return his look of love with a joyful response of love. . . . The Church has always taught that we must pay for our sins, that we shall be judged and punished according to our sinfulness. But I cannot believe that God wants punishment to go on interminably any more than does a loving parent. The entire purpose of loving punishment is to teach, and it lasts only as long as is needed for the lesson. And the lesson is always love" (p. 97). One should note that Madeleine L'Engle does not give biblical arguments or reasons. Her book is not an exposition of Scripture. Rather it is a creative expression of her own opinions ("I cannot believe that . . ."). I regard it as a great loss that unlike C. S. Lewis some of our most creative Christian writers today seem indifferent to close allegiance to the specifics of Scripture and impatient with the humdrum activity of careful biblical interpretation.

5. C. S. Lewis, *George MacDonald: An Anthology* (London: Geoffrey Bless: The Centenary Press, 1946), 18, 20.

6. These and the following biographical details of MacDonald's life I am taking from Rolland Hein's "Introduction" to *George MacDonald: Creation in Christ*, ed. Rolland Hein (Wheaton: Harold Shaw Publishers, 1976), 7-12.

7. From a sermon entitled "Justice" in *Creation in Christ*, 81.

8. All the page references in the text refer to Ibid.

9. See note 4 on Thomas Talbott and Madeleine L'Engle.

10. It is an awesome and fearful thing to believe in such a hell. But it is even more awesome and fearful *not* to believe in it if it is real. The Bible makes it an inescapable reality as the following texts show.

> "And many of those who sleep in the dust of the earth shall awake, some to everlasting life, and some to shame and *everlasting contempt*" (Daniel 12:2).

The Hebrew *'olam* need not always mean "everlasting," but in this context it seems to because it points to a decisive division into joy or misery after death and resurrection.

> "His winnowing fork is in His hand, and He will clear His threshing floor and gather His wheat into the granary, but the chaff He will burn with *unquenchable fire*" (Matthew 3:12; see Luke 3:17).

This is John the Baptist's prediction of the judgment that Jesus would bring in the end. He pictures a decisive separation, and the term "unquenchable fire" (*puri asbestō*) implies a fire that will not be extinguished, and therefore a punishment that will not end. This is confirmed in Mark 9:43-48.

> "And if your hand causes you to sin, cut it off; it is better for you to enter life maimed than with two hands to go to hell, to the *unquenchable fire*. And if your foot causes you to sin, cut it off; it is better for you to enter life lame than with two feet to be thrown into hell. And if your eye causes you to sin, pluck it out; it is better for you to enter the kingdom of God with one eye than with two eyes to be thrown into hell, *where their worm does not die, and the fire is not quenched*" (Mark 9:43-48).

Here the "unquenchable fire" is clearly hell, and the last line shows that the point is the unending misery of those who go there ("their worm does not die"). If annihilation (the teaching that some simply cease to exist after death) were in view, why would the stress be laid on the fire not ever being quenched and the worm never dying? This focus on duration is confirmed in Matthew 18:8.

> "And if your hand or your foot causes you to sin, cut it off and throw it from you; it is better for you to enter life maimed or lame than with two hands or two feet to be thrown into the *eternal fire*" (Matthew 18:8).

Here the fire is not only unquenchable, but more explicitly, "eternal" (*to pur to aiōnion*). That this fire is not merely a purifying fire of "the age" to come (as some take *aiōnion* to mean) will be shown in the subsequent sayings of Jesus, especially the one on the unforgivable sin. (See below, Matthew 12:32.)

"And do not fear those who kill the body but cannot kill the soul; rather fear Him who can destroy both soul and body in hell" (Matthew 10:28; see Luke 12:4-5).

The "destruction" referred to here is decisive and final, but it does not have to mean obliterate or annihilate. The word *apolumi* frequently means "ruin" or "lose" or "perish" or "get rid of" (Matthew 8:25; 9:17; 10:6; 12:14). It is eternal ruin. (See 2 Thessalonians 1:9 below).

"Then He will say to those at His left hand, 'Depart from me, you cursed, into the *eternal fire* prepared for the devil and His angels. . . . And they will go away into *eternal punishment*, but the righteous into eternal life" (Matthew 25:41, 46).

Here the eternal fire is explicitly "punishment." And its opposite is eternal life. It does not honor the full import of "eternal life" to say that it only refers to a quality of life without eternal connotations. So it would fall short of truth to say that "eternal punishment" has no reference to eternal duration.

"The Son of man goes as it is written of Him, but woe to that man by whom the Son of man is betrayed! *It would have been better for that man if he had not been born*" (Matthew 26:24).

If Judas were destined for glory eventually, or even destined for annihilation, it is difficult to imagine why it would have been better for him not to have been born. In John 17:12 he is called the "son of perdition" (*huios tēs apōleias*)—a term related to the word for destroy in Matthew 10:28.

"Whoever blasphemes against the Holy Spirit never has forgiveness, but is guilty of an *eternal sin*" (Mark 3:29).

"And whoever says a word against the Son of Man will be forgiven; but whoever speaks against the Holy Spirit will not be forgiven, either in this age or in the age to come" (Matthew 12:32).

This rules out the idea that after a time of suffering in hell, sinners will then be forgiven and admitted to heaven. Matthew says that there will be no forgiveness in the age to come for the unforgivable sin, and so Mark calls it an *eternal* sin, which shows that the word "eternal" is indeed a word of duration and not just a word referring to a limited period in the age to come.

"And besides all this, between us and you a great chasm has been fixed, in order that those who would pass from here to you may not be able, and none may cross from there to us" (Luke 16:26).

These are the words of Abraham in heaven speaking to the rich man in Hades. The point is that the suffering there cannot be escaped. There is no way out.

"For God will render to every man according to his works: to those who by patience in well-doing seek for glory and honor and immortality, He will give eternal life; but for those who are factious and do not obey the truth, but obey wickedness, there will be wrath and fury" (Romans 2:6-8).

This text is significant because wrath and fury are the alternative to "eternal life." This seems to imply that the wrath and fury keep one out of life "eternally"—for ever.

> "They will suffer the punishment of *eternal destruction* and exclusion from the presence of the Lord and from the glory of His might, when He comes on that day to be glorified in His saints, and to be marveled at in all who have believed" (2 Thessalonians 1:9).

The word for "destruction" (*olethros*) means "ruin" (1 Timothy 6:9; 1 Corinthians 5:5). The picture is not of obliteration but of a ruin of human life out of God's presence for ever.

> "Let us leave the elementary doctrines of Christ and go on to maturity, not laying again a foundation of repentance from dead works and of faith toward God, with instruction about ablutions, the laying on of hands, the resurrection of the dead, and *eternal judgment*" (Hebrews 6:1-2).

> "These are blemishes on your love feasts . . . wild waves of the sea, casting up the foam of their own shame; wandering stars for whom the nether gloom of darkness has been reserved *forever*" (Jude 12-13).

> "And the smoke of their torment goes up *forever and ever*, and *they have no rest*, day or night, these worshipers of the beast and its image, and whoever receives the mark of its name" (Revelation 14:11).

There is no stronger Greek expression for eternity than this one: *eis aiōnas aiōnōn*.

> "Once more they cried, 'Hallelujah! the smoke from her goes up *forever and ever*'" (Revelation 19:3).

> "And the devil who had deceived them was thrown into the lake of fire and brimstone where the beast and the false prophet were, and they will be tormented *day and night forever and ever*" (Revelation 20:10).

Again the strongest of expressions for everlasting duration: *eis tous aiōnas tōn aiōnōn*.

11. See note 2 above.

12. I have tried to show that the biblical view of hell is not unjust and that there is a just correspondence between what a person deserves and the punishment he receives. See Piper, *Desiring God*, 46.

13. MacDonald's followers (with many others who have never heard of MacDonald) continue to say, "It is not God who needs to be reconciled to us; it is we who need to be reconciled to him" (Thomas Talbott, "What Jesus Did for Us," 10). But this statement is based not only on an oversimplified idea of God's grace, as though he could not feel wrath and mercy toward a sinner at the same time; but it is also based on a misunderstanding of the key biblical texts (Romans 5:10-11; 2 Corinthians 5:18-20). MacDonald and others assume that when Paul says, "We were reconciled to God," or, "Be reconciled to God," it must mean that the only change accomplished is in us. But this is not necessarily what the Greek phrase "be

reconciled" means, and the contexts show that the removal of God's wrath against sin is included. Roger Nicole shows this persuasively from the idea of reconciliation in Matthew 5:24.

> It is also argued, from the language of Scripture, that it is never God who is said to be "reconciled," but man. But this argument too is specious. In the first place, in Greek the use of the word is precisely the reverse of what it is in English and French. This could be illustrated from many passages, but this one is especially clear. In Matthew 5 [vv. 23-24] Jesus says: *If you are offering your gift at the altar, and there remember that your brother has something against you, leave your gift there in front of the altar; first go and be reconciled to your brother, then come and offer your gift.* Who is being reconciled to whom here? Let's say that the worshiper is A, and the brother is B. It is clear that B has the grievance: "Your brother has something against you." Yet it is A that must be reconciled. Therefore, when Paul says, "Be reconciled to God," it is God who has the grievance, and the exhortation means to be sure that God does not hold his just grievance against you. The reconciliation of which the Scripture speaks is a reconciliation by which God in his mercy dismisses the grievance which he justly holds against us for our sin. And this he can do because of the intervention of Jesus Christ; God was in Christ, providing for the setting aside of the grievance.

That this is what Paul really means is clear from the contexts of both of the important passages [Romans 5:10-11; 2 Corinthians 5:18-20]. Romans 5:9 says explicitly that we are saved by Christ from the wrath of God. Not saved from our own wicked disposition, but from the wrath of God. In 2 Corinthians 5:19 Paul explains that in reconciliation God was "not counting their sins against them." So it is primarily the reconciliation of God to us that the Scripture is describing. [Roger Nicole, "The Achievement of the Cross, Part One: The Biblical Variety of Language," *Sola,* 2, No. 6 (December 1989), 3.]

14. William Childs Robinson, "Reconciliation," *Baker's Dictionary of Theology,* ed. Everett F. Harrison (Grand Rapids: Baker Book House, 1960), 437-438

15. Quoted in Vernon Grounds, "Atonement," *Baker's Dictionary of Theology,* 77.

16. Thomas Talbott says, "Many are those who represent God as a grea Monarch whose chief aim is to defend his own honor and to pursue his own glory, but that is not the God revealed in Jesus Christ. In Christ we encounter the true character of God—his love, his humility, his meekness." (Talbott, "What Jesus Did for Us," 12.) But these two things cannot be played off against each other—the imperial rights of God and his great condescension. Again I say that the profound insights of Jonathan Edwards have neither been attained nor overturned by MacDonald or his followers. In his discourse on *The Excellency of Christ,* Edwards paints a picture of Christ and his work which is untouched by Talbott's efforts to divide the Monarch from the meek Lamb of God. Edwards opens for us the truth that "there is an admirable conjunction of diverse excellencies in Jesus Christ." He shows with abundant biblical evidence that in Christ there is infinite

highness and infinite condescension, infinite justice and infinite grace, infinite glory and lowest humility, infinite majesty and transcendent meekness, deepest reverence for God and equality with God, infinite worthiness of good and the greatest patience under suffering of evil, a wonderful spirit of obedience with supreme dominion over heaven and earth, absolute sovereignty and perfect resignation, self-sufficiency and entire trust and reliance on God. Once a person has seen such a Christ portrayed from Scripture, the reconstructions of Talbott and MacDonald lose much of their appeal. *The Excellency of Christ, The Works of Jonathan Edwards,* 1 (Edinburgh: Banner of Truth Trust, 1974), 680-689.

17. Both these works are found in Edwards, *Works,* 1-2 (Edinburgh: Banner of Truth Trust, 1974).

The Lord, your God, is in your midst,
a warrior who gives victory;
he will rejoice over you with gladness,
he will be quiet in his love;
he will exult over you with loud singing.

Zephaniah 3:17

His delight is not in the strength of the horse,
nor his pleasure in the legs of a man;
But the Lord takes pleasure in those who fear him,
in those who hope in his steadfast love.

Psalm 147:10-11

Chapter 7

The Pleasure of God in Doing Good to All Who Hope in Him

Can you imagine what it would be like to hear God singing?

A mere *spoken* word from his mouth brought the universe into existence. What would happen if God lifted up his voice and not only spoke but sang! Perhaps a new heaven and a new earth would be created.

> Behold, I create a new heavens and a new earth. . .
> I create Jerusalem a rejoicing,
>   and her people a joy.
>
> Isaiah 65:17-18

What do you hear when you imagine the voice of God singing?

I hear the booming of Niagara Falls mingled with the trickle of a mossy mountain stream. I hear the blast of Mt. St. Helens mingled with a kitten's purr. I hear the power of an East Coast hurricane and the barely audible puff of a night snow in the woods. And I hear the unimaginable roar of the sun, 865,000 miles thick, 1,300,000 times bigger than the earth, and nothing but fire, 1,000,000 degrees centigrade on the cooler surface of the corona. But I hear this unimaginable roar mingled with the tender, warm crackling of logs in the living room on a cozy winter's night.

Dumbfounded

And when I hear this singing I stand dumbfounded, staggered, speechless that he is singing over me—one who has dishonored him so many times and in so many ways. It is almost too good to be true. He is rejoicing over my good with all his heart and with all his soul. He virtually breaks forth into song when he hits upon a new way to do me good. I would not dare say this on my own authority. Nor could I say it if I had not seen another foundation for his joy than my own righteousness. But I have it on the authority of the prophet Jeremiah.

> 39) I will give them one heart and one way, that they may fear me for ever, *for their own good* and the good of their children after them. 40) I will make with them an everlasting covenant, that *I will not turn away from doing good to them*; and I will put the fear of me in their hearts, that they may not turn from me. 41) *I will rejoice in doing them good*, and I will plant them in this land in faithfulness, *with all my heart and with all my soul* (Jeremiah 32:39-41).

You can't escape the happiness of this text by thinking it was promised to Israel and not to you. God won't let you get away from his goodness that easily. When Jeremiah speaks of an "everlasting covenant" that God will make with his people (v. 40), he means the "new covenant" described just one chapter earlier, "I will make a new covenant with the house of Israel. . . . I will put my law within them, and I will write it upon their hearts. . . . I will forgive their iniquity and I will remember their sins no more" (Jeremiah 31:31-34). But this new covenant is the covenant Jesus sealed with his blood. Remember how at the last supper he said, "This cup is the *new covenant* in my blood" (1 Corinthians 11:25; cf. Mark 14:24; Hebrews 8:6-13). So the benefits of this covenant reach as far as the blood of Jesus reaches. Paul said his whole ministry *among Jews and Gentiles* was the ministry of the "new covenant" (2 Corinthians 3:6). That means that "the Gentiles are fellow heirs [with Israel], members of the same body, and partakers of the promise in Christ Jesus through the gospel" (Ephesians 3:6). So you can't escape the happiness of Jeremiah's promise by saying you are not a Jew. By faith in Christ, through the blood of the covenant, you can *be* a "true Jew" (Romans 2:29). "If you are Christ's, then you are Abraham's offspring, heirs according to promise" (Galatians 3:29).

Now think about it for a moment. Don't run your eyes over the promises of God like the wrong pages in a phone book. God

Almighty, Maker of heaven and earth, said, *"I will not turn away from doing good to them.* . . . *I will rejoice in doing them good* . . . *with all my heart and with all my soul."* Let all three promises sink in.

1. God will not turn away from doing you good. He will keep on doing good. He doesn't do good to his children sometimes and bad to them other times. He keeps on doing good and he never will stop doing good for ten thousand ages of ages. When things are going "bad" that does not mean God has stopped doing *good.* It means he is shifting things around to get them in place for more good, if you will go on loving him. He works all things together for good "for those who love him" (Romans 8:28). "No good thing does he withhold from those who walk uprightly" (Psalm 84:11). "Lo, it was for my welfare that I had great bitterness" (Isaiah 38:17). "It is good for me that I was afflicted, that I might learn your statutes" (Psalm 119:71, cf. v. 67).

The Goodness of God in George Mueller's Tragedy

George Mueller, the great man of prayer, who built orphanages and inspired the faith of thousands, shows us how to lay hold on this great truth that God will not turn away from doing good to us. In July of 1853, Lydia Mueller, his only child, was struck with typhoid fever. She came to the brink of death but through the prayers of many she was spared. Mueller's description of this trial is full of wisdom and faith.

> While I was in this affliction, this great affliction, besides being at peace, so far as the Lord's dispensation was concerned, I also felt perfectly at peace with regard to the cause of the affliction. Once on a former occasion, the hand of the Lord was heavily laid on me in my family. I had not the least hesitation in knowing, that it was the Father's rod, applied in infinite wisdom and love, for the restoration of my soul from a state of lukewarmness. At this time, however, I had no such feeling. Conscious as I was of manifold weaknesses, failings, and shortcomings, so that I too would be ready to say with the Apostle Paul, "O wretched man that I am;" yet I was assured that this affliction was not upon me in the way of the fatherly rod, but for the trial of my faith. . . . Parents know what an only child, a beloved child is, and what to believing parents an only child, a believing child, must be. Well, the Father in heaven said, as it were, by this His dispensation, Art thou willing

to give up this child to Me? My heart responded, As it seems good to Thee, my Heavenly Father. Thy will be done. But as our hearts were made willing to give back our beloved child to Him who had given her to us, so He was ready to leave her to us, and she lived. *"Delight thyself also in the Lord; and He shall give thee the desires of thine heart"* (Psalm 37:4). The desires of my heart were, to retain the beloved daughter, if it were the will of God; the means to retain her were, to be satisfied with the will of the Lord.

Of all the trials of faith that as yet I have had to pass through, this was the greatest; and by God's abundant mercy, I own it to His praise, I was enabled to delight myself in the will of God; for I felt perfectly sure, that, if the Lord took this beloved daughter, it would be best for her parents, best for herself, and more for the glory of God than if she lived: this better part I was satisfied with; and thus my heart had peace, perfect peace, and I had not a moment's anxiety.[1]

Before you respond to this by saying, "It's easy to speak of God's goodness when you get your daughter back," listen to the rest of the story. On February 6, 1870, George Mueller's wife, Mary, died of rheumatic fever. They had been married thirty-nine years and four months. He was sixty-four years old. Shortly after the funeral he was strong enough to preach a "funeral sermon" as he called it. What text would he choose when God had taken his best beloved? He chose Psalm 119:68, "You are good, and do good." His three points were:

1. The Lord was good, and did good, in giving her to me.
2. The Lord was good, and did good, in so long leaving her to me.
3. The Lord was good and did good, in taking her from me.[2]

Under this third point he recounts how he prayed for her during her illness.

Yes, my Father, the times of my darling wife are in Thy hands. Thou wilt do the very best thing for her and for me, whether life or death. If it may be, raise up yet again my precious wife—Thou art able to do it, though she is so ill; but howsoever Thou dealest with me, only help me to continue to be perfectly satisfied with Thy holy will.[3]

As he looked back on the way God had answered his prayer he said,

Everyday I see more and more how great [is] her loss to the orphans. Yet, without an effort, my inmost soul habitually joys in the joy of that loved departed one. Her happiness gives joy to me. My dear daughter and I would not have her back, were it possible to produce it by the turn of the hand. God Himself has done it; we are satisfied with Him.[4]

God never stops doing good to his covenant people. And if an enemy is temporarily given the upper hand, we can say, straight into the muzzle of the gun, "You mean evil against me, but God means it for good" (Genesis 50:20). Since God is sovereign and has promised *not to turn away from doing good to his covenant people*, we can know beyond all doubt, in tribulation and distress and persecution and famine and nakedness and peril and sword, that we are more than conquerors through him who loved us (Romans 8:35-37).

He Rejoices to Do You Good

2. But the promise is greater yet. Not only does God promise not to turn away from doing good to us, he says, "*I will rejoice in doing them good*" (Jeremiah 32:41). "The Lord will again *take delight* in prospering you" (Deuteronomy 30:9). He does not bless us begrudgingly. There is a kind of eagerness about the beneficence of God. He does not wait for us to come to him. He seeks us out, because it is his pleasure to do us good. "The eyes of the Lord run to and fro throughout the whole earth, to show his might in behalf of those whose heart is whole[5] toward him" (2 Chronicles 16:9). God is not waiting for us, he is pursuing us. That, in fact, is the literal translation of Psalm 23:6, "Surely goodness and mercy shall *pursue* me all the days of my life." I have never forgotten how a great teacher once explained it to me. He said God is like a highway patrolman pursuing you down the interstate with lights flashing and siren blaring to get you to stop—not to give you a ticket, but to give you a message so good it couldn't wait till you get home.

God loves to show mercy. Let me say it again. God loves to show mercy. He is not hesitant or indecisive or tentative in his desires to do good to his people. His anger must be released by a stiff safety lock, but his mercy has a hair trigger. That's what he meant when he came down on Mount Sinai and said to Moses,

"The Lord, the Lord, a God merciful and gracious, *slow to anger*, and *abounding in steadfast love*" (Exodus 34:6). The point is the contrast between the sluggishness of his anger and the effusiveness of his love.

God Is Never Bored

God is never irritable or edgy. He is never fatigued or depressed or blue or moody or stressed out. His anger never has a short fuse.[6] He is not easily annoyed. He is above any possibility of being touchy or cranky or temperamental. Instead he is infinitely energetic with absolutely unbounded and unending enthusiasm for the fulfillment of his delights. This is hard for us to comprehend, because we have to sleep every day just to cope, not to mention thrive. We go up and down in our enjoyments. We get bored and discouraged one day and feel hopeful and excited another. We are like little geysers that gurgle and sputter and pop erratically. But God is like a great Niagara—you look at it and think: surely this can't keep going at this force for year after year after year. It seems like it would have to rest. Or it seems like some place up stream it would run dry. But, no, it just keeps surging and crashing and making honeymooners happy century after century. That's the way God is about doing us good. He never grows weary of it. It never gets boring to him.

> Let those who desire my vindication
> shout for joy and be glad,and say evermore,
> "Great is the Lord,
> *who delights in the welfare of his servant!*"
> Psalm 35:27

His Delight Demonstrates His Greatness

God delights in the welfare of his servant because it shows his greatness. "*Great* is the Lord, who delights in the welfare of his servant." God has overcome every obstacle that would keep him from lavishing kindness on us forever. That is what the last chapter was all about. Christ was bruised to bear the condemnation that stood like a dam between the desert valley of our lives and the trillion-ton, cool, clear, deep, freshwater reservoir of God's goodness. But now there is no condemnation to those who are in Christ Jesus (Romans 8:1). He carried our griefs and bore our sorrows and triumphed over death "so that in the coming ages he might show the immeasurable riches of his grace in kindness toward us in Christ Jesus" (Ephesians 2:7). The watergates of the dam are opening wider and wider—up to our ability to bear the blessing of God's glory. God is not like an insecure bully, who likes to show off his strength by putting weaker people down. God loves to show off his greatness by being an inexhaustible source of strength to build weak people up. His exuberance in delighting in the welfare of his servant is the measure of the immensity of his resources—what the Bible calls, "the riches of his glory." "My God will supply all your needs *according to his riches in glory* in Christ Jesus" (Philippians 4:19). For the Lord takes pleasure in his people; he adorns the humble with victory (Psalm 149:4).

Another way to translate that last line of Psalm 149:4 would be, "He beautifies the meek with salvation." God's pleasure in his Son is the pleasure he has in the breathtaking panorama of his own perfections reflected back to him in the countenance of Christ. God is an infinitely beautiful person. If you have ever loved any beauty you can begin to feel this. For all beauty in the universe is a spin-off of the original beauty in God. One of the ways God expresses his delight in this beauty is by giving it away to his people. He takes pleasure in them by adorning them or beautifying them with his own beauty. He does it partly now in wonderful works of grace called the fruit of the Spirit—love, joy, peace, patience, kindness, goodness, faithfulness, gentleness, self-control (Galatians 5:22). And he will complete the beautification process at the resurrection when the whole creation stands up to celebrate "the glorious liberty of the children of God" (Romans 8:21) and all believers "will shine like the sun in the kingdom of their Father" (Matthew 13:43). No joy, however great, that men and women have known in their happiest moments can compare with the joy of God in beautifying his people.

In this process of beautifying his people God rejoices to take away every pain and sorrow and misery.

I will rejoice in Jerusalem,
and be glad in my people;
no more shall be heard in it the sound of weeping
and the cry of distress.

Isaiah 65:19

For a season on the earth it was necessary that "through many tribulations we enter the kingdom" (Acts 14:22). There are good reasons for this, and they are reasons for our good. But God will rejoice when the lessons are over and the final exams are passed and the vacation has begun. When he sees us perfectly whole, with no tears, no pain, no blemish, no disability, no defect, he will break forth into song. And our joy in the beauty of the new earth and the beauty of our new bodies and the beauty of perfect holiness will be joy in the beautiful rejoicing of God.

With All His Heart and All His Soul

3. But still the promise is greater. First, God promises not to turn away from doing us good. Then he promises that he will do this good with rejoicing. Finally, he promises that this rejoicing over the good of his people will be with all his heart and with all his soul. "*I will rejoice in doing them good*, and I will plant them in this land in faithfulness, *with all my heart and with all my soul*" (Jeremiah 32:41).

How do you describe the joy of doing something "with all your heart?" One way is to use comparisons that awaken in everybody the kind of emotions this would involve. For example, Isaiah uses one to help us feel the fullness of God's joy over us as his people. "You shall no longer be termed Forsaken, and your land shall no more be termed Desolate; but you shall be called My delight is in her, and your land Married; for the Lord delights in you. . . . *As the bridegroom rejoices over the bride, so shall your God rejoice over you*" (Isaiah 62:4-5). When God does good to his people it is not so much like a reluctant judge showing kindness to a criminal whom he finds despicable (though that analogy has truth in it); it is like a bridegroom showing affection to his bride.

The Honeymoon Never Ends

Sometimes we joke and say about a marriage, "The honeymoon is over." But that's because we are finite. We can't sustain a honeymoon level of intensity and affection. We can't foresee the irritations that come with long-term familiarity. We can't stay as fit and handsome as we were then. We can't come up with enough new things to keep the relationship that fresh. But God says his joy over his people is like a bridegroom over a bride. He is talking about honeymoon intensity and honeymoon pleasures and honeymoon energy and excitement and enthusiasm and enjoyment. He is trying to get into our hearts what he means when he says he rejoices over us *with all his heart.*

And add to this, that with God the honeymoon never ends. He is infinite in power and wisdom and creativity and love. And so he has no trouble sustaining a honeymoon level of intensity; he can foresee all the future quirks of our personality and has decided he will keep what's good for us and change what isn't; he will always be as handsome as he ever was, and will see to it that we get more and more beautiful forever; and he is infinitely creative to think of new things to do together so that there will be no boredom for the next trillion ages of millenniums.

Dignified Men Don't Run

Jesus uses another comparison to help us feel the force of what it means to have the Father rejoice over us *with all his heart.* In Luke 15 he says two times that "there is more joy in heaven over one sinner who repents than over ninety-nine righteous persons who need no repentance" (vv. 7,10). Then he illustrates what happens in heaven by telling a story about a father who had a wayward son who left home and squandered all his inheritance. The son comes to his senses while feeding pigs in a far country, and decides to go home and seek mercy from his father. He heads home and prepares a speech as he goes something to this effect: "Father, I'm not worthy to be called your son; so maybe you would let me live in the servants' quarters and work and eat with them?"

As Jesus tells this story you can feel the energy of love building as he shows how the father rejoices "with all his heart" over the boy's arrival. While the boy is still a long way off the Father sees him and his heart warms with compassion (v. 20). He doesn't hold back and watch to see what the boy looks like; he bursts out the front door and starts running down the road. Now don't miss the force of this scene. Well-to-do, dignified, aristocratic, aging men don't run, they walk. They keep their composure. They show that they are on top of their emotions. But not in Jesus' story about God's joy over his people.

The father runs. Can you see them running? Or maybe the boy was too stunned to run. Perhaps he couldn't believe his eyes. Maybe the smell of pigs was still on him. Maybe the thought flashed through his mind to turn and escape this utterly unexpected demonstration of affection. But he does not turn. Jesus says the father embraced him and kissed him—pig smell and all. Can you see that embrace without feeling the emotion? I can't. Maybe that's because I have four sons. And as I write this, three of them are on short term mission projects between four hundred and ten thousand miles away. I can still feel the strong embrace each gave me at the airport. And I can feel the embrace that's coming.

But I think the emotion goes deeper than that. I know I am that son in Jesus' story. And I cannot comprehend that the Father in heaven—the great and glorious Creator of all the universe and Sovereign over all things—throws to the wind all dignified self-consciousness and runs to me and embraces me and kisses me, as though—no! it is no fiction—rather, *because* he is happy with me. He is glad *with all his heart* that I am part of the family. This is why I cannot see that embrace without pausing to let my eyes and my throat recover.

But Jesus is not finished with the story. We still do not feel all that is meant by the words "with all my heart." The father cuts off the boy's speech before he can get to the part about coming back as a slave. None of that! Instead, the father orders the best robe to replace the rags; he calls for a beautiful family ring; he fits him with new shoes, even though the old ones were used to run away; and, to top it all off, the father gives a great banquet with the best food and a band of minstrels to fill the air with happy music.

This is the message Jesus has for any who will turn home to the Father and seek their joy in the wonders of his love. The message is not new. It is as old as the prophets. One of them puts the message in the form of a magnificent and almost unbelievable promise of God's singing over his people:

> The Lord, your God, is in your midst,
> a warrior who gives victory;
> he will rejoice over you with gladness,
> he will be quiet in his love;
> *he will exult over you with loud singing.*
>   Zephaniah 3:17

I say this is almost too good to believe—that when the father calls the minstrels to sing at the banquet, it is he himself that leads the singing, and the song has to do with how glad he is that we are there. In fact it is too good for some people to believe, and they, tragically, cannot believe it. But Zephaniah labors under the wonderful inspiration of God to overcome every obstacle that would keep a person from believing—really feeling and enjoying—the unspeakable news that God exults over us with singing. Suppose you struggle, as a weak and damaged soul, to believe this and cannot. Let me speak for Zephaniah for a moment and ask you a few questions.

What If You Can't Believe Such Goodness

I ask "Can you feel the wonder of this today—that God is rejoicing over you with loud singing?"

"No," you say, "I can't, because I am too guilty. I am unworthy. My sin is too great, and the judgments against me are too many. God could never rejoice over me."

But I say, "Consider Zephaniah 3:15. God foresees your hesitancy. He understands. So his prophet says, 'The Lord has taken away the judgments against you!' Can you not feel the wonder that the Lord exults over you with loud singing today, even though you have sinned? Can you not feel that the condemnation has been lifted because he bruised his own Son in your place, if you will only believe?"

"No," you say, "I can't, because I am surrounded by enemies. Obstacles press me in on every side. There are people who never let me believe this. There are people at work who would make my life miserable if God were my treasure. There are people in my family who would ostracize me. I have friends who would do everything to drag me down. I could never go on believing. I would have too many enemies. The oppression would be too much to bear, I could never do it."

But I say, "Consider Zephaniah 3:17, 'The Lord is a warrior who gives victory;' and verse 19, 'Behold, at that time I will deal with your oppressors (says the Lord);' and verse 15, 'He has cast out your enemies.' Can you feel the wonder that God is doing everything that needs to be done for you to enjoy his own enjoyment of you? Can you see that the enemies and the oppressors are not too strong for God? Nothing can stop him, when he exults over you with loud singing. Can you feel the wonder of it now? Can you believe that he rejoices over *you*?"

"No," you say, "still I can't, because he is a great and holy God and I feel like he is far away from me. I am very small. I am a nobody. The world is a huge place with many important people. There are major movements and institutions that he is concerned with and happy about. I am too small. God is like the president. He is far away in Washington, busy with big things."

But I say, "Consider Zephaniah 3:15, 'The king of Israel, the Lord, is in your midst;' and verse 17: 'The Lord, your God, is in your midst.' He is not far from you. Yes, I admit that this staggers the imagination and stretches credibility almost to the breaking point—that God can be present personally to everyone who comes to him and believes on him. But say to yourself, again and again, He is God! He is God! What shall stop God from being close to me if he wants to be close to me? He is God! He is God! The very greatness that makes him seem too far to be near, is the greatness that enables him to do whatever he pleases, including being near to me. Has he not said, for this very reason, 'I dwell in a high and holy place, *and also with him who is of a contrite and humble spirit*' (Isaiah 57:15)? Can you not then feel the marvel that God makes merry over you—even with loud singing—when you come to him and believe him?"

But still you say, "No, you just don't understand. I am the victim and the slave of shame. I have been endlessly belittled by my parents (see Zephaniah 2:8,10). I have been scoffed at and threatened and manipulated and slandered. Inside this cocoon of shame even the singing of God sounds faint and far away and indecipherable. It is as though my shame has made me deaf to anyone's happiness with me, especially God's. I cannot feel it."

But I say, "I am sure I do not feel all that you feel. I have not been through what you have been through. But God is no stranger to shame. Unbelievable shame was heaped on his Son (Hebrews 12:2), terrible slander, repeated belittling, even from his own townsfolk (Matthew 13:55-58). Therefore, 'We do not have a High Priest who is unable to sympathize with our weaknesses.' I know I have never walked in your shoes. I did not have to live with the family you lived with. But Jesus knows. He feels it with you. And best of all his Father says right here in Zephaniah 3:19, 'I will save the lame and gather the outcast, and *I will change their shame into praise and renown in all the earth.*' Is it not amazing how well God knows you? Can you not feel the warmth of his heart as he makes provision for every question you have? Do you not yet hear the singing of God as you draw near?"

Does He Delight in Me Or in Himself?

And now you say, "Almost I can feel this unspeakable wonder that God exults over me—even me—with loud singing. But there remains one obstacle. You have said that God loves his own glory above all things. You have said that God takes pleasure in his own fame and the honor of his name. I do not understand how this could be consistent with loving me. I have not honored him as I should. In fact, I have dishonored him all my life in one way or another—sometimes just forgetting about him, sometimes indifferent to his presence, sometimes distrusting his promises, sometimes angry at his way of running the world. I do not see how he could go on taking infinite pleasure in his own glory and still get so excited about me—even exult over me with loud singing."

And I say, "If that is your last obstacle then make ready to sing! For the answer is given in Zephaniah 3:12. You are right that God delights in the glory of his name above all things. That's the point of this book. Nor would we want God to be an idolater and find his joy in any lesser beauty than the infinite beauty of God. We would not want an unrighteous God who valued anything more than what is most valuable—who tried to trick the market by bidding on silver when he knew all along that gold is best. Yes, you are right, God is infinitely holy and overwhelmingly happy in the immeasurable worth of his own perfections.

"But now ask yourself this question: If you wanted to be folded into the very joy that God has in his own glorious name, and be a part of that very pleasure of God, where would you go? Where would you seek refuge from the displeasure of God? Zephaniah 3:12 gives the answer: The Lord says, 'For I will leave in the midst of you a people humble and lowly. *They shall seek refuge in the name of the Lord.*' Here is the connection between God's delight in his name and his delight in you. When you take refuge in his name, he exults over you with loud singing. Seeking refuge in the name of God honors God, and when God is honored he rejoices."

Jesus Is the Name of God

Today, on this side of the New Testament, we know that taking refuge in God's name means taking refuge in Jesus. He came in his Father's name (John 5:43); he died to glorify and vindicate the Father's name (John 12:28); he manifested the Father's name to his disciples, and kept them in the Father's name (John 17:6, 12). And now Christ himself has been given a name above every name (Philippians 2:9), and God the Father means for his name today to be glorified through the name of his Son (John 14:14), not apart from the Son. There is no other refuge than Jesus today. "There is no other *name* under heaven given among men by which we must be saved" (Acts 4:12). And everyone who confesses that Jesus is Lord brings glory to God the Father (Philippians 2:11). Christ welcomes desperate sinners for the glory of his Father (Romans 15:7). The Father bruised the Son so that sinners could take refuge in the awesome name, and that "the nations might glorify God for his mercy" (Romans 15:9).

If you humble yourself and seek the glory of God and if you hide your name in the name of God (spelled J E S U S), then your heavenly Father who loves his name above all things will reward you beyond all imaginings and exult over you with loud singing. Think of it like this. Even though we have sinned and desecrated the glory of God, Jesus has been bruised to repair the injury we have done to God's glory. The iniquity of us all has been laid on him. This means that when we take refuge in him, we appeal for salvation not on the basis of our track record, which has fallen so far short of God's glory, but on the basis of Jesus' vindication of the Father's glory. In this way, even though we are sinners who have dishonored God's glory, the glory of God becomes the foundation of our appeal—for we are hiding in the one who lived and died and rose again to glorify the passion of God for his name and the mercy of God to save.

This is what the little word "just" means in 1 John 1:9: "If we confess our sins, he is faithful and *just*, and will forgive our sins, and cleanse us from all unrighteousness." This text says God would be *unjust* (not merely unmerciful) not to forgive us if we confess our sins. Why is that? Why is forgiveness now a matter of justice and not merely a matter of mercy? The answer is that Jesus has shed his blood (1 John 1:7) to make a just recompense for all who confess their sins and take refuge in him. Thus God would be unjust not to forgive them, *not* because they have honored him by their sinless lives, but because they take refuge in the name of Jesus. The death of Jesus so honored the Father and so vindicated the glory of his name that God is bound by his justice, not just his mercy, to forgive all who stake their lives on the worth of Jesus. "Your sins are forgiven *for the sake of his name*," John says (1 John 2:12).

Christ's name, and therefore God's name and God's honor, is at stake whenever we fly to Jesus for refuge and bank on his worth instead of our own. This is why there is no contradiction in saying that God loves his name above all things, and yet is committed with all his heart to the good of his people—the people who hope in Jesus. He will not turn away from doing good to them. He rejoices in doing this good for them. And—for all who can believe it—he exults over us with loud singing.

How Do We Please God?

Linger with me for a few moments to clarify something that has been assumed in this chapter—indeed in the whole book. I have repeatedly assumed that the benefits of God's promises and the purchase of Jesus' death and resurrection are for the people of God. I have also assumed that the mark of this people is not merely that they are "chosen before the foundation of the world," but that they have willingly responded to God in a certain way. In this chapter I have focused mainly on God's pleasure in the good of his people. He rejoices in doing us good with all his heart and with all his soul. But it has become clear that, in order to explain this, I have had to raise the question of our proper response to God. God does not rejoice to do good to everyone in the same way. Though his sun rises on the just and the unjust (Matthew 5:45), there is a saving grace that abounds to those who hope in his love. "God opposes the proud, but gives grace to the humble. . . . Draw near to God and he will draw near to you" (James 4:6, 8).

It is fitting therefore that we dwell on this for a while. God's pleasure in the good of his people is inseparably connected with his pleasure in a certain kind of response that defines who his people are. The truth of chapter 5 (The Pleasure of God in Election) does not nullify the teaching of Scripture that no one is saved who does not respond to the invitations and commands of the gospel. God will see to it that his elect hear the invitation and respond the way they should (Deuteronomy 30:6; Ezekiel 11:19-20; 36:27; Matthew 11:27; John 6:37, 44, 65; 10:16; 11:52; Acts 13:48; 16:14; 18:10; 1 Corinthians 2:23-24; 1 Thessalonians 1:4-5; 2 Thessalonians 2:13; 2 Timothy 2:25). But he does not do this in a way that lessens our accountability to hear and believe. "He who believes in him is not condemned; he who does not believe is condemned already" (John 3:18). Our response to God is utterly crucial. And God has pleasure in a certain kind of response.

This Chapter Is a Turning Point

The present chapter marks a turning point, because up till now we have not focused on what kind of human attitudes and actions God delights in. We have focused first on God's pleasure in his own glory. I believe this order is very important. We need to see first and foremost that God is God—that he is perfect and complete in himself, that he is overflowingly happy in the eternal fellowship of the Trinity, and that he does not need us to complete his fullness and is not deficient without us. Rather *we* are deficient without *him*. The all-sufficient glory of God, freely given in fellowship through his sacrificed Son, is the stream of living water that we have thirsted for all our lives.

Unless we begin with God in this way, when the gospel comes to us, we will inevitably put ourselves at the center of it. We will feel that *our* value rather than *God's* value is the driving force in the gospel. We will trace the gospel back to God's need for *us* instead of tracing it back to the grace that rescues sinners who need *him*.

But the gospel is the good news that God is the all-satisfying end of all our longings, and that, even though he does not need us, and is in fact estranged from us because of our God-belittling sins, he has, in the great love with which he loved us, made a way for sinners to drink at the river of his delights through Jesus Christ. And we will not be enthralled by this good news unless we feel that he was not obliged to do this. He was not coerced or constrained by our value. *He* is the center of the gospel. The exaltation of *his* glory is the driving force of the gospel. The gospel is a gospel of *grace!* And grace is the pleasure of God to magnify the worth of God by giving sinners the right and power to delight in God without obscuring the glory of God.

Take a Test

There is a test here because the children of God love the centrality of God in the gospel. They love to say with Paul, "From him and through him and to him are all things; to him be glory forever and ever" (Romans 11:36). They love to make their boast only in the Lord (1 Corinthians 1:31). They love to say that God is the beginning and middle and end in the affair of salvation. They love to say they were *chosen* for the glory of his grace (Ephesians 1:6), and *called* from darkness to light to declare the wonders of his grace (1 Peter 2:9), and *justified* because Christ died to vindicate the holiness of God's grace (Romans 3:25-26), and will one day be *swallowed up in life*, and glory (2 Corinthians 5:4; Romans 8:30).

And so for seven chapters we have focused on the pleasures that God has in himself and in the freedom of his work, so that it would be unmistakable that God is the center of the gospel. We have only suggested occasionally the kind of *response* that would bring God pleasure. But now we are ready. Now we will be able to see why the human responses which God demands and enjoys come as good news to sinners, and yet keep God at the center of his own affections. If the gospel demands a response from sinners, then the demand itself must be good news instead of an added burden, otherwise the gospel would not be gospel. And if the true biblical gospel always has God at the center, then the response it demands must magnify him and not us.

What Kind of Command Can Be Good News?

Now what kind of response can accomplish both of these things: good news for sinners and glory to God? The answer is given clearly in Psalm 147:10-11:

> His delight is not in the strength of the horse,
> nor his pleasure in the legs of a man;
> but the Lord takes pleasure in those who fear him,
> in those who hope in his steadfast love.

Consider with me first, from verse 11, why God takes pleasure in "those who fear him and hope in his love." Then we will turn to verse 10 and refine our answer by asking why God does *not* delight in "the strength of the horse and the legs of a man."

Fear and Hope at the Same Time

Does it strike you as strange that we should be encouraged to *fear* and *hope* at the same time and in the same person? "The Lord takes pleasure in those who *fear* him, in those who *hope* in his steadfast love." Do you hope in the one you fear and fear the one you hope in? It's usually the other way around: if we fear a person, we hope that someone *else* will come and help us. But here we are supposed to fear the one we hope in and hope in the one we fear. What does this mean?

I think it means that we should let the experience of hope penetrate and transform the experience of fear. In other words, the kind of fear that we should have toward God is whatever is left of fear when we have a sure hope in the midst of it.

Greenland Glacier

Suppose you were exploring an unknown glacier in the north of Greenland in the dead of winter. Just as you reach a sheer cliff with a spectacular view of miles and miles of jagged ice and mountains of snow, a terrible storm breaks in. The wind is so strong that the fear rises in your heart that it might blow you over the cliff. But in the midst of the storm you discover a cleft in the ice where you can hide. Here you feel secure. But, even though secure, the awesome might of the storm rages on, and you watch it with a kind of trembling pleasure as it surges out across the distant glaciers.

At first there was the fear that this terrible storm and awesome terrain might claim your life. But then you found a refuge and gained the hope that you would be safe. But not everything in the feeling called fear vanished from your heart. Only the life-threatening part. There remained the trembling, the awe, the wonder, the feeling that you would never want to tangle with such a storm or be the adversary of such a power.

And so it is with God. In the same Psalm we read, "He gives snow like wool; he scatters hoarfrost like ashes. He casts forth his ice like morsels; who can stand before his cold?" (verses 16-17). The cold of God is a fearful thing—who can stand against it! And verses 4-5 point to the same power of God in nature: "He determines the number of the stars, he gives to all of them their names. Great is our Lord, and abundant in power; his understanding is beyond measure."

In other words, God's greatness is greater than the universe of stars, and his power is behind the unendurable cold of arctic storms. Yet he cups his hand around us and says, "Take refuge in my love and let the terrors of my power become the awesome fireworks of your happy night-sky." The fear of God is what is left of the storm when you have a safe place to watch right in the middle of it. And in that place of refuge we say, "This is amazing, this is terrible, this is incredible power; Oh, the thrill of being here in the center of the awful power of God, yet protected by God himself! O, what a terrible thing to fall into the hands of the living God without hope, without a Savior! Better to have a millstone tied around my neck and be thrown into the depths of the sea than to offend against this God! What a wonderful privilege to know the favor of this God in the midst of his power!"

And so we get an idea of how we feel both hope and fear at the same time. Hope turns fear into a trembling and peaceful wonder; and fear takes everything trivial out of hope and makes it earnest and profound. The terrors of God make the pleasures of his people intense. The fireside fellowship is all the sweeter when the storm is howling outside the cottage.

Now why does God delight in those who experience him in this way—in people who fear him and hope in his love?

Surely it is because our fear reflects the greatness of his power and our hope reflects the bounty of his grace. God delights in those responses which mirror his magnificence. This is just what we would have expected from a God who is all-sufficient in himself and has no need of us—a God who will never give up the glory of being the fountain of all joy, who will never surrender the honor of being the source of all safety, who will never abdicate the throne of sovereign grace. God has pleasure in those who hope in his love because that hope highlights the freedom of his grace. When I cry out, "God is my only hope, my rock, my refuge!" I am turning from myself and calling all attention to the boundless resources of God.

The Command That Is Good News for Sinners

We asked a few moments ago, What kind of response can God demand from us so that the demand gives good news to us and glory to him? This is the answer: the demand to hope in his love with an earnest, profound sense of his awesome power.

As a sinner with no righteousness of my own, standing before a self-sufficient and holy God, what command would I rather hear than this: "Hope in my love!" If we only knew it, every one of us is stranded on an ice face in Greenland, and the wind is blowing fiercely. Our position is so precarious that even if we inhale too deeply our weight will shift and we will plunge to our destruction. God comes to us and says in that moment, "I will save you, and protect you in the storm. But there is a condition." Your heart sinks. You know you can't meet conditions. Your face is flat against the ice. Your fingernails are dug in. You can feel yourself giving way. You know that if all you do is move your lips you're going to fall. You know that there is nothing you can do for God!

Then he speaks the gospel command: "My requirement," he says, "is that you hope in me." Now I ask, Is this not good news? What could be easier than to hope in God when all else is giving way? And that is all he requires. That's the gospel.

But it is not only good news for us sinners. It is also the glory of God to make only this demand upon us. Why? Because when you hope in God you show that he is strong and you are weak; that he is rich and you are poor; that he is full and you are empty. When you hope in God you show that *you* are the one who has needs, not God (Psalm 50:10-15; 71:4-6,14). You are the patient, he is the doctor. You are the thirsty deer in the forest, he is the overflowing spring. You are the lost sheep, he is the good shepherd.

The beauty of the gospel is that in one simple demand ("Put your hope in God!") *we* hear good news and *God* gets the glory. That is why God takes pleasure in those who hope in his love— because in this simple act of hope *his grace* is glorified and *sinners* are saved. This is the command of the gospel that keeps God at the center—the center of his affections and ours.

What's Wrong with Horses and Legs?

Now we must ask why God does *not* take pleasure in horses and legs as it says in verse 10:

> His delight is not in the strength of the horse,
> nor his pleasure in the legs of a man.

The point here is not that strong horses and strong legs are bad. After all, God made them. In fact we saw in chapter 3 that he rejoices in the strength and freedom of mighty horses. For example, he asks Job,

> Do you give the horse his might?
> Do you clothe his neck with strength?
> Do you make him leap like the locust?. . .
> He paws in the valley, and exults in his strength;
> He goes out to meet the weapons.

> He laughs at fear, and is not dismayed;
> he does not turn back from the sword. . .
> he cannot stand still at the sound of the trumpet.
> When the trumpet sounds, he says, "Aha!"
> He smells the battle from afar,
> the thunder of the captains, and the shouting.
>
> Job 39:19-25

Clearly God exults in the strength of the horse that he alone has made. Job can't take credit for any of the horse's wonderful powers. No, the point is not that this glorious animal is bad. The point is this: in the day of battle men put their hope in horses instead of putting their hope in God. But Proverbs 21:31 says, "The horse is made ready for the day of battle, but the victory belongs *to the Lord*." Therefore Psalm 20:7 says, "Some boast in chariots, and some in horses; but we boast of the name of the Lord our God." And Psalm 33:17 says, "The war horse is a vain hope for victory, and by its great strength it cannot save."

God is not displeased with the strength of a horse and the legs of a man as good things that he has made. He is displeased with those who *hope* in their horses and in their legs. He is displeased with people who put their hope, for example, in missiles or in make-up, in tanks or tanning parlors, in bombs or body-building. God takes no pleasure in corporate efficiency or balanced budgets or welfare systems or new vaccines or education or eloquence or artistic excellence or legal processes, when these things are the treasure in which we hope, or the achievement in which we boast. Why? Because when we put our hope in horses and legs, then horses and legs get the glory, not God.

Where We Love For God To Be

Thus when we say that God exults over his people with loud singing, we mean that he exults over those who hope in his love. In this way God maintains his rightful place—the place we love for him to have—at the center of the gospel. There is a condition we must meet in order to know him as our God and be a part of the wonderful covenant in which he never turns away from doing us good but rejoices over us with all his heart and all his soul. That condition is to put our hope in him as the all-satisfying

Refuge and Treasure. God takes pleasure in this response with all his heart, because it magnifies the glory of his grace and satisfies the longing of our soul.

Notes

1. George Mueller, *Autobiography of George Mueller*, compiled by G. Fred. Bergin (London: J. Nisbet and Co., 1906), 424.
2. Ibid., 431.
3. Ibid., 442.
4. Ibid., 440.
5. The Hebrew word *shalēm* (be whole, perfect, complete) does not mean that you have to be sinlessly perfect for God to do you good. The Old Testament shows God doing good to people who have gotten themselves into terrible trouble because of their own sin. See especially Psalm 107:10-13. The point of saying that our hearts need to be "whole" toward God is that we can't be divided in our allegiance. God has to be our only God. We can't look partly to God but, doubting him, look partly to another source of help. The point seems to be the same as in James 1:5-6 and Matthew 6:24. The Lord is on the prowl to bless people who despair of themselves and look wholly to him for the help they need.
6. This is not contradicted by the RSV translation of Psalm 2:11, "His wrath is *quickly* kindled." The point here is not that God acts impetuously or that he shows anger without extensive provocation. This is plain from verses 4-5. God endures the sins of proud secular rulers a long time before he "terrifies them in his fury." The point of verse 11 is that these rulers should not presume upon the patience of God because at any moment his anger could suddenly break out against them. The NIV gets at the idea when it says, "His wrath can flare up in a moment."

*The sacrifice of the wicked
is an abomination to the Lord,
but the prayer of the upright
is his delight.*

Proverbs 15:8

Chapter 8

The Pleasure of God
in the Prayers
of the Upright

Dwight L. Moody, the famous nineteenth century evangelist, was preaching once to a crowded meeting of children in Edinburgh, Scotland. To get their attention he posed a question: "What is prayer?"—expecting to answer the question himself. But to his amazement scores of little hands went up all over the hall. So Moody asked one young fellow to give his answer. The boy spoke out with clear and confident tones, "Prayer is an offering up of our desires unto God for things agreeable to His will, in the name of Christ, with confession of our sins and thankful acknowledgment of His mercies." Moody's amazed response was, "Thank God, my boy, that you were born in Scotland!"[1]

In those days in Scotland parents still believed it was their solemn duty to teach their children biblical truth in the form of a catechism. But it is likely that very few of my readers grew up in homes with that kind of pedagogical rigor. And it is likely that we all have much to learn about prayer—and even more to learn about the kind of God who has pleasure in prayer. We know we have much to learn when we linger in the presence of those who have learned to pray.

For example, George Mueller has taught me much about patience and perseverance in prayer:

I am now, in 1864, waiting upon God for certain blessings, for which I have daily besought Him for 19 years and 6 months, without one day's intermission. Still the full answer is not yet given concerning the conversion of certain individuals. In the meantime, I have received many thousands of answers to prayer. I have also prayed daily, without intermission, for the conversion of other individuals about ten years, for others six or seven years, for others four, three, and two years, for others about eighteen months; and still the answer is not yet granted, concerning these persons [whom I have prayed for nineteen-and-a-half-years]. . . . Yet I am daily continuing in prayer and expecting the answer. . . . Be encouraged, dear Christian reader, with fresh earnestness to give yourself to prayer, if you can only be sure that you ask for things which are for the glory of God.[2]

The Power That Wields the Weapon

The longer I meditate on the meaning of prayer and the more I try to learn from Jesus in the private "school of prayer," the more convinced I become that prayer is given to us primarily as a means of power in the service of the spiritual weapon of God's Word. I preached a sermon once during a week of prayer under the title: "The Power that Wields the Weapon." In the last half of this chapter it will become clear why I think this connection between the Word of God and prayer is so crucial. In my own experience outside Scripture, no one has shown me more graphically the passion with which the ministry of prayer can serve the ministry of the Word than John Hyde. Often known as "Praying Hyde," he was a missionary to India who took up his foreign ministry in 1892. His story is told by Captain E. G. Carré who gives us a glimpse of John Hyde's inspiring commitment to serve the Word with the power of prayer.

> I owe him more than I owe to any man, for showing me what a prayer-life is, and what a real consecrated life is. I shall ever praise God for bringing me into contact with him. . . . The first time I met him was at Ludhiana in the Punjab, where he lived at the time. I had been invited to speak a few words on the Revival in the Khassia Hills to the Conference of the United States Presbyterian Mission, who had their annual session at the time there. I had traveled by night from Allahabad to Ludhiana, and reached there early in the morning. I was taken to have a cup of tea with the delegates and others, and I was introduced across the table to Mr. Hyde. All that he said to me was, "I want to see you; I shall wait for you at the door." There he was waiting, and his first word was,

"Come with me to the prayer room, we want you there." I do not know whether it was a command or a request. I felt I had to go. I told him that I had traveled all night, and that I was tired, and had to speak at four o'clock, but I went with him. We found half-a-dozen persons there, and Hyde went down on his face before the Lord. I knelt down, and a strange feeling crept over me. Several prayed, and then Hyde began, and I remember very little more. I knew that I was in the presence of God Himself, and had no desire to leave the place; in fact, I do not think that I thought of myself or of my surroundings, for I had entered a new world, and I wanted to remain there.

We had entered the room about eight o'clock in the morning; several had gone out, others had come in, but Hyde was on his face on the floor, and had led us in prayer several times. Meals had been forgotten, and my tired feeling had gone, and the Revival account and message that I was to deliver, and concerning which I had been very anxious, had gone out of my mind, until about three-thirty, when Hyde got up, and he said to me, "You are to speak at four o'clock; I shall take you to have a cup of tea." I replied that he must need a little refreshment, too, but he said, "No, I do not want any, but you must have some." We called in at my room and washed hurriedly, and then we both had a cup of tea, and it was full time for the service. He took me right to the door, then took my hand, and said, "Go in and speak, that is your work. I shall go back to the prayer room to pray for you, that is my work. When the service is over, come into the prayer room again, and we shall praise God together." What a thrill, like an electric shock, passed through me as we parted. It was easy to speak, though I was speaking through an interpreter. What I said, I do not know. Before the meeting was over, the Indian translator, overcome by his feelings, and overpowered by the Spirit of God, failed to go on, and another had to take his place. I know the Lord spoke that night. He spoke to me, and spoke to many. I realized then the power of prayer; how often I had read of blessing in answer to prayer, but it was brought home to me that evening with such force that ever since I try to enlist prayer warriors to pray for me whenever I stand up to deliver his messages. It was one of the most wonderful services I ever attended, and I know that it was the praying saint behind the scenes that brought the blessing down on me.

I went back after the service to him, to praise the Lord. There was no question asked by him, whether it was a good service or not, whether men had received a blessing or not; nor did I think of telling him what blessing I had personally received and how his prayers had been answered. He seemed to know it all, and how he

praised the Lord, and how easy it was for me to praise the Lord
and speak to Him of the blessing He had given.[3]

We will return to the relationship between prayer and the
Word. But something else must come first. It is crucial that we
not be more fascinated, more gripped, by the prayers of a man
than by the pleasures of God. How easy it is to be more thrilled
by radical devotion than by divine beauty. It is a subtle danger. To
help avoid this pitfall we will meditate first on God's own pleasure
in the prayers of the upright, and then turn to the awesome place
of prayer in the worldwide ministry of the Word.

How the Book Has Shifted Focus

The focus has been gradually shifting in the last three chapters.
The earlier focus was on the pleasures of God in his own perfections
and his own works of creation and providence. We stressed his self-
sufficiency and his overflowing fullness of joy and his sovereign
freedom from coercion or constraint or bribery. Then, with the
chapters on election, the bruising of the Son and the good of God's
people, we have been shifting our focus more and more toward
God's pleasure in the kind of response he means for his people to
have. As from the beginning, our question still remains: What is the
measure of *God's* worth and excellency? *He* is our main focus, not
ourselves. Nevertheless, the worth of a soul's beauty is measured by
the object of its love. Therefore we must focus on what it is that
God loves in us. We have begun to do this especially in chapter 7,
and we will continue this focus to the end of the book. So even if
we concentrate on what God requires of *us*, the reason is always the
deeper question: why does he? Or: what does this requirement
reveal about God's own worth and excellency?

This focus corresponds to a tremendously important practical
question we should have, namely, how we, as sinners, can *please* a
holy God. What can we feel or think or do that would bring him
pleasure? We know that this is a legitimate biblical question
because Paul said in 2 Corinthians 5:9 that whether he was in
heaven or on earth he would make it his aim to *"please the Lord."*
This is a crucial question because even if God would allow us into
heaven as persons displeasing to him, heaven would not be

heaven. It would be a miserable thing if there were nothing we could do that delighted the heart of God. A joyful personal relationship with God in Heaven is inconceivable if there is no way for us to please him.

So someone may ask, "If this is such an important practical question, why did you spend so many chapters writing about God's delight in himself instead of getting right to the practical matter of how *we* can delight the heart of God?" The answer is that the vision of God developed in those earlier chapters is the foundation of my hope that I—sinner though I am—may yet be able to please God. And an amazing hope like that needs a deep, deep foundation! How we view God will determine our idea of how we can please God. And how a person decides to try to please God is the most fateful decision a person can ever make.

What if you discovered (like the Pharisees did), that you had devoted your whole life to trying to please God, but all the while had been doing things that in God's sight were abominations (Luke 16:14-15)? Someone may say, "I don't think that's possible; God wouldn't reject a person who has been trying to please him." But do you see what this questioner has done? He has based his conviction about what would please God on his idea of what God is like. That is precisely why we must begin with the character of God. That is why we had to begin with the pleasures of God in himself.

What we saw in those early chapters was that God has no needs that I could ever be required to satisfy. God has no deficiencies that I might be required to supply. He is complete in himself. He is overflowing with happiness in the fellowship of the Trinity. The upshot of this is that God is a mountain spring, not a watering trough. A mountain spring is self-replenishing. It constantly overflows and supplies others. But a watering trough needs to be filled with a pump or bucket brigade. So if you want to glorify the worth of a watering trough you work hard to keep it full and useful. But if you want to glorify the worth of a spring you do it by getting down on your hands and knees and drinking to your heart's satisfaction, until you have the refreshment and strength to go back down in the valley and tell people what you've found.

You do not glorify a mountain spring by dutifully hauling water up the path from the river below and dumping it in the spring. What we have seen is that God is like a mountain spring, not a watering trough. And since that is the way God *is*, we are not surprised to learn from Scripture—and our faith is strengthened to hold fast—that the way to *please* God is to come to him to get and not to give, to drink and not to water. He is most glorified in us when we are most satisfied in him.

My Hope in Death Valley Deserts

My hope as a desperate sinner, who lives in a Death Valley desert of unrighteousness, hangs on this biblical truth: that God is the kind of God who will be pleased with the one thing I have to offer—my thirst. That is why the sovereign freedom and self-sufficiency of God are so precious to me: they are the foundation of my hope that God is delighted not by the resourcefulness of bucket brigades, but by the bending down of broken sinners to drink at the fountain of grace.

> From of old no one has heard or perceived by the ear,
> No eye has seen a God besides you,
> Who works for those who wait for him.
> Isaiah 64:4

In other words, this unspeakably good news for helpless sinners—that God delights not when we offer him our strength but when we wait for his—this good news that I need to hear so badly again and again, is based firmly on a vision of God as sovereign, self-sufficient and free. If we do not have this foundational vision of God in place when we ask how we can please him, it is almost certain that our efforts to please him will become subtle means of self-exaltation, and end in the oppressive bondage of legalistic strivings. A lifelong hope in the overflowing grace of God to meet all our needs ("according to the riches of his *glory*"!) simply will not stand without a deep foundation in the doctrine of God.

I tried to make clear in chapter 7 that whatever God requires of us in response to the good news must itself be good news. If God provided salvation for us in Christ, but then required us to carry an unbearable burden and work under an intolerable yoke, the gospel would not be good news. If God demanded, as the basis of his delight in us, the end of *our* delight rather than its true beginning, there would be no gospel. So in this chapter our aim is to expand the good news of what kind of response God delights in. This chapter and the next are specific applications and outworkings of chapter 7. There we saw that God takes pleasure in those who *hope* in his love. Now we will see that hope in God gives rise to prayer and obedience.

More Pleasure in Meeting Needs Than Making Demands

We take our starting point from Proverbs 15:8,

The sacrifice of the wicked
  is an abomination to the LORD,
but the prayer of the upright
  is his delight.

My hope is that the effect of this chapter will not only be that you feel encouraged to pray, but mainly that the nature of God as a fountain of free grace will be reaffirmed—that God is the kind of God who delights most deeply not in making demands but in meeting needs. Prayer is his delight because prayer shows the reaches of *our* poverty and the riches of *his* grace. Prayer is that wonderful transaction where the wealth of God's glory is magnified and the wants of our soul are satisfied. Therefore God delights in the prayers of the upright.

Abominable Religion

Meditate with me for a few moments on Proverbs 15:8 by asking some questions and probing why it is that God abominates the sacrifices of the wicked and enjoys the prayers of the upright. My first question is this: How can something as good as a sacrifice to God, which God ordained in the book of Leviticus, become an abomination to the Lord? The first half of Proverbs 15:8 says, "The sacrifice of the wicked is an abomination to the LORD."

The answer seems to be that an act which is good in itself can become displeasing to God when it is done with the wrong inner disposition. An outward act that looks pious to us can look horrible in God's eyes because the pious act comes from a heart that is wrong. There seems to be a principle implied here that would go something like this: in God's eyes the beauty (and hence enjoyableness) of an act is the outworking of inward beauty, and the ugliness of an act is the outworking of an inward ugliness. Since God always looks on the heart (1 Samuel 16:7), he always sees our outward acts not as man sees them, but as extensions of what he sees on the inside. Whether our acts are immoral, like stealing and lying and adultery, or whether our acts are moral like church attendance and community service, both may be abominable in God's eyes if the heart is not right.

Paul teaches the same thing when he says in Romans 14:23, "Whatever is not from faith is sin." The inner beauty of hoping in God, of trusting him for help and guidance, makes the external act beautiful. And if this faith is not there motivating the act, the act is not pleasing to the Lord; it is sin. Hebrews 11:6 teaches this when it says, "Without faith it is impossible to please God." Mere external righteousness does not please God. In fact we will see it is not righteousness at all if it does not come from faith. In the near context of Hebrews 11:6 the very same issue of sacrifices is addressed that we have here in Proverbs 15:8. Hebrews 11:4 says, "*By faith* Abel offered to God a more acceptable sacrifice than Cain." Why was Abel's sacrifice pleasing to God and not Cain's? The reason is that Abel's sacrifice was offered *by faith*, but Cain's wasn't; and without faith it impossible to please God.

So I answer our first question by saying that the reason a "good" act (like a sacrifice) can be an abomination to God is that an act is viewed by God as an outworking of the condition of the heart. If the heart did not give rise to the act from an impulse of faith, the act is not pleasing to God, no matter how "religious" or "moral."

Another way to say this would be to say that if our behavior does not glorify God, it is not pleasing to God. What makes behavior glorify God most is when it is done out of a great confidence that God is meeting every need. "Abraham grew strong in his *faith*, giving *glory to God*, and fully convinced that God was able to do what he had promised" (Romans 4:20-21). Trusting in the promises of God and acting out of that trust (hope) glorifies the trustworthiness of God and his ability and wisdom and power to do what he promises. We glorify God when our service comes from faith in his strength, because the one who gives the strength gets the glory. This is the plain statement of 1 Peter 4:11, "Let him who serves serve in *the strength that God supplies* in order that in everything *God may get the glory.*" So God has pleasure in an act that comes from faith because he has pleasure in the demonstration of his glory. Acts that do not come from faith are not God-centered in this way and cannot please the God we have come to know in Scripture.

Objection

There is a possible objection to this. Someone might say that when you read the prophets like Isaiah and Amos the reason God despises the sacrifices and the prayers of the wicked is not their inner disposition but their outer behavior during the week between Sabbaths. For example, in Isaiah 1:13 the prophet says, "Bring no more vain offerings; incense is an abomination to me. New moon and Sabbath and the calling of assemblies—I cannot endure iniquity and solemn assembly." Then in verses 15 and 16 Isaiah tells why God is so displeased with the worship of his people: "Your hands are full of blood. Wash yourselves; make yourselves clean; remove the evil of your doings from before my eyes; cease to do evil, learn to do good; seek justice, correct oppression, defend the fatherless, plead for the widow." So the question is: Doesn't God abominate the sacrifices of the wicked simply because he hates the inconsistency of someone being crooked during the week and pious on Sunday?

Answer

The problem with this objection is that it does not go to the heart of the matter. Yes, God hates that inconsistency. But when a wicked person comes to God and makes a sacrifice *with a heart of penitence*, his sacrifice *is* accepted. That is the whole purpose of the guilt offering. A person who has been sinful during the week *can* be accepted through the sacrifice when it is accompanied by a broken, humble, repentant heart.

So what Isaiah is really saying is that the reason God abominates the sacrifices of the unjust is not merely the inconsistency of external behavior during the week, but that they come before the Lord with hearts that are not broken for their sin, and with no true intention of forsaking it. And *this heart condition* of stubbornness and impenitence is why their sacrifices are an abomination to God. The sacrifice is *meant* to be an occasion of forgiveness for sinners. So the sin of the people in itself is not a sufficient answer for why their sacrifice is rejected.

Therefore, I think our conclusion stands: the sacrifices of the wicked are an abomination because God sees all our acts as extensions or outworkings of the heart, and where the heart is bad the deed is bad, whether secular or religious.

So my second question is: what is the essence of the badness of this heart? Or more importantly, what is the opposite of this bad heart? What makes a person upright instead of wicked in heart so that his prayers will delight God instead of being an abomination to him? Here we turn to the second half of Proverbs 15:8:

> The sacrifice of the wicked
>   is an abomination to the Lord,
> but the prayer of the upright
>   is his delight.

Two characteristics of the upright heart show clearly why its prayers are a delight to God.

Trembling at the Word of the Lord

The first mark of the upright heart is that it *trembles* at the word of the Lord. I get this from Isaiah 66, which deals with this very same problem of some who worship in a way that pleases God and some who worship in a way that doesn't. Isaiah 66:3 describes the wicked who bring their sacrifices: "He who slaughters an ox is like him who kills a man; and he who sacrifices a lamb, like him who breaks a dog's neck." Their sacrifices are an abomination to God—on a par with murder. Why? In verse 4 God explains: "When I called, no one answered, when I spoke they did not listen." Their sacrifices were abominations to God because the people were deaf to his voice.

But what about those whose prayers God heard? God says in verse 2, "This is the man to whom I will look, he that is humble and contrite in spirit, *and trembles at my word.*" So I conclude from this that the first mark of the upright, whose prayers are a delight to God, is that they tremble at God's word. These are the people to whom the Lord will look. So the prayer of the upright that delights God comes from a heart that at first feels precarious in the presence of God. It trembles at the hearing of God's word, because it feels so far from God's ideal and so vulnerable to his judgment and so helpless and so sorry for its failings.

This is just what David said in Psalm 51:17, "The sacrifice acceptable to God is a broken spirit; a broken and contrite heart, O God, you will not despise." This is also what the Lord said to Solomon in 2 Chronicles 7:14. The first thing that makes a prayer acceptable to God is the brokenness and humility of the one who prays: "If my people who are called by my name *humble themselves* and pray . . . I will hear from heaven." So the first mark of the upright heart whose prayers please the Lord is brokenness, contrition, humility, trembling. In other words, what makes a heart upright and what makes prayers pleasing to God is a felt awareness of our tremendous need for mercy.

The other thing that marks the upright heart is *trust* in the willingness and power of God to give the mercy we need. Psalm 4:5 says, "Offer *right sacrifices*, and put your *trust* in the Lord." I take that to mean that an essential part of the upright heart whose sacrifices are *not* an abomination is trust.

Upright Does Not Mean Perfect

We could easily make the mistake of thinking that when the Old Testament speaks of the "upright" or the "righteous" it cannot mean us because we are still sinners. But the righteous and the upright are not perfect. They are persons who confess their sin, hate it and trust God for forgiveness and help. One of the best places to see this is Psalm 32. It begins, "Blessed is he whose transgression is forgiven, whose sin is covered." So the psalm is about forgiven sinners, not about perfect people. Then at the end of the psalm, the wicked are distinguished from the righteous and upright. What is the difference? Verses 10 and 11 describe it like this:

> Many are the pangs of the *wicked*;
>   but steadfast love surrounds him
>   who *trusts in the Lord.*
> Be glad in the Lord, and rejoice, O *righteous*,
>   and shout for joy, all you *upright* in heart!

Verse 10 contrasts "the wicked" with those who "*trust* in the Lord." Then verse 11 calls them *righteous* and *upright* in heart. In this psalm, then, the upright are not sinless people. They are the blessed "whose transgression is forgiven, whose sins are covered." So if you are trusting Christ and coming to him for forgiveness, broken for your sin and hating it, you should think of yourself as "the upright."

And the word for "upright" in Psalm 32 is the same word used in Proverbs 15:8, "The prayer of the *upright* is [God's] delight." So I conclude that there are at least these two essential marks of the upright heart. First, it *trembles* at the word of God. It feels precarious and helpless and in tremendous need of mercy. Then, second, it *trusts* the mercy of God to forgive and help and save.

Why God Delights in the Prayer of the Upright

Why then does God delight in the prayers of the upright? He delights in their prayers for the same reason that he abominates the sacrifices of the wicked—because the prayers of the upright are the extension and outworking of the heart; but, unlike the heart of the wicked, the heart of the upright magnifies the power and grace of God. The prayer of the upright is a delight to God because it expresses those affections of the heart which call attention to the all-sufficiency of God.

So this chapter takes us a step beyond chapter 7. There we saw from Psalm 147:11 that "The Lord takes pleasure in those who *hope* in his love." Here we see that the Lord takes pleasure in prayers that give expression to that hope. The reason our hope is a pleasure to God is because it shows that all our joy comes from the bounty of his grace. And the reason our prayers are a pleasure to God is because they express this God-exalting hope. It is a precious thing beyond all words—especially in the hour of death—that we have a God whose nature is such that what pleases him is not our *work for* him but our *need of* him.

The intensity of God's pleasure in prayer becomes more and more obvious as we look at the connection between prayer and the other things that God is committed to with all his heart.

For example, God loves to magnify his glory in the lives of his people. So he designed prayer as a way for this to happen. Jesus says, "Whatever you ask in my name, I will do it, *that the Father may be glorified in the Son*" (John 14:14). So God has designed prayer as an occasion when he and the Son will be glorified as the source and agent in doing good to his people. This is one of the reasons Revelation describes the prayers of the saints as golden bowls of incense before the throne of God (Revelation 5:8). God delights in the aroma of his own glory as he smells it in the prayers of his people.

The Aroma of God's Favorite Food

It is as though God has a favorite food. When we pray, he smells the aroma from the kitchen as you prepare his special dish. When God hungers for some special satisfaction, he seeks out a prayer to answer. Our prayer is the sweet aroma from the kitchen ascending up into the King's chambers making him hungry for the meal. But the actual enjoyment of the meal is his own glorious work in answering our prayer. The food of God is to answer our prayers. The most wonderful thing about the Bible is that it reveals a God who satisfies his appetite for joy by answering prayers. He has no deficiency in himself that he needs to fill up, so he gets his satisfaction by magnifying the glory of his riches by filling up the deficiencies of people who pray.

This seems to be the point of Psalm 50:13-15. "Do I eat the flesh of bulls, or drink the blood of goats?" says the Lord. No. Therefore "offer to God a sacrifice of thanksgiving . . . and call upon him in the day of trouble, and he will deliver you, and *you shall glorify* [*him*]." The demonstration of the glory of God in answered prayer is God's special feast. So if we want to feed him with the only kind of joy he is capable of, we hold up the empty cup of prayer and let him show the riches of his glory by filling it. Thus the intensity of God's delight in his glory is the measure of his pleasure in the prayers of his people.

Prayer and Election

Another example to illustrate God's passion for the prayers of his people is the connection between prayer and election. In chapter 5 we unfolded the biblical teaching about God's delight in freely and unconditionally choosing a people for his own possession. We saw that God has the freedom and the sovereign right to save—really save—any and all lost sinners that he pleases—and that he indeed must do this if his elect are to inherit their appointed blessing. What we can see now, as we reflect on God's pleasure in prayer, is that prayer for the salvation of the lost is rooted in election. Prayer is one of God's appointed means of bringing the elect to faith. Thus God loves such prayers with the very passion that moved him to choose a people for his glory.

Until we embrace the sovereignty of God in election (and, therefore, in conversion), we cannot really pray consistently that God would actually save lost sinners. We cannot pray the way Paul describes his own praying in Romans 10:1, "Brothers, my heart's desire and prayer to God for them is that they might be saved." Paul's heart's desire is for the salvation of his fellow Jews. And when our hearts ache for something, we pray for it. And so he says that his prayer to God is that they be saved. He wants something accomplished in his mission—the salvation of Jews as he preaches in the synagogues. So he prays to God that this would happen. He asks God to save them. "O God, that they might be saved! Do it, God! Do what you need to do to save my kinsmen!"

But that kind of praying is inconsistent if you do not believe in the sovereignty of God in election and conversion. The sovereignty of God is his right and power to save unbelieving, unrepentant, hardened sinners. There are a lot of people who do not believe God has that right. They do not believe that God has the right to intrude upon a person's rebellion, and overcome it, and draw that person effectually to faith and salvation. They do not believe that God has the right to exert himself so powerfully in grace as to overcome all the resistance of a hardened sinner. Instead they believe that man himself has the sole right of final determination in the choices and affections of his heart toward God. Every person, they say, has final self-determination in whether they will overcome the hardness of their hearts and come to Christ. And so it is finally in the hands of man, not God, who will be saved and how many will inhabit the kingdom.

The effects on prayer for such people are devastating if they try to pray consistently with this rejection of the sovereignty of God in election and conversion. It means they can't ask God to actually fulfill many of his promises and effectually save anybody.

> They can't pray, "God, take out my friend's heart of stone and give him a new heart of flesh" (Ezekiel 11:19).
>
> They can't pray, "Lord, circumcise my daughter's heart so that she loves you" (Deuteronomy 30:6).
>
> They can't pray, "Father, put your Spirit within my dad and cause him to walk in your statutes" (Ezekiel 36:27).
>
> They can't pray, "Lord, grant my teacher repentance and a knowledge of the truth" (2 Timothy 2:25-26).
>
> They can't pray, "Open my sister's eyes so that she will believe the gospel" (Acts 16:14).

The reason they can't pray this way is that all these prayers give God a right that they have reserved for man—namely the ultimate, decisive determination of man's destiny. If you ask God to do any of these things, he would be the one who actually saves. How then does one pray if one really believes that man, not God, must make the ultimate decisions about individual salvation (and thus the ultimate decisions about the size and makeup of heaven's population)?

Prayer to a God Not Sovereign in Conversion

I take an example from a well-known book on prayer that seems to reject God's sovereignty in the salvation of sinners. This writer says that the way to pray is to "Ask God to cause a specific person . . . to begin questioning whom they can really trust in life."[4] But my question then is: Why is it right for God to *cause* a person to think a question and wrong for God to cause that person to think an answer? Why is it legitimate for God to take control of a person to the degree that he causes the person to ask a question he would not have otherwise asked, but it is not legitimate for God to exert that same influence to cause the person to give an answer that he would not otherwise have given—namely, that Jesus should be trusted?

Here is another example of how this writer says we should pray for unbelievers: "Pray that God will plant in the hearts of these people . . . an inner unrest, together with a longing to know the 'Truth.'" Now my question is: If it is legitimate for God to "plant a longing" in a person's heart, how strong can the longing be that God chooses to plant? There are two kinds of longings God could plant in an unbeliever's heart. One kind of longing is so strong that it leads the person to pursue and embrace Christ. The other kind of longing is not strong enough to lead a person to embrace Christ. Which should we pray for? If we pray for the strong longing, then we are praying that the Lord would work effectually and get that person saved. If you pray for the weak longing, then we are praying for an ineffectual longing that leaves the person in sin (but preserves his self-determination).

Do you see where this leads? People who really believe that man must have the ultimate power of self-determination, can't consistently pray that God would convert unbelieving sinners. Why? Because if they pray for divine influence in a sinner's life they are either praying for a successful influence (which takes away the sinner's ultimate *self*-determination), or they are praying for an unsuccessful influence (which is not praying for *God* to convert the sinner). So either you give up praying for God to convert sinners or you give up ultimate human self-determination.

Prayer to a God Who Effectively Saves

Paul leaves no doubt where he stands on that issue in Romans 9:16, "It depends not upon man's will or exertion, but upon God's mercy." So he prays that God would convert Israel! He prays for her *salvation*! He does not pray for ineffectual influences, but for effectual influences. And that is how we should pray too. We should take the new covenant promises of God and plead with God to bring them to pass in our children and our neighbors and on all the mission fields of the world.

"God, take out of their flesh the heart of stone and give them a new heart of flesh" (Ezekiel 11:19).

"Lord, circumcise their heart so that they love you" (Deuteronomy 30:6).

"Father, put your Spirit within them and cause them to walk in your statutes" (Ezekiel 36:27).

"Lord, grant them repentance and a knowledge of the truth that they may escape from the snare of the devil" (2 Timothy 2:25-26).

"Father, open their hearts so that they believe the gospel" (Acts 16:14).

When we believe in the sovereignty of God—in the right and power of God to elect and then bring hardened sinners to faith and salvation—then we will be able to pray with no inconsistency, and with great biblical promises for the conversion of the lost. Thus God has pleasure in this kind of praying because it ascribes to him the right and honor to be the free and sovereign God that he is in election and salvation.

Prayer in His Name to Spread His Fame

Another way to sense God's pleasure in the prayers of his people is to see the connection they have with God's awesome passion for the spread of his fame. We pondered that passion in chapter 4. But what we will see now is that God's passion for the spread of his fame is the measure of his pleasure in the prayers behind it. Second Thessalonians 3:1-2 makes this connection strikingly clear:

Finally, brothers, pray for us, that the word of the Lord may run and be glorified, as [it was] with you, and that we may be delivered from wicked and evil men; for not all have faith.

This text gives tremendous significance to prayer in God's purposes to spread his fame around the world. What it says is that *through prayer* the word of the Lord overcomes obstacles and reaches a glorious victory. The word is pictured as an athlete running in a race to attain the prize of glory. An athlete is glorified when he wins and is recognized and acclaimed as superior to all the others in the race. So the word of the Lord is running in the world. It will one day win the race of words—the race of philosophies and theories and world views. It will be recognized and acclaimed as superior to all other words and philosophies—*if* we pray! "*Pray* for us that the word of the Lord may run and be glorified."

The extraordinary significance of prayer for the spread of God's fame will not be felt until we see clearly how everything hangs on the triumph of the Word of the Lord. Prayer should never be exalted above the Word in the mission of the church. The proclamation of the gospel in word and deed is the crucial front-line weapon in world missions. Prayer is the power that wields the weapon of the Word; but the Word itself is the weapon by which the nations will be brought to faith and obedience. God's purpose to spread his fame to all the peoples, and fill the earth with the knowledge of his glory, will triumph by the spread of God's Word and not without it.

> Everyone who calls upon the name of the Lord will be saved. But how are they to call upon him in whom they have not believed? And how are they to believe in him of whom they have never *heard* and how are they to *hear* without a *preacher* . . . . Faith comes by *hearing* and hearing by the *word* of Christ (Romans 10:13-17).
>
> The *gospel* is the power of God unto salvation (Romans 1:16).
>
> You have been born anew not of perishable seed, but of imperishable, through the living and abiding *Word of God* (1 Peter 1:23).
>
> This *gospel of the Kingdom* will be *preached* throughout the whole world, as a testimony to all nations; and then the end will come (Matthew 24:14).

The Word of God, the gospel of the kingdom, is the weapon that God designs to use in penetrating the kingdom of darkness and gathering the children of light from all the nations. His whole redemptive plan for the universe hangs on the success of his word. If the preaching of the Word aborts, the purposes of God fail. But that cannot happen.

> For as the rain and the snow come down from heaven,
>   and return not thither but water the earth,
> making it bring forth and sprout,
>   giving seed to the sower and bread to the eater,
> *so shall my word be that goes forth from my mouth;*
>   *it shall not return to me empty,*
> *but it shall accomplish that which I purpose,*
>   *and prosper in the thing for which I sent it.*
>   (Isaiah 55:10-11)

God is sovereign. Though he makes all his plans for universal fame hang on the success of his Word, his purposes cannot fail. The gospel *will* run and be glorified. We see this confidence everywhere in the Scripture. Let me illustrate it with the effect it had on one stream of Christian history.

The Puritan Hope

The first missionary endeavor of the Protestants in England burst forth from the soil of Puritan hope. The Puritans, you remember, were those pastors and teachers in England (and then New England), roughly between the years 1560 and 1660, who wanted to purify the Church of England and bring it into theological and practical alignment with the biblical teachings of the Reformation. They had a view of God's sovereignty that produced an undaunted hope in the victory of God's Word over all the world. They really believed the promises of God's triumph over all the nations.

In you shall *all* families of the earth be blessed.
Genesis 12:3

To him shall be the obedience of the peoples.
Genesis 49:10

All the ends of the world shall remember
   and turn unto the Lord:
and all the families of the nations
   shall worship before you.
For dominion belongs to the Lord,
   and he rules over the nations.
Psalm 22:27

O you who hear prayer,
Unto you shall all men come.
Psalm 65:2

All the earth shall worship you,
   and shall sing praises to you;
   they will sing praises to your name.
Psalm 66:4

There is none like you among the gods, O Lord,
   nor are there any works like yours.
All the nations you have made shall come and bow down
   before you, O Lord,
   and shall glorify your name.
Psalm 86:8-9

This tremendous confidence that the Word of Christ would one day penetrate all the nations, and be glorified by every people on earth, gave birth to the first Protestant missionary endeavor in the English-speaking world, and it happened 150 years before the modern missionary movement began with William Carey in 1793.

Between 1627 and 1640, 15,000 people emigrated from England to America, most of them Puritans, carrying this great confidence in the worldwide reign of Christ. In fact, the seal of the colonists of Massachusetts Bay had on it a North American Indian with these words coming out of his mouth: "Come over into Macedonia and help us" taken from Acts 16:9. What this shows is that in general the Puritans saw their emigration to America as part of God's missionary strategy to extend his kingdom among the nations.

The Enthrallment of John Eliot

One of those hope-filled Puritans who crossed the Atlantic in 1631 was John Eliot. He was twenty-seven years old at the time, and a year later became the pastor of a new church in Roxbury, Massachusetts, about a mile from Boston. But something happened that made him more than a pastor.

According to Cotton Mather, there were twenty tribes of Indians in that vicinity. He specifically calls them "nations" to emphasize the missionary significance ("make disciples of all *nations*"). John Eliot could not avoid the practical implications of his theology: if the infallible Scriptures promise that all nations will one day bow down to Christ, and if Christ is sovereign and able by his Spirit to subdue all opposition to his promised reign, then there is good hope that a person who goes as an ambassador of Christ to one of these nations will be the chosen instrument of God to open the eyes of the blind and set up an outpost of the kingdom of Christ.

And so when he was slightly over forty years old Eliot set himself to study Algonquin. He deciphered the vocabulary and grammar and syntax and eventually translated the entire Bible as well as books that he valued like Richard Baxter's *Call to the Unconverted*. By the time Eliot was eighty-four years old, there were numerous Indian churches, some with their own Indian pastors. It is an amazing story of a man who was enthralled by the inevitable triumph of world evangelization.

This is what gripped the Puritan mind and eventually gave birth to the modern missionary movement in 1793. William Carey, the "father of modern missions," was nourished on this tradition, as were David Brainerd and Adoniram Judson and Alexander Duff and David Livingstone and John Paton and a host of others who gave their lives to reach the unreached peoples of the world. The modern missionary movement did not arise in a theological vacuum. It grew out of a conviction that put the sovereignty of God square in the center of human life and it nourished itself daily on the infallible promises that the word of God would run and be glorified among all the nations.

The Awesome Place of Prayer

But now we are ready to see the awesome place of prayer, and why it is such a sweet aroma to God who loves the triumph of his gospel and the spread of his fame. John Eliot did not labor in his own strength. He once said, "Prayers and pains through faith in Christ Jesus will do any thing!"[5] Prayers came before pains and in pains and after pains. And the key to bearing the pains until he died at age eighty-four was the prayers.

God has made the spread of his fame hang on the preaching of his Word; and he has made the preaching of his Word hang on the prayers of the saints. This is the awesome place of prayer in the purposes of God for the world. The triumph of the Word will not come without prayer. How do we know this?

We know it by the way the apostle Paul pleads for prayer in the ministry of the Word. Three times he appeals for prayer from the churches so that the Word he preaches will succeed in its intended mission. *"Pray also for me*, that utterance may be given me in opening my mouth boldly to proclaim the mystery of the *gospel"* (Ephesians 6:19). *"Pray for us also*, that God may open to us a door for the *Word*, to declare the mystery of Christ" (Colossians 4:3). "Finally, brothers, *pray for us*, that the *word of the Lord* may run and be glorified" (2 Thessalonians 3:1).

A Wartime Walkie-talkie, Not a Domestic Intercom

Prayer is the walkie talkie on the battle-field of the world. It calls on God for courage (Ephesians 6:19). It calls in for troop deployment and target location (Acts 13:1-3). It calls in for protection and air cover (Matthew 6:13; Luke 21:36). It calls in for fire power to blast open a way for the Word (Colossians 4:3). It calls in for the miracle of healing for the wounded soldiers (James 5:16). It calls in for supplies for the forces (Matthew 6:11; Philippians 4:6). And it calls in for needed reinforcements (Matthew 9:38). This is the place of prayer—on the battlefield of the world. It is a wartime walkie talkie for spiritual warfare, not a domestic intercom to increase the comforts of the saints. And one of the reasons it malfunctions in the hands of so many Christian soldiers is that they have gone AWOL.[6]

Almighty God has spoken. If he is God, it is sure that his Word will accomplish all his purpose. God's truth *must* win the spiritual war of the ages. But 2 Thessalonians 3:1 says, "*Pray* that the Word will triumph!" I take this to mean that God will indeed cause his Word to be glorified. But he does not intend to win without prayer. God will be duly glorified when the knowledge of his glory fills the earth like the waters cover the sea (Habakkuk 2:14). And the earth will be filled with the knowledge of his glory when the Word of the Lord triumphs among all the peoples of the earth. And the Word will triumph through mighty, prevailing prayer.[7] Therefore the intensity of God's pleasure in prayer is proportionate to the intensity of his passion that all his purposes be complete. If he loves his Son, if he loves his sovereignty, if he loves his creation, and his fame, and his electing grace, and his redeeming work, and the good of his people, and the ingathering of all the children of God, then he must love prayer with all his heart.

For I am more convinced than ever that this gift is no mere convenience with which we settle in more nicely to this world. Rather God has given us prayer because Jesus has given us a mission. God's pleasure in the prayers of his people is proportionate to his passion for world evangelization. We are on this earth to press back the forces of darkness, and we are given access to Headquarters by prayer in order to advance this cause. When we try to turn it into a civilian intercom to increase our material comforts, it malfunctions, and our faith begins to falter.

Materialistic Evangelical Praying

David Bryant, founder of Concerts of Prayer International, tells about a young Hindu social worker who came to America and stayed at his house. He and his wife Robyne took her one evening to dinner at a friend's home. On the way the Hindu woman "witnessed" to David and Robyne. She showed them a picture of a guru who had died forty-five years ago. She and her family now worship him and pray to him.

When Bryant blurted out, "But he's dead!" she disagreed, and said that in response to her prayers he has given her a very good life and surrounded her with many blessings.

When they got to the home where they would eat dinner, David Bryant hoped that his Christian friend would help bear a credible witness to this Hindu woman. But he was dismayed when at the dinner table his host said, "Great house, isn't it? I know I put a lot more into it than I can ever hope to get out of it. But I don't mind. We plan to be here the next forty-five years anyway, God willing. We're so thankful. The Lord has blessed us in so many ways. I don't know what we'd do without him."

Bryant sat in his back yard the next morning asking himself: Is that the point of prayer—to treat God like Coke? Some say things go better with Coke. Some say things go better with Christ. Some say things go better with a guru. A bird splashed into a nearby birdbath and sent Bryant's mind to Matthew 6. "Yes," he thought, "we are supposed to be as free and peaceful as the birds. But why? To seek first the Kingdom!"[8]

A Closing Appeal for Wartime Praying

The crying need of the hour—every hour—is to put the churches on a wartime footing. Mission leaders are crying out, "Where is the church's concept of militancy, of a mighty army willing to suffer, moving ahead with exultant determination to take the world by storm? Where is the risk-taking, the launching out on God alone?"[9]

The answer is that it has been swallowed up in a peace-time mentality. Thousands of Christians do not hear the diabolic bombs dropping and the bullets zinging overhead. They don't smell the hellish Agent Orange in the whitened harvest of the world. They don't cringe or weep at the thousands who perish every week. They don't reckon with spiritual hosts of wickedness in heavenly places and the world rulers of this present darkness. In fact, it is not dark, they say. It is bright and comfortable and cheery—just look at my home and car and office and cabin and boat. And listen to my new disc-player and look at my new video equipment.

The need of the hour is a global wartime mentality. I say "wartime" because life is war (1 Timothy 6:12; Ephesians 6:10ff; 2 Corinthians 10:3-5). I say "global" because "the field is the world" (Matthew 13:38). And because thousands of unreached peoples are scattered around the globe.

"Peoples," not just people. The command to the church is not to win every person before the Lord comes, but to win some from every people. This is the great unfinished task!

"To him shall be the obedience of the *peoples*" (Genesis 49:10). "Let the *peoples* praise you, O God, let all the *peoples* praise you" (Psalm 67:3). "Behold, I made him a witness to the *peoples*, a leader and commander for the *peoples*" (Isaiah 55:4).

How will we come to feel the extraordinary Satanic devastation being wreaked among the remaining unreached peoples of the world? How can our people come to see the irrationality of a persistently bouncy, peacetime, Disneyland mentality when the days are evil (Ephesians 5:16), and the god of this world is blinding billions (2 Corinthians 4:4), and Satan is filled with rage because his time is short (Revelation 12:12), and the stakes are infinitely higher than any conceivable nuclear World War III or any environmental disaster (Luke 12:4-5).

How can a sense of urgency and vigilance and passion and zeal become part of the Christian ethos today? How can the sweaty, bruised, thrilling courage of wartime camaraderie become as deeply ingrained in our mind-set as the warm and comfortable images of family and flock? How might we ever get our conference meetings out of the posh, luxurious hotels and convention centers and meet in something fitting for the Calvary Road—something that says wartime austerity, and radical sacrifice, and Spartan readiness to go anywhere and do anything at any pain for the King?

The crying need for the last decade of this millennium is a global wartime mentality among all the pastors and churches and believers of the Christian Church.

And this is doubly true because the sufferings on the home front are so great. (Yes, even in the bouncy, positive, air-conditioned, video-equipped dens of America!) In the time that it has taken me to write this special appeal I have received a call from a man in our church weeping because his wife is divorcing him and taking the children. I have met him and prayed. I have called her and made an appointment. Now I am back trying to write the closing part of this chapter.

Just hours later a woman called to say that her father was dying. I left the writing again and drove thirty minutes to his bedside and prayed. Two hours later he died.

Again I am back at the keyboard trying to grasp the need of the world. Trying to feel the Satanic devastation not only of my own sin-sick church and city but also of the cities where there aren't 1,000 churches like there are in the Twin Cities.

The phone rings off the hook. Your own kids fight and get sick. The marriage twists with unfulfilled expectations and self-pitying pouting. A hundred people have different ideas about the new church building, and the organ, and the parking lot.

And many say this is the real battle. Divorce, death, disagreement. But I don't believe it. Oh yes, it's real. And, yes, it's a battle. But it's not the main battle. Is the field hospital the main reason for having troops on the field? What's the main reason sergeants are in the trenches? To settle soldiers' disputes? Do chaplains come along just to bury the dead? Or is there a war to be won?

There is. And the victory is near. But it will not be easy or cheap. The awesome mission is clear: "This gospel of the kingdom will be preached throughout the whole world, as a testimony to all nations, and then the end will come" (Matthew 24:14). Christ has his elect from every people, tribe, tongue and nation (Revelation 5:9). They are held captive by the Enemy (2 Timothy 2:26). And so the mine fields must be crossed, the barbed wire cut, the snipers evaded, and gospel antidotes for Satan's mind-altering drugs administered against immense opposition (Luke 21:12-19).

So again I ask, How will the church ever come to think this way? How will millions of lukewarm church-goers be brought to wartime readiness and put on military alert? How can the massive mentality of American prosperity, and peace with the world, and family comfort, ever be overcome?

I believe the answer, beneath and behind the renewed empowering of the Word of God, is a movement of persevering, believing, expectant prayer. Because it is prayer that opens our hearts to the surpassing worth of God (Ephesians 1:17f.), and makes us feel the height and depth of Christ's love (Ephesians 3:18). It's prayer that makes us love lost people (1 Thessalonians 3:12) and have a passion for righteousness (Philippians 1:11). It's prayer that opens doors for the gospel (Colossians 4:3) and brings in the recruits (Matthew 9:38), and makes them bold (Ephesians 6:19). It's prayer that protects from the Enemy (Romans 15:31; Matthew 6:13) and makes the Word of God run and be glorified (2 Thessalonians 3:1).

And only when the people of God "cry to him day and night" will God come forth with power and vindicate his cause in the world (Luke 18:7f.) and bring in the Kingdom (Matt. 6:10). In this great hope the Church may pursue its work with indomitable joy. May the Lord awaken us to the terrible war, the triumphant Christ, the awesome power of prayer and the strategic priority of unreached peoples as a corporate mission.

One hundred years ago, A. T. Pierson said, "Every new Pentecost has had its preparatory period of supplication. . . . God has compelled his saints to seek Him at the throne of grace, so that every new advance might be so plainly due to His power that even the unbeliever might be constrained to confess: 'Surely this is the finger of God!' "[10] This is the fame that gives God pleasure, and therefore the measure of his passion for our prayer.

Patrick Johnstone sounds the urgent battle cry in his utterly strategic book, *Operation World*. In his words we see clearly the response God demands of us and the response in which the Lord delights. What then is the worth and excellency of such a God?

> It is a solemn thing to intercede for the nations of the world! Let us mobilize prayer! We can tip the scales of history. Christians can be the controlling factor in the unfolding drama of today's world—let us not allow ourselves to be chased around by the enemy, but let us go up at once and take the kingdoms of this

world for Jesus (Numbers 13:30; Daniel 7:18)—He is delighted to give them to us (Daniel 7:22, 27; Luke 12:32). In practical terms, may these truths make our prayer lives as individuals, and in prayer meetings, outward-looking, Satan-shaking, captive-releasing, kingdom-taking, revival-giving, Christ-glorifying power channels for God![11]

Notes

1. The account is told in the anonymously written *The Kneeling Christian* (Grand Rapids: Zondervan Publishing House, 1945), 51.

2. George Mueller, *Autobiography of George Mueller*, compiled by G. Fred. Bergin (London: J. Nisbet and Co. 1906), 296.

3. *Praying Hyde*, ed. Captain E. G. Carré (South Plainfield, N.J.: Bridge Publishing, Inc., n.d.), 67-69.

4. Let me say immediately that I have gotten much benefit from this book, and I believe God is using it and the other ministries of its author for great good in world evangelization. The fact that I think he is wrong on this matter, and that it is indeed harmful to be wrong, does not mean that I put myself above him spiritually or that I deny God's grace and power in his life. I am referring to Dick Eastman, *The Hour that Changes the World*, (Grand Rapids: Baker Book House, 1979). On page 158 he says, "Of course we know that every person has a will to choose or reject the message of Christ's love. Therefore we cannot ask God to force unbelievers . . . to believe on him." So he goes on to suggest that our prayers for the lost should be in the form of asking God to cause these people to ask six questions: Whom can I trust? What is my purpose? When will I really be free? Why do people hate religion? How can I cope? Where will I go when I die? I think this is very good advice. My difference is that I would also encourage people to pray that God overcome all resistance and effectually bring people to the point where they willingly give the right answer to these questions and believe. You are not "forcing" faith when you cause someone to want to believe.

5. Cotton Mather, *Great Works*, 1 (Edinburgh: Banner of Truth Trust, 1979, orig. published, 1702), 562.

6. It is crucial that all Christians see their life as a warfare. That is not all that it is. But it is that, always. We see this in Scripture. When Paul came to the end of his life, he said in 2 Timothy 4:7, "I have fought the good fight, I have finished the race, I have kept the faith." And in 1 Timothy 6:12 he tells Timothy, "Fight the good fight of faith; lay hold on eternal life to which you were called." So life is war because the maintenance of our faith and the laying hold on eternal life is a constant fight. Paul makes clear in 1 Thessalonians 3:5 that the number one target of Satan is faith. If we endure to the end we will be saved, Jesus said (Mark 13:13), and Satan is fighting always to bring us to ruin by destroying our faith.

Concerning his own life of warfare Paul said earlier, "I do not run aimlessly, I do not box as one beating the air; but I pommel my body and subdue it, lest after preaching to others I myself should be disqualified" (1 Corinthians

9:26-7). Concerning his ministry he said, "Though we live in the world we are not carrying on a worldly war, for the weapons of our warfare are not worldly but have divine power to destroy strongholds. We destroy arguments and every proud obstacle to the knowledge of God, and take every thought captive to obey Christ" (2 Corinthians 10:3-5). So life is war and ministry is war. (See Revelation 12:17; 17:14.)

Probably the most familiar passage on the warfare we live in daily is Ephesians 6:12-3. "We are not contending against flesh and blood, but against the principalities, against the powers, against the world rulers of this present darkness, against the spiritual hosts of wickedness in the heavenly places. Therefore take the whole armor of God." Many other passages could be brought in, but perhaps this is enough to make the urgent point that life is war and we need to develop a wartime mentality and a wartime lifestyle.

7. See Wesley L. Duewel, *Mighty, Prevailing Prayer* (Grand Rapids: Francis Asbury Press, 1990).

8. David Bryant, "Aggression: Is It for the Birds?" *World Christian*, 3, No. 5 (September/October, 1984): 36-37.

9. Jim Reapsome, "What's Holding up World Evangelization?" *Evangelical Missions Quarterly*, April 1988, 118.

10. A. T. Pierson, *The New Acts of the Apostles* (New York: The Baker & Taylor Co., 1894), 352ff.

11. Patrick Johnstone, *Operation World* (Kent: STL Books and WEC International, 1986), 21-22.

Has the Lord as great delight in burnt offerings
and sacrifices,
as in obeying the voice of the Lord?
Behold, to obey is better than sacrifice,
and to hearken than the fat of rams.

1 Samuel 15:22

A false balance is an abomination to the LORD,
but a just weight is his delight.

Proverbs 11:1

Chapter 9

The Pleasure of God
in Personal Obedience
and Public Justice

In chapters 7 and 8 we have emphasized the good news that God is a mountain spring and not a watering trough. He is self-replenishing, and does not need a bucket brigade to meet his needs. We do not serve him, therefore, as though he needed anything (Acts 17:25). Rather we honor his overflowing fullness when we thrive on the water of Life. God is most glorified in us when we are most satisfied in him. This means that whenever I am most thirsty and desperate for help, I can encourage my soul not only with the truth that there is a merciful impulse in the heart of God, but also with the truth that the source and power of that impulse is the zeal of God to act for the glory of his own name. I can plead with the psalmists, *"For your name's sake, O Lord,* pardon my guilt, for it is great" (Psalm 25:11). I can cry out in distress, "Help us, O God of our salvation *for the glory of your name,* and deliver us" (Psalm 79:9). I can ask for light in the night, *"For your name's sake,* lead me and guide me" (Psalm 31:3).

The last two chapters have shown us that God's passion for the glory of his own name is the measure of his pleasure in those who *hope* in his love and *pray* in his name. When we *hope in God* we glorify God as the fountain of deep and lasting joy. And when we *pray* we give expression to that God-glorifying hope. In this chapter we go one step further and say that *obedience* to God makes this God-glorifying hope visible and proves that it is real in our lives. Obedience is the irrepressible public relations project of those who have tasted and seen that the Lord is good (Matthew 5:16).

Two Key Questions

We begin with Samuel's words to Saul in 1 Samuel 15:22, "Has the LORD as great delight in burnt offerings and sacrifices, as in obeying the voice of the Lord?" The answer is clearly *no*. The Lord delights far more in obedience than in the performance of worship ceremonies without it. The two questions I pose as I listen to this text are 1) Why does God delight in obedience? And 2) Is this good news? Is it good news to hear that what pleases God is obedience, or is it a discouraging burden? Many hear the biblical call for obedience as something very different from the gospel. They hear the ominous tones of legalism and "works" and insecurity. And so they make every effort to keep the gospel call for faith and the call for obedience in radically separate categories. They believe that, if the call for obedience were mixed with the gospel call for faith, salvation by faith would be contaminated by "works" and the gospel would be destroyed. Is this true? Before we focus on these two questions let's be sure we have the setting of 1 Samuel 15 clear in our minds.

When Israel came out of Egypt and passed through the wilderness the Amalekites attacked them. You can read about it in Exodus 17:8-16. God gave the Israelites victory, but this wicked mistreatment was never forgotten. In Deuteronomy 25:17-19 God said,

> Remember what Amalek did to you on the way as you came out of Egypt, how he attacked you on the way, when you were faint and weary, and [how he] cut off at your rear all who lagged behind you; and he did not fear God. Therefore when the Lord your God has given you rest from all your enemies round about, in the land which the Lord your God gives you for an inheritance to possess, you shall blot out the remembrance of Amalek from under heaven; you shall not forget.

Finally the time appointed for judgment comes and the Lord commands Saul, the first king of Israel, to execute the sentence against the Amalekites. The command is given in 1 Samuel 15:2-3:

> Thus says the Lord of hosts, "I will punish what Amalek did to Israel in opposing them on the way, when they came up out of

Egypt. Now go and smite Amalek, and utterly destroy all that they have; do not spare them, but kill both man and woman, infant and suckling, ox and sheep, camel and ass."

So Saul gathered his army and went against the city of Amalek. He warned the Kenites to get out if they wanted to spare their lives (1 Samuel 15:6). And then he destroyed the Amalekites from Havilah as far as Shur, east of Egypt. But verse 9 describes the fatal disobedience of Saul:

> But Saul and the people spared Agag, and the best of the sheep and of the oxen and of the fatlings, and the lambs, and of all that was good, and would not utterly destroy them; all that was despised and worthless they utterly destroyed.

The Lord saw this disobedience and he repented[1] that he had made Saul king (1 Samuel 15:11). Samuel is angry at this turn in God's attitude toward Saul and he cries out to God all night (1 Samuel 15:11, see also 12:23). The result of his night of prayer is a firm resolve to do what God says. He rises early in the morning and finds out that Saul has gone to Carmel, set up a monument for himself and proceeded to Gilgal where he was first made king (1 Samuel 11:15). So Samuel goes to meet Saul, and is met with the ingratiating words, "Blessed are you to the Lord; I have performed the commandment of the Lord" (1 Samuel 15:13).

Samuel asks what the sound of bleating sheep and lowing oxen means if Saul really destroyed everything the way God said. But Saul blames it on the people: "*They* have brought them from the Amalekites; for the *people* spared the best of the sheep . . ." (1 Samuel 15:15). But nothing Saul says will work now. He has disobeyed the commandment of the Lord and he finally admits it in verse 24: "I have sinned; for I have transgressed the commandment of the Lord and your words."

Now with this situation clearly in view we can take up our first question: Why is God so displeased with disobedience? Or to put the question positively, Why does God take so much delight in obedience?

Why God Delights in Obedience

I see at least five reasons in this story why God hates disobedience and takes pleasure in obedience. I will mention them in order from what seems to me the least to most serious.

First, God has pleasure in obedience because disobedience shows a misplacement of fear. In 1 Samuel 15:24, "Saul said to Samuel, 'I have sinned; for I have transgressed the commandment of the Lord and your words, *because I feared the people* and obeyed their voice.'" Why did Saul obey the people instead of God? Because he feared the people instead of God. He feared the human consequences of obedience more than he feared the divine consequences of sin. He feared the displeasure of the people more than the displeasure of God. And that is a great insult to God. Samuel had said twice to Saul and to the people, "Fear the Lord, and serve him faithfully with all your heart" (1 Samuel 12:14, 24). But now the leader himself has feared man and turned away from following God (1 Samuel 15:11).

It is a great biblical truth that to fear a thing is to do homage to it. In Isaiah 8:12-13 the prophet warns against the very mistake Saul made:

> Do not call conspiracy all that this people call conspiracy, and do not fear what they fear, nor be in dread. But the Lord of hosts, *him you shall regard as holy*, let him be your fear, and let him be your dread.

If our lives are guided by the same fears that unbelievers have then we do not "regard God as holy." We do not honor him and revere him as greater than all things. In fact, Isaiah says, it is a kind of pride to be afraid of what man can do while we disregard the promises of God. He quotes God with this piercing question: "I, I am he that comforts you; *who are you that you are afraid of man* who dies, of the son of man who is made like grass, and have forgotten the Lord, your Maker?" (Isaiah 51:12-13). Fear of man may not feel like pride, but that is what God says it is: "Who do you think you are to fear man and forget me your Maker!"

The apostle Peter takes up this teaching of Isaiah and applies it to the Christian life. He says, "If you suffer for righteousness' sake, you will be blessed. Have no fear of them, nor be troubled, but in your hearts reverence Christ as Lord" (1 Peter 3:14-15). Isaiah said, "Don't fear man, regard God as holy." Peter said, "Don't fear man, reverence Christ as Lord." The word behind "regard as holy" and "reverence" is basically the same in both cases. The point is this: if you fear man, you have begun to deny the holiness, the worth, of God and his Son Jesus. God is infinitely stronger. He is infinitely wiser and infinitely more full of reward and joy. To turn from him out of fear of what man can do is to discount all that God promises to be for those who fear him. It is a great insult. And in such an insult God can take no pleasure. On the other hand when we hear the promises[2] and trust him with courage, fearing the reproach brought upon God by our unbelief, then he is greatly honored. And in that he has pleasure.

Second, God has pleasure in obedience because disobedience shows a misplacement of pleasure. Saul tried to persuade Samuel that it was a noble intention that led him to disobey God and keep the best sheep and oxen alive (1 Samuel 15:21). He said they wanted to sacrifice these to the Lord in Gilgal. But the Lord had given Samuel insight into the true motive of Saul and the people. We see it in 1 Samuel 15:19: "Why then did you not obey the voice of the Lord? Why did you *swoop on* the spoil, and do what was evil in the sight of the Lord?"

They "swooped" down on the spoil like hungry birds eager to fill their bellies. This word "swoop" is used in 1 Samuel 14:32 to describe how the people fell on the spoil when the Philistines were defeated. It says, "The people flew upon the spoil, and took sheep and oxen and calves, and slew them on the ground; and the people ate them with the blood."

When Samuel says, "Why did you *swoop* on the spoil, and do what was evil in the sight of the Lord?" he implies that the people were driven by an overweening desire for the pleasures of all that meat. Their pleasure was misplaced. It should have been in God. But they delighted more in the meat of sheep and oxen than they did in the smile and fellowship of God. This is, of course, a great insult to God, and therefore very displeasing in his sight. But to look to the promises of God and the prospect of his awesome presence, and delight more in that than in the fleeting pleasures of disobedience, is a great honor to God. And in that he has pleasure.

Third, God has pleasure in obedience because disobedience shows a misplacement of praise. When Saul had defeated the Amalekites the first thing he did was build himself a monument.

First Samuel 15:12: "It was told Samuel, Saul came to Carmel and behold, he set up *a monument for himself.*" Evidently Saul was more interested in getting a name for himself than in making a name for God through careful obedience to his word. He misplaced praise from God to himself.

This sin becomes even worse when you read 1 Samuel 15:17-18:

> And Samuel said, "Though you are little in your own eyes, are you not the head of the tribes of Israel? The Lord anointed you king over Israel. And the Lord sent you on a mission, and said, Go, utterly destroy the sinners, the Amalekites, and fight against them until they are consumed. Why then did you not obey the voice of the Lord?"

Earlier in 1 Samuel 9:21 Saul had seemed amazed that God would choose him to be king over Israel even though he was from the smallest tribe, the tribe of Benjamin, and from the least of the families of his tribe. And he *should* have been amazed! If he wanted honor, he should have been amazed and satisfied with the honor that God had given him. This is Samuel's point here in verse 17—why are you driven by a lust for human glory when God has in fact given you a glorious privilege as the head of the tribes of Israel and the anointed king of God's people?

But Saul was not content with the glory of God and the honor of being his chosen king. He wanted his own glory and his own praise. And the submissive path of obedience does not offer that kind of praise and glory. And so he did things his own way in order to get his own glory.

Fourth, God has pleasure in obedience because disobedience is as the sin of divination. This is the very reason Samuel gives why disobedience is displeasing to God in 1 Samuel 15:22-23. "Behold, to obey is better than sacrifice, and to hearken than the fat of rams. *For rebellion is as the sin of divination.*"

Back in Deuteronomy 18:10, God had put divination in the same category with horrible things that he hates:

> There shall not be found among you any one who burns his son or his daughter as an offering, any one who practices *divination*, a soothsayer, or an augur, or a sorcerer, or a charmer, or a medium, or a wizard, or a necromancer. For whoever does these things is an abomination to the Lord.

Why are rebellion and disobedience like the sin of divination? Divination is seeking to know what to do in a way that ignores the word and counsel of God. It discounts the guidance and revelation of God, or regards them as wrong or insufficient. And that is exactly what disobedience is based on. God says one thing, and we say, "I think that I will consult another source of wisdom." In the case of divination the added source of wisdom is a medium of some sort. But most often in the case of disobedience the added source of wisdom is simply oneself! Disobedience of God's word puts my own wisdom in the place of God's and thus insults God as the only sure and reliable source of wisdom. What does it say about your doctor if he writes the prescription for three pills a day and you decide to take them once a day? It says that you put yourself above your doctor. You distrust his skill and competence and good will. It is a great insult, and he could not take pleasure it that—and you won't get well.

Fifth, God has pleasure in obedience because disobedience is idolatry. This is what Samuel says in 1 Samuel 15:23: "For rebellion is as the sin of divination, and *stubbornness is as iniquity and idolatry.*" When God says one thing and we consult the little wizard of our own wisdom and then stubbornly choose to go our own way we are, in effect, idolaters. We have not only chosen to consult ourselves as an alternative to God, and thus become guilty of divination, but we go beyond that and actually *esteem* the direction of our own mind over God's direction, and become guilty of idolatry. Worst of all, the idol is our own self.

So it stands to reason that God will be displeased with disobedience because at every point it is an attack on his glory. It puts the fear of man in the place of the fear of God. It elevates pleasure in things above pleasure in God. It seeks a name for itself instead of a name for God. It seeks out additional guidance besides God's, instead of resting in the wisdom of God. And it sets more value on the dictates of self than on the dictates of God and thus attempts to dethrone God by giving allegiance to the idol of the human will.

But obedience, being the exact opposite, in all these things enthrones and honors God. Therefore God has great pleasure in obedience. He beams like any father would when his children are courageous because they know their daddy's strong arm is behind them. He takes pleasure in us when our obedience shows that we put our treasure in him and not the enticements of sin. He delights in the meekness and humility of our submission that loves to make a name for God and not man. He rejoices over the resting of our souls in the sufficiency of his wisdom. And he exults over us with singing when we enthrone his will as more precious than all the ways of the world.

But Is This Good News?

Yes, God takes great pleasure in obedience, but can we? Is it good news to hear that God is pleased by obedience? Or is this a burden we thought we had escaped when we heard the gospel of forgiveness and justification by faith? I believe it is good news that God delights in obedience. There are at least four reasons.

First, God's pleasure in obedience is good news because it means he is praiseworthy and reliable. If God did not delight in obedience he would be a living contradiction. He would love his glory above all things and yet not take pleasure in the acts that make his glory known. He would, in effect, be two-faced and double-tongued. His beauty would vanish, and with it all our happy praise! And he would be unreliable because you can't trust a God whose values are so fickle that he exalts himself one minute and approves of insults the next. If God is praiseworthy and reliable he must exult in the tribute of obedience. And there is no greater news than the assurance that God is worthy of praise and worthy of trust.

Second, God's pleasure in obedience is good news because everything God commands is for our good. Jesus is the great physician, not the great dictator. "Those who are well have no need of a physician, but those who are sick; I have not come to call the righteous, but sinners to repentance" (Luke 5:31-32). Jesus dictates. He commands. But all his commands are like a doctor's prescription, or a physician's therapy. They are not arbitrary. They are meant to make us well and happy. If they have some painful side effects, that is not because the doctor is unkind or unwise. It is because the disease is so bad that severe medicines may be required. Every command from Jesus is meant for our good.

But not only are the commands of *Jesus* for our good; so were *all* the commandments of the law in the Old Testament for the good of Israel. They were not a cruel burden. They were the loving guidelines of an infinitely wise heavenly Father for the good of his people.

> The Lord commanded us to do all these statutes, to fear the Lord our God, *for our good always,* that he might preserve us alive, as at this day (Deuteronomy 6:24).
>
> And now, Israel, what does the Lord your God require of you, but to fear the Lord your God, to walk in all his ways, to love him, to serve the Lord your God with all your heart and with all your soul, and to keep the commandments and statutes of the Lord which I command you this day *for your good* (Deuteronomy 10:12-13).

When the Bible tells us that God takes pleasure in obedience we should rejoice, because that means the doctor cares whether we get well. If he took no pleasure in our doing the tasks assigned to make us well, he would not be a God of love. So it is good news indeed, not only that he has given us commandments for our good, but also that he rejoices to see them done.

Third, God's pleasure in obedience is good news because his commandments are not too hard for us. Moses said it very clearly in Deuteronomy 30:11, "This commandment which I command you this day *is not too hard for you.*" The Old Testament law was not the kind of arrangement where God stood over his people with a scowl and a club waiting for someone to make a tiny slip. At the very birthplace of the law on Mount Sinai, the Law-Giver identified himself like this: "The Lord, the Lord, a God merciful and gracious, slow to anger, and abounding in steadfast love and faithfulness, keeping steadfast love for thousands, forgiving iniquity and transgression and sin . . ." (Exodus 34:6-7). The law had an elaborate provision for forgiveness and restoration rooted in the heart of God. So the law as a whole could be fulfilled even by those who needed repeated forgiveness. It is not an all-or-nothing demand for perfection. Therefore it is "not too hard for you."

Jesus put it this way, "Come to me, all who labor and are heavy laden, and I will give you rest. Take my yoke upon you, and learn from me; for I am gentle and lowly in heart, and you will find rest for your souls. For *my yoke is easy, and my burden is light*" (Matthew 11:28-30). This does not mean there is no yoke and no burden. It means that there is something about Jesus that makes his demands (even when they sever us from home and wealth and life itself) "light" and "easy." The apostle John found this to be true in practice for many decades, and then wrote, "This is the love of God, that we keep his commandments. *And his commandments are not burdensome*" (1 John 5:3).

God's pleasure in obedience is not like the sadistic pleasure of a heartless coach who likes to see his recruits sweat and strain under impossible conditioning exercises. In fact he pronounces a curse on such moral taskmasters: "Woe to you teachers of the law! For you load men with burdens hard to bear, and you yourselves do not touch the burdens with one of your fingers" (Luke 11:46). God is not like that. With every command, he lifts not just his finger, but all his precious promises and all his omnipotent power and puts them at the service of his child. "No eye has seen a God besides you, who works for those who wait for him" (Isaiah 64:4). His commands are only as hard to obey as his promises are hard to believe. This leads us to the fourth reason God's pleasure in obedience is good news.

Fourth, God's pleasure in obedience is good news because the obedience he loves is the obedience of faith. This concept is so widely misunderstood today that some people cannot see how faith and obedience are necessarily connected as root and branch. So you often find in many churches and ministries the cultivation of an implicit two-stage Christianity: a faith stage and then (maybe) an obedience stage. But this is not the way the Bible pictures the life of faith. The separation of faith and obedience, as though faith were necessary for salvation and obedience were optional, is a mistake owing to a misunderstanding of what faith really is. True saving faith is not the kind of belief in the facts of the gospel that leaves the heart and life unchanged. If it were, then God's pleasure in obedience would indeed be bad news. He would be saying that we are saved by faith, and then, to please him with obedience, we must move beyond faith to something else in order to produce good behavior. This is not good news. The good news is that saving faith is by its nature a life-changing power.

Obedience Is Not "By Works"

This is evident in numerous biblical passages. For example, in Romans 9:31-32 Paul explains that the reason Israel did not attain the righteousness taught in the law of Moses (which, remember, "is not too hard for you") is because Israel did not pursue this obedience "by faith."

> Israel, pursuing a law of righteousness, did not arrive at that law. Why? Because *they did not pursue it by faith*, but as though it were by works (NASB).

They made the same mistake some are making today. They thought that obeying the law is not a matter of faith, but a matter of works. Note very carefully, "works" is not synonymous with obeying the law. That's plain because Paul says you can pursue obedience to the law either by faith or by works. But God never meant for obedience to be pursued "by works." That's clear from the little phrase, "*as though* it were by works." "As though" means obedience is not by works but by faith. So "works" is not simply efforts to obey the law of God. Works is a way of trying to bring about the fruit of obedience without making faith the root. Such "workers" did not attain the righteousness taught in the law because "they did not pursue it by faith." Let me say it again: "works" is not the effort to obey God. That effort is good, but works are bad. What makes works bad is that they are efforts to obey that are not rooted in faith.

It is a great irony that the people who cultivate a two-stage Christianity do so in the name of grace, but in effect nullify grace. They say there is a faith stage necessary for getting to heaven, and then an obedience stage not necessary for getting to heaven. This looks like grace because they say obedience is not mandatory like faith is. But in fact the whole Christian life is gradually transformed into an experience of second stage "works." Having cut the root of faith away from obedience in order to make obedience optional and exalt grace, in effect, they define the life of obedience as a life of "works" which we are to produce not by the effectual power of saving faith, but by some other kind of effort. But this effort to obey by some other power than faith is not an event of grace. For Paul makes clear that "works" and grace are opposites (Romans 11:6).

Grace Is Power, Not Just Pardon

Underlying this mistake is a misunderstanding of grace. Grace is not simply leniency when we have sinned. Grace is the enabling gift of God not to sin. Grace is power, not just pardon. This is plain, for example, in 1 Corinthians 15:10. Paul describes grace as the enabling power of his work: "By the *grace* of God I am what I am, and his *grace* toward me did not prove vain; but I labored harder than all of them, yet not I, but the *grace* of God which is with me." Grace is not simply the pardon of Paul's sins, it is the power to press on in obedience. Therefore the effort we make to obey God is not an effort done in our own strength, but "in the strength which God supplies, that in everything God may get the glory" (1 Peter 4:11). And doing something by relying on the strength which God supplies simply means doing it by faith. Therefore the obedience which gives God pleasure is by grace through faith. It is the obedience of faith.

Paul confirms this in 2 Thessalonians 1:11-12 by calling our acts of goodness "works *of faith*" and by saying that the glory this brings to Jesus is "according to the *grace* of God" because it happens "by [his] power." "To this end we always pray for you, that our God may make you worthy of his call, and may fulfill every good resolve and *work of faith by [his] power*, so that the name of our Lord Jesus may be glorified in you, and you in him, *according to the grace of our God* and the Lord Jesus Christ." The obedience that gives God pleasure is produced by the *power* of God's *grace* through *faith*. The same dynamic is at work at every stage of the Christian life. The power of God's grace that saves through faith (Ephesians 2:8) is the same power of God's grace that sanctifies through faith.

"Saved Through Sanctification"

The reason for this is that sanctification is part of salvation. It is a great mistake to think of salvation as stage one in the Christian life and sanctification (or holiness, or obedience) as stage two. Salvation is the big biblical term that describes all God's saving work for us and in us, past, present and future. We "have been saved" (Ephesians 2:8), "are being saved" (1 Corinthians 1:18) and "will be saved" (Romans 13:11; 1 Peter 1:5). Salvation is not one stage in the Christian life. It *is* the Christian life. And sanctification is one essential part of it.

So Paul says in 2 Thessalonians 2:13-14, "We are bound to give thanks to God always for you, brothers, beloved by the Lord, because God chose you from the beginning *to be saved, through sanctification* by the Spirit and *belief in the truth*" (see also 1 Thessalonians 4:7-8; 1 Peter 1:2). Notice two things. First, we are not saved apart from sanctification. "God chose you to be saved, *through sanctification.*" It is an *essential* part of salvation, not an optional stage after salvation. Second, this process of salvation through sanctification happens "through belief in the truth."[3] That is, sanctification is by faith. Or to put it most plainly, the obedience which pleases God is the obedience of faith, and the obedience of faith is an essential part of salvation. We are chosen to be saved *through sanctification*, which is the same as the obedience of faith.

How Does Faith Produce Obedience?

But how does faith produce obedience? When you trust Christ to take care of your future ("faith is the assurance of things hoped for"), the inevitable result is that sinful strategies to ·gain happiness sink in the peaceful confidence that God will make a greater joy for you in his own way. Therefore moral conformity to the image of Christ (Romans 8:29) is the fruit of faith.

Martin Luther saw this so clearly! In the two years between October 1518 and October 1520 the indomitable reformer had a respite from the Roman siege. He worked feverishly, not knowing how long his safety would last. One of the works that came from this period was the walloping little pamphlet called *The Freedom of a Christian.* Even in translation, and four centuries later, it vibrates with the passion of this ignited man.

It captures (or I should say releases!) the connection between faith and holiness—between confidence in the promises of Christ and conformity to the person of Christ. Luther wrote,

> It is a further function of faith that it honors him whom it trusts with the most reverent and highest regard, since it considers him truthful and trustworthy. . . . So when the soul firmly trusts God's promises, it regards him as truthful and righteous. . . . When this is done, the soul consents to his will. Then it hallows his name and allows itself to be treated according to God's good pleasure for, clinging to God's promises, it does not doubt that he who is true, just, and wise will do, dispose, and provide all things well.
>
> Is not such a soul most obedient to God in all things by this faith? What commandment is there that obedience has not completely fulfilled? . . . This obedience, however, is not rendered by works, but by faith alone.[4]

We should never think of obedience as something unattached to saving faith as though the one could exist for long without the other. Obedience to Christ is the necessary result of true faith.[5]

But to make crystal clear why it is that faith begets obedience, or practical likeness to Christ, we should draw out the essential meaning of saving faith even more clearly than we have so far. We will see in a moment from Hebrews that the *future* dimension of saving faith is essential if faith is to have its sanctifying effect. Trusting in God to meet our needs breaks the power of sin's promise to make us happier. But what we need to see here is that *the essence of faith is being satisfied with all that God is for us in Christ.*

This statement emphasizes two things. One is the God-centeredness of faith. It is not merely the *promises* of God that satisfy us. It is all that *God himself* is for us. Faith embraces God—not just his promised gifts—as our treasure. Faith banks its hope not just on the real estate of the age to come, but on the fact that *God* will be there (Revelation 21:3). And even *now* what faith embraces most earnestly is not just the reality of sins forgiven (as precious as that is) but the presence of the living Christ in our hearts and the fullness of God himself (Ephesians 3:17-19).

The other thing emphasized in defining faith as *being satisfied with all that God is for us* is the term *satisfaction*. Faith is not just believing facts about God. It is not just intellectual assent. Faith is the quenching of the soul's thirst at the fountain of God. The biblical evidence for this can be seen most easily in John 6:35. "Jesus said to them, 'I am the bread of life; he who *comes* to me shall not hunger, and he who *believes* in me shall never thirst.'" "Believing" means "coming" to Jesus to eat and drink the "bread of life" and the "living water" (John 4:10,14) which are nothing other than Jesus himself.[6] And when we eat this food and drink this water we are satisfied with Jesus. That is the meaning of faith. We rest in him. Here is the secret of the power of faith to break the enslaving force of sinful attractions. If the heart is satisfied with all that God is for us in Jesus, the power of sin to lure us away from the wisdom of Christ is broken. And we will love holiness because it is an expression of the personality of the One who brings us so much satisfaction.[7]

The Source of Moses' Obedience

The writer to the Hebrews works this out for us in some practical illustrations. For example, he shows that Moses' obedience and love was produced by this kind of faith.

> By faith Moses, when he was grown up, refused to be called the son of Pharaoh's daughter, choosing rather to share ill-treatment with the people of God than to enjoy the fleeting pleasures of sin. He considered abuse suffered for the Christ greater wealth than the treasures of Egypt, for he looked to the reward (Hebrews 11:24-26).

Here we see the key to the triumph of obedience over disobedience. The key is confidence that what Christ offers is better than the "fleeting pleasures of sin." Moses looked to the reward of God's promises, he weighed that against the rewards of unrighteousness, and he rested satisfied in God. With that, the power of sin was broken and he was freed to love a rebellious people for forty years. The writer of Hebrews calls this liberating contentment "faith." "*By faith* Moses . . . chose to share ill-treatment with the people of God."

The definition of faith behind this usage is given in Hebrews 11:1: "Faith is the assurance of things hoped for." In other words, faith is the satisfied assurance that God will work things out in the future far better than I could work them out by relying on myself or by departing from the path of obedience—even if obedience means suffering now. Being satisfied with all that God is for me in Christ—past, present and future—is the power to resist the alluring temptations of disobedience.

The Power to Be Plundered in Love and Joy

The writer to the Hebrews gives another, even more graphic illustration of the way faith produces obedience. He tells the story of how in the early days of their faith the Christians showed great love to the imprisoned saints by visiting them at great cost to themselves. What was the powerful source of this obedience to the command to "remember those who are in prison" (Hebrews 13:3)?

> Recall the former days when, after you were enlightened, you endured a hard struggle with sufferings sometimes being publicly exposed to abuse and affliction, and sometimes being partners with those so treated. For you had compassion on the prisoners, and *you joyfully accepted the plundering of your property, since you knew that you yourselves had a better possession and an abiding one.* Therefore do not throw away your confidence which has great reward (Hebrews 10:32-36).

In these Christians' lives the power to love was the confidence that God would take care of their future. So their obedience was the obedience of faith. The cost of obedience—which was immense—was not so great as the offsetting promise of God. The assurance of things hoped for was the source of the obedience of love. This is what Paul meant in Galatians 5:6 when he said, "In Christ Jesus neither circumcision nor uncircumcision is of any avail, but *faith working through love.*" Faith works through love because faith is satisfied with all that God is for us in Christ, and so faith breaks the alluring power of selfish temptations.

This stress on satisfaction shows the secret of the psychological dynamics of why faith produces obedience. When we are satisfied with our counselor we will do what he counsels. But more than that. True faith delights in all that Jesus is—his character, his personality, his nature. This means that his counsel itself will be beautiful to us. We will love holiness because it is an expression of the personality of the One whose personality we cherish.

There are many questions raised these days about how faith and works are related. Sometimes the debate is described in terms of whether you can have Jesus as your Savior if you do not have him as your Lord. This is another way of describing the cultivation of the two-stage Christianity—a Savior stage (faith) and a Lordship stage (obedience). I find this development in evangelicalism very troubling. Instead of carrying this chapter any further from its main aim to show obedience as the pleasure of God, I have decided to devote an Appendix at the end of this book to the issues clustering around the Lordship of Christ. I encourage you to consult the Appendix, "Letter to a Friend," to see what the issues are, and to see a long list of Scriptures to show that the obedience which pleases God is not an optional second stage, but an essential part of our salvation as evidence of true and saving faith.

We Are his Pleasure When He Is Our Treasure

The point I have been laboring to clarify here is that God's pleasure in obedience is good news because that obedience that pleases him is the obedience *of faith*. Another way to put it would be to say that God is happy with our obedience when our obedience is the overflow of our happiness with God. God is delighted with our obedience when it is the fruit of our delight in him. Our obedience is God's pleasure when it proves that God is our treasure. This is good news, because it means very simply that the command to obey is the command to be happy in God. The commandments of God are only as hard to obey as the promises of God are hard to believe. The Word of God is only as hard to obey as the beauty of God is hard to cherish.

The Pleasure of God in Public Justice

Before leaving this chapter I want to make explicit that God's pleasure in obedience extends into the public sphere of life. I want to relate God's pleasure to the issues of public justice. In the last three chapters we have been moving from the inside to the outside of life. God rejoices over those who *hope* in his love. God takes pleasure in the *prayers* of the upright. God delights in *obedience* more than in sacrifice. You can see the movement here from inner to outer experience. *Hope* is deepest within. Then it expresses itself more or less openly in *prayer*. And this prayerful reliance on God gives rise to *obedience*.

But so far we have not stressed the public, or secular dimension of this obedience. You might call this the business part of your life. It includes things like filling up your gas tank and buying antiques and punching a time card and paying your taxes. Does God take delight in the way you do things at the store or the office or the shop or the kitchen? Is any wrong behavior in these non-religious areas so significant that God would even call them an abomination?

With this concern we have moved out just about as far as we can go: from hope to prayer to general obedience to specific forms of obedience in the non-religious, business part of life. But there is one more step we could take, and I want to take it in the last part of this chapter. We could ask, Does God have any delight in the behavior of non-Christian people in the non-religious areas of life?

So we really have two areas to examine briefly before leaving this chapter: the non-religious, business life of Christians, and the non-religious, business life of non-Christians. What sort of action does God delight in here? And why does he?

"A Just Weight Is His Delight"

Proverbs 11:1 is a decisive pointer in answering these questions. The verse doesn't say whether believers or unbelievers are in view. It simply says, "A false balance is an abomination to the LORD, but a just weight is his delight."

The implications here are far-reaching. Suppose you were a merchant in Old Testament times and you sold corn meal. And suppose that in those days ten cents a pound was a fair price. Someone comes to you and asks to buy five pounds of corn meal. So you reach for your five-pound stone and place it in the dish on one side of the scales. Then you take your bag of meal and start pouring it into the dish on the other side of the scale. You pour until the two dishes swing at the same level. Then you pour the dish full of meal into your customer's container, and he knows that he has been given the right amount of grain. The size of a five-pound stone is common knowledge.

But then suppose that during the night you took a sharp, hard blade and dug a small hole in the side of the stone and worked it around hollowing out the inside until it weighed only four pounds. Then you covered the little hole over with clay the same color as the stone and let it dry. The next day you don't use it on the educated and strong, because they might make a fuss over the smaller pile of meal, and might even examine the stone. But when the child comes on behalf of his mother, or when the widow comes who is partially blind, you use your hollow stone. Our text says that this is utterly reprehensible to God: "A false balance is an abomination to the Lord."

Today's False Balances

Now, what sorts of acts in our day are implied in the phrase, "false balance"? I'll mention four categories, which are really two different ways of dividing the acts into two categories.

First, this verse refers to sellers and it refers to buyers:

1. It includes acts of *selling* when the seller does not give goods or services worth the price or the fee that he is charging. You can imagine a gasoline pump that reads a penny more per gallon than it should, or a scale at the grocery store that reads high, or a medicine label that claims too much, or a realtor who doesn't tell a buyer about a flooding problem in the house he is selling, or a college teacher who hasn't written a new lecture in ten years and spends his time remodeling his basement.

2. It includes acts of *buying* when the buyer schemes to pay less than the goods or services are really worth. You can see what God thinks of such an act in Proverbs 20:14, " 'It is bad, it is bad,' says the buyer; but when he goes away, then he boasts." This would include paying some poor vendor in Tijuana a ridiculously small sum for a quality rug he had made because he is desperate for a sale and you can take it or leave it. It would include not paying the late penalty on my water bill by dating my check before the deadline.

The other way to categorize the acts denounced in Proverbs 11:1 is to notice that **it refers to acts of deceit and it refers to acts of injustice.**

3. It includes acts that involve *deceit* in transactions with other people. And so the act expresses a lie. For example, as you do your income tax returns this verse has something definite to say about whether your reporting is a delight to God or an abomination to him. Or you might file an insurance claim and lie about the extent of the damages in order to get a better settlement.

4. The other side of this category is that such acts of deceit always do an *injustice* to another person. A person does not get what is his due. For example, you might stick a person with a lemon of a car by not being truthful about its condition when you sell it. Or you might rush a refugee family into signing a lease for an unseen apartment and charge them exorbitant rent and leave the apartment in poor condition with no improvements.

I hope you can see that all such things are implied in Proverbs 11:1, "A false balance is an abomination to the LORD, but a just weight is his delight." You can be a deceitful seller or a deceitful buyer. And you can do an injustice to a buyer and you can do an injustice to a seller.

The Secular Interests of God

One lesson to be learned already from this is that God has an interest in all our non-religious life. All our business transactions are his concern. God is not so distant or even so "religious" that he only cares about what happens at church and during devotions. Every square inch of this earth is his and every minute of our lives is a loan from his breath. He is much more secular than we often think.

At the second Lausanne Congress on World Evangelization in Manila in 1989, Os Guiness gave a powerful message on the challenges of modernity. He spoke of the modern secular spirit and its infiltration into the church. He warned that we could take on so many features of the world that we could "win the world and lose our own soul." He exposed the shallow religiosity of many American church-goers by comparing it to the sentiment of one high-ranking executive of the McDonald's Corporation. He is supposed to have said, "I believe in God, family, and McDonald's. And when I get to the office I reverse the order." Guiness said this is not submission to the Lordship of Christ. He quoted Abraham Kuyper: "There is not an inch of any sphere of life over which Jesus Christ does not say, 'Mine.'" God is passionately concerned with the way we do our business.

Charles Bridges, an evangelical pastor in the Church of England a century ago, asks this searching question: "Is it not a solemn thought, that the eye of God marks all our common dealings of life, either as an *abomination or a delight*?"[8] We should test ourselves. Are we being shaped more by the secular spirit of the world or by the Spirit of God? The test is this: do we feel that minor business misrepresentations are only part of the game rules of the day or are they an abomination to God? Is God's will the first and foremost concern in all our political and business dealings, or only in some personal and domestic areas? God's pleasure in obedience extends passionately to the public sphere of life.

Why is the justice of believers in the public sphere a pleasure to God? The answer should be clear from what we have said earlier in this chapter about obedience being the outworking of faith. The obedience of public justice glorifies God when it grows out of a heart that is trusting in his promises and is satisfied in his protection and care. It is especially pleasing to God because he is passionately concerned with his fame, as we saw in chapter 4. He wants the glory that comes to him when his people are publicly righteous and loving. "Let your light so shine before men that they might see your good deeds and give glory to your Father in heaven" (Matthew 5:16). Just and honest dealings make the saving, satisfying lordship of God visible.

Proverbs 20:17 says, "Bread gained by deceit is sweet to a man, but afterward his mouth will be full of gravel." In other words, when we use false balances or lie on our tax returns or misrepresent the facts in our dealings, we are declaring that the fleeting sweetness of sin is more to be desired than the everlasting peace of God. This is no honor to God and therefore no pleasure to his heart. "A false balance is an abomination to the LORD, but a just weight is his delight."

The Honest Work of Unbelievers

But what about unbelievers? Does God delight in their just dealings, even though this does not come from faith? There are unbelievers who order their business lives in honest and just ways. Is this a delight to God?

The answer is no and yes, because God looks at the honesty of unbelievers in two different ways. When God looks at their honesty and justice as an outworking of their inner life of unbelief he does not delight in it because it is sinful. Romans 14:23 says, "Whatever is not from faith is sin."

Honest unbelievers are like a rebellious teenage son who rejects his parents and everything they stand for, and goes to another city. But to make it in the real world, he decides to play by some of their rules. So he gets a job as a cook at a restaurant. Months later his parents happen to visit that city and go to that restaurant. Without knowing he is there, they order one of their favorite delights (call it "just balances" or "honest scales"). And without knowing it, their own son makes the meal they enjoy. But back there in the kitchen he is as rebellious as ever. He is not doing it for their sake at all. And so even this act of fixing what they have ordered is an expression of rebellion. And if his parents could be told the truth, they would not rejoice and say, "Oh, how wonderful, our son is now a delight to us, because he made our favorite meal!"

So God does not delight in the honesty and the justice of unbelievers when he sees it as an expression of their rebellious and unbelieving hearts. Acts done without any trust in God's grace or any love for his glory are not a delight to God.

Vestiges of God's Upright Image

But there is a sense in which God does delight in the just balances and honest weights of unbelievers, namely, when he looks at their honesty and justice as fragments of his own divine work expressing a vestige of his own upright image.

This seems to be implied in Proverbs 16:11. "A just balance and scales are the LORD's; all the weights in the bag are his work." I think this means that wherever you find just scales and a bag of honest weights you find the work of God. Justice is God's creation. Honesty is God's design. Integrity is the work of God— even in unbelievers—just like their head and heart and hands and feet are his work.

Theologians call this common grace. It isn't saving grace. It doesn't get a person to heaven. It is the same grace that makes the sun come up every day on the good and the evil and sends rain on the just and the unjust (Matthew 5:43-47; see also Matthew 22:10). It is the grace that keeps a society from sinking into anarchy. And when God sees the work of his own common grace holding the world back from premature ruin, and giving at least some outward expression to his purposes of justice and honesty, he delights in what he sees.

The honesty and justice of unbelievers is like a seashell washed up on the beach. There's no life in it. But it does have a kind of beauty. There is some sturdiness to it and symmetry and order. Life is more enjoyable because this shell exists. It has its uses: you could plant a flower in it; or you could use it to stud your rock wall, or you could teach things from it at school—like the fact that this shell took its form from life.

So it is with the integrity of unbelievers. It is the leftover shell of holiness, the vestige of the image of God, the residue of something glorious and beautiful in the heart of God. It is the very work of his grace preserving and keeping this fallen humanity back from the precipice of anarchy and chaos. When God looks on the honesty and justice of his unbelieving and rebellious creatures *in this way*, he delights in their justice and takes pleasure in their honesty. It is the work of his own hands, and the gift of his grace.

God's Pleasure in Persevering Political Engagement

Since the partial external conformity of unbelievers to God's designs of justice and honesty does in one way delight the heart of God, it was right for William Wilberforce to devote twenty years of his life in Parliament to the abolition of English slave trading, even though the great majority of those merchants who gave up the trade did it under constraint and not for any holy reasons at all. It was the work of God's grace that rid England of the barbarisms of the African slave trade. And therefore the Lord looked down *with delight* on February 22, 1807, when the House of Commons passed the decisive bill. The same will be true when persevering pro-life forces bring an end to wanton, legalized child-killing in America.

Yes, God delighted most in the living *power of holiness* in the life of Wilberforce and Henry Thornton as they embraced one another and frolicked in the snow like schoolboys outside the chamber. And, in a different and mysterious way, God also delighted in the *shell of holiness* that took shape in English society when it was purged of the slave trade once and for all. For he delights in the work of his hands.

John Wesley, the great evangelist, wrote to Wilberforce to strengthen his hand in God. He said,

> Unless God has raised you up for this very thing, you will be worn out by the opposition of men and devils, but if God be for you who can be against you? Are all of them together stronger than God? Oh, be not weary in well-doing. . . .[9]

My prayer is that the truth of God's pleasure in public justice will inspire many in our day to take up the mantle of William Wilberforce and wear it into the battle against the manifold injustices of our day. Few of these injustices will give way before brief spurts of outrage. It will take a deep commitment, like Wilberforce's. May the vision of God's passion for the obedience of faith and for public justice in an unbelieving society sustain our passion until "justice rolls down like waters, and righteousness like an ever-flowing stream" (Amos 5:24).

Where All the Pleasures of God Are Leading

All the pleasures of God are leading irrevocably to the establishment of a kingdom where disobedience and unbelief will be no more. God will reign in righteousness and justice and peace, and all of life will be the obedience of faith and joy.

• God's pleasure in his Son is leading to the kingdom of

obedience because God wills to conform all its inhabitants to the image of Christ (Romans 8:29).

- God's pleasure in his sovereign freedom is leading to the kingdom of obedience because he will omnipotently cause us to walk in his statutes and observe all his ordinances (Ezekiel 36:27).

- God's pleasure in creation is leading to the kingdom of obedience because creation waits with eager longing for the revealing of the children of God; creation itself will mirror the majesty of God perfectly when the world is filled with righteousness and faith (Romans 8:19-22).

- God's pleasure in his fame is leading to the kingdom of obedience because he has an awesome passion to remove the reproach of his name that comes from our transgression (Isaiah 48:9-11; Ezekiel 36:22-23).

- God's pleasure in election is leading to the kingdom of obedience because he chose us in Christ before the foundation of the world "that we should be holy and blameless before him" (Ephesians 1:4).

- God's pleasure in bruising the Son is leading to the kingdom of obedience because Christ died for the church "that he might sanctify her . . . and present the church to himself in glory without spot or wrinkle, or any such thing" (Ephesians 5:25-27; Titus 2:14; Hebrews 10:10).

- God's pleasure in those who hope in his love is leading to the kingdom of obedience, because the internal light of hope shines brightest in the external rays of righteousness and love (Colossians 1:4-5; Hebrews 10:34-36).

- And God's pleasure in the prayers of the upright is leading to the kingdom of obedience because the sum of every prayer is "Hallowed be your name; your kingdom come, your will be done on earth as it is in heaven" (Matthew 6:9-10).

Notes

1. Just a brief word in passing about this divine "repentance." Samuel says in 1 Samuel 15:29 that "the Glory of Israel will not lie or repent; for he is not a man, that he should repent." I take this to mean that the repenting which God does (for example, in v. 11) is not like the repenting man does. In fact, it is so different that in one sense it is not a repenting at all, as verse 29 says. It is

not based on ignorance or deceit. The repenting of God is the turning of his heart in a new direction but not one that was unforeseen. God does not repent because he is caught off guard by some turn of events. That would indeed be like man. But the Glory of Israel is not a man that he should repent. When the Bible says that God repents, it means that he expresses a different attitude about something than he expressed before, not because any turn of events was unexpected, but because the turn of events makes it fitting to express a different attitude now because of a change of circumstances.

2. "He has said, 'I will never leave you nor forsake you.' Hence we can confidently say, 'The Lord is my helper, I will not be afraid; what can man do to me?' " (Hebrews 13:5-6).

3. The Lord Jesus said this same thing to Paul on the Damascus Road, "I send you to open the eyes [of the Gentiles], that they may turn from darkness to light and from the power of Satan to God, that they may receive forgiveness of sins and a place among those who are *sanctified by faith in me.*"

4. Martin Luther, *The Freedom of a Christian,* in: *Three Treatises* (Philadelphia: Fortress Press, 1960), 284-285.

5. This is denied by many people today in the name of a two-stage Christianity that cultivates a distinction between the first necessary stage of faith and the second optional stage of obedience (or discipleship). The debate is sometimes described in terms of whether one must have Jesus as Lord in order to also have him as Savior. I have addressed this issue partly in chapter 9 and more extensively in the Appendix, "Letter to Friend."

6. Jesus pushes this image all the way in John 6:53, "So Jesus said to them, 'Truly, truly, I say to you, unless you eat the flesh of the Son of man and drink this blood, you have no life in you.' " I take the meaning of these images to be this: Jesus wants to be the satisfaction of our deepest hunger and thirst. So coming to him for this satisfaction is like eating and drinking the life-giving food that is offered to us freely through his broken body and shed blood. Additional evidence that we are on the right track in equating *coming to Jesus for satisfaction* with *faith* is found in John 7:37-38, "Jesus stood up and proclaimed, 'If any one *thirst,* let him *come* to me and drink. He who *believes* in me, as the Scripture has said, "Out of his heart shall flow rivers of living water."' " See also John 6:64-65 for the equating of *coming* to Jesus and *believing* on Jesus.

7. Henry Scougal represents a great Christian tradition in seeing faith in terms of the satisfaction of the soul in spiritual beauties. He says, "The root of the divine life [in the human soul] is faith. . . . Faith hath the same place in the divine life, which sense hath in the natural, being indeed nothing else but *a kind of sense, or feeling persuasion of spiritual things*" (italics added). *The Life of God,* Scougal, 46.
Jonathan Edwards is part of the tradition too. And he shows that the tradition has its roots firmly in scripture in his essay, "Concerning Faith," *Works,* 2 (Edinburgh: Banner of Truth Trust, 1974), 578-595. He says that faith "is a belief of the truth, from a spiritual taste and relish of what is excellent and divine" (p. 578). He notes that "love is what faith arises from, or is included in faith," because of John 3:18-19, "He who does not *believe* is condemned already . . . and this is the condemnation, that men *loved*

darkness rather than light." He sees the same implication in John 5:1-4 where faith and love are shown to be the victory that overcomes the difficulty of obedience. He comments, "Our love enables us to overcome the difficulties that attend keeping God's commands: which shows that love is the main thing in saving faith, the life and power of it, by which it produces great effects" (p. 586).

Edwards admits that short definitions of faith are all inadequate to express the whole reality: "The difficulty in giving a definition of faith is, that we have no word that clearly and adequately expresses the whole act of acceptance, or closing of the soul or heart with Christ. Inclination expresses it but partially; conviction expresses it also but in part; the sense of the soul does not do it fully. And if we use metaphorical expressions, such as embrace, love, etc. they are obscure, and will not carry the same idea with them to the minds of all" (p. 582).

8. Charles Bridges, *Proverbs* (Edinburgh: Banner of Truth Trust, 1968), 112.

9. Quoted in Charles Colson, "Standing Tough against All Odds," *Christianity Today*, 6 September 1985, 29.

"Fear not, little flock,
for it is your Father's pleasure
to give you the kingdom."

Luke 12:32

Almost Too Good to Be True

A Final Word of Hope

"But for Jesus I'd Have Gone Mad"

John G. Paton was born on May 24, 1824, in Dumfries County, Scotland. His father was a godly weaver who kept his stocking frames in a back room of the house and his Bible on the front table. Paton's biographer says that the Scottish traditions of church-going and Bible stories and Shorter Catechism were "not tasks but pleasures" in the Paton home.

John had to quit school when he was twelve to help his father support the family of eleven children. When he was seventeen he had a deep experience of conversion that brought all the teaching and love of his parents home to his own heart. Soon the call to Christian service became irresistible and Paton worked for ten years as a city missionary in Glasgow among the poor children of the slums.

At thirty-two he accepted the call to missionary service in the New Hebrides in the South Pacific. In March of 1858 he married Mary Ann Robson, and on April 16 they sailed together for the cannibal island of Tanna. In less than a year they had built a little home and Mary had given birth to a son. But on March 3, 1859, one year after their marriage, Mary died of the fever, and in three weeks the infant son died. John Paton buried them alone, and wrote, "But for Jesus . . . I'd have gone mad and died beside that lonely grave."

One of the gifts that Jesus had given him to sustain him in those days were the words his wife spoke shortly before her death. She did not murmur against God in her final sickness, or resent her husband bringing her to the New Hebrides. Rather she spoke these incredible words: "I do not regret leaving home and friends. If I had it to do over, I would do it with more pleasure, yes, with all my heart."[1]

Here Is a Great Soul

These final words of Mary Ann Paton take us back to the source and inspiration of this book—to the words of Henry Scougal: "The worth and excellency of a soul is to be measured by the object of its love." When we hear Mary Paton tell us that she would do it all again "with more pleasure, yes, with all my heart," we sense intuitively that here is a great soul. Her soul was great because its pleasure came from a great purpose. In her last letter to friends at home, dated December 28, 1858, she grieved over the lostness of the people around her in Port Resolution, then said, "Still we trust that the cloud which has so long enveloped Tanna will soon be rolled away, and the light of the Sun of Righteousness irradiate this dark land."[2] Her soul was big with the dream that the glory of Christ would be revealed, and the kingdom of God would come to the New Hebrides with light and life and everlasting joy.

We feel it intuitively—that her soul was worthy and excellent and admirable. But when God reveals to us that he is moved by the same dream and the same passion—to give us the kingdom with light and life and everlasting joy—we hesitate. Something hinders the release of wonder. Something confines our affections. Something makes us fear that this is just too good to be true. Oh, how complex are the obstructions of belief! The way our parents treated us, the cultic curiosities of a grandmother, the deadening force of poverty or wealth, the anesthesia of televised worldliness, the boredom of trivial business, the wilderness of lonely wedlock, the heartbreak of wayward kids, the never-ending ache of arthritic joints, the memories of lovelessness and fragile hope—how many ways the enemy of our souls can make us fear that the God and Father of Jesus Christ is too good to be true.

Jesus Battles Our Unbelief

But Jesus will not sit by and let us disbelieve without a fight. He takes up the weapon of the Word and speaks it with power for all who struggle to believe: "Fear not, little flock, for it is your Father's pleasure to give you the kingdom" (Luke 12:32). His aim is to defeat the fear that God is not the kind of God who really wants to be good to us—that he is not really generous and helpful and kind and tender, but is basically irked with us—ill-disposed and angry.

Sometimes, even if we believe in our heads that God is good to us, we may feel in our hearts that his goodness is somehow forced or constrained, perhaps like a judge who has been maneuvered by a clever attorney into a corner on some technicality of court proceeding, so he has to dismiss the charges against the prisoner whom he really would rather send to jail. But Jesus is at pains to help us not feel that way about God. He is striving in this verse to describe for us the indescribable worth and excellency of God's soul by showing the unbridled pleasure he takes in giving us the kingdom. "Fear not, little flock, for it is your Father's *pleasure* to give you the kingdom."

Every little word of this stunning sentence is intended to help take away the fear that Jesus knows we struggle with, namely, that God begrudges his benefits; that he is constrained and out of character when he does nice things; that at bottom he is angry and loves to vent his anger. This is a sentence about the nature of God. It's about the kind of heart God has. It's a verse about what makes God glad—not merely about what God *will* do or what he *has* to do, but what he *delights* to do, what he *loves* to do and takes *pleasure* in doing. Every word counts.

> Fear not, little flock,
> for it is your Father's pleasure
> to give you the kingdom.

What God Really Wants To Do

Take the word "pleasure." In Greek it is a verb: "to be a pleasure," or, "to be pleased by." You could translate it: "it pleased God," or, "God chose it gladly," or, "it was a pleasure to him."

The noun form of this verb is used in Philippians 1:15 like this: "Some indeed preach Christ from envy and rivalry, but others from *good will*"—or we could say, "from *pleasure*." Paul describes two motives driving the preachers in Rome where he is in prison. One group of preachers is being driven to preach not because they love Paul or because they love the preaching of the gospel, but because they hope to increase Paul's affliction (Philippians 1:17). But the other group is preaching because they really love to preach the gospel and because they love Paul. They are doing what they really love to do. It is out of "gladness" that they preach. It is their pleasure. Their heart is not divided. Preaching is not a cloak for envy or rivalry. It is what they really love to do. That's the meaning of the word.

And that is what Jesus means when he says, "It is God's *pleasure* to give you the kingdom." In other words, God is not acting in this generous way in order to cloak and hide some malicious motive. The word "pleasure" utterly rules that out. He is not saying inside, "I will have to be generous for a while even though I don't want to be, because what I really want to do is bring judgment on sinners."

The Lord's meaning is inescapable: God is acting here in freedom. He is not under constraint to do what he doesn't really want to do. At this very point, when he gives his flock the kingdom, he is acting out his deepest delight. This is what the word means: God's joy, his desire, his want and wish and hope and pleasure and gladness and delight is to give the Kingdom to his flock. "Fear not, little flock, it is your Father's pleasure—not his duty, not his necessity, not his obligation, but his *pleasure*—to give you the kingdom." That is the kind of God he is. That is the measure of the greatness of his heart.

What Is the True Father Like?

Second, let's look at the phrase "your Father." "Fear not, little flock, it is *your Father's* pleasure to give you the kingdom." Jesus does not say, "It is your employer's pleasure to give you your salary." He does not say, "It is your slave master's pleasure to give you your lodging." He does not even say—which we would have expected him to say—"It is your King's pleasure to give you the kingdom." He chooses every word in this sentence to help us get rid of the fear that God is ill-disposed to us—that he is begrudging in his generosity, or constrained in his kindness. So he calls God "your Father."

Now, not all of us have had fathers who patterned their lives after God. And so for you the word "father" may not be full of peace the way Jesus means it to be. If that is your experience, then you may have to relearn from God's own revelation of himself what a father is supposed to be like.

One of the most insightful and mature men of our church grew up in a home where his father was almost constantly abusive. I recall one evening in a small prayer group listening to this man pray. Tears came to my eyes as I heard him quote a passage from Hebrews that I had never heard anyone else recite from memory. The passage included these words: "We have had earthly fathers to discipline us and we respected them. Shall we not much more be subject to the Father of spirits and live: for they disciplined us for a short time at their pleasure, but he disciplines us for our good, that we may share his holiness" (Hebrews 12:9-10). I could tell from his prayer and the deep emotion of his voice that this text had been a key of hope in his own life. His own father had "disciplined" him in cavalier and cutting ways that left deep wounds. But over the years, since his conversion, God had begun to teach him what a true Father is like.

In fact the discoveries of grace were so profound in his college days that he had virtually memorized the book of Romans. It is not hard to see why, when you come to the climax of that greatest of books and read, "You did not receive the spirit of slavery to fall back into fear, but you have received the Spirit of *sonship.* When we cry, '*Abba, Father,*' it is the Spirit himself bearing witness with our spirit that we are *children of God,* and if children, then heirs, heirs of God and fellow heirs with Christ . . . Creation waits with eager longing for the revealing of the *sons of God.* . . . If God is for us, who can be against us?" (Romans 8:15-17,19,31). This man and many others have discovered that it is possible to learn again what it really means to have a Father in heaven who loves to give the kingdom to his children.

Jesus Rebuilds the Meaning of Fatherhood

Jesus said, "He who has seen me, has seen the Father" (John 14:9). The incarnation of the Son of God was God's way of rebuilding the meaning of Fatherhood for millions who could not know it any other way. Perhaps the apostle John cherished more than others learning what it meant to have a Father and to be a father. His gospel is radiant with the wonderful relationship between Jesus and his Father in heaven. And again and again in John's letters he calls his church, "my children." It was he who opened the fatherly heart of Jesus most fully on the night of his betrayal. "Having loved his own who were in the world, he loved them to the end" (John 13:1). When Jesus says that it is our *Father's* pleasure to give us the kingdom, he means that his whole heart is in it. It is not merely a matter of justice or obligation or duty. It is the desire of his heart. He is our Father, and if we who are evil know how to give good things to our children, how *much more* will our Father in heaven give the kingdom to those who ask him (cf. Matthew 7:11).

He Loves to Give, Not Sell

Third, consider the word "give." "It is your Father's pleasure to *give* you the kingdom." Jesus does not say, *sell* you the kingdom, or *trade* you the kingdom. He says it is the Father's pleasure to *give* you the kingdom.

We have seen it again and again in these chapters—and Oh, how I pray it sinks in—that God is a mountain spring and not a watering trough. He delights to overflow—to give and give and give! And therefore the gospel is the good news that God does not need a bucket brigade; he wants people who will *drink!* The qualification for receiving his kingdom is not strength but thirst. It is our Father's pleasure to give us the kingdom, freely. It cannot be bought or bartered or earned in any way. There is only one way to have it, and it is the easiest way of all—the gospel way: "Truly, I say to you, whoever does not *receive* the kingdom of God like a child shall not enter it." God is not stingy. He is not a Scrooge. He is not miserly or tight-fisted or parsimonious. He is liberal and generous and ungrudging and bountiful. It is his pleasure to *give* us the kingdom (see Luke 8:10).

The Pleasure of Our Shepherd-God

Fourth, consider the word "flock." "Fear not, little *flock*, for it is your Father's pleasure to give you the kingdom." Look how Jesus is piling up the metaphors. God is our *Father*. And, since he gives us a kingdom, he must be our *King*. And since we are his flock, he must be our *Shepherd*. Jesus is at pains to choose every word he can to make his point clear: God is not the kind of God who begrudges his blessings.

What does it mean to be the flock of God? It means Psalm 23! It means the promise of green pastures and still waters. It means guidance in the light of life and comfort in the shadow of death. It means triumph over enemies and overflowing cups of gladness and omnipotent goodness and mercy pursuing us every day of our lives forever and ever.

And now we have met our Shepherd-God face to face in Jesus. And we have learned that the good Shepherd lays down his life— he purchases the kingdom—for the sheep. Does he do this begrudgingly? Does he do it under some kind of oppressive constraint? Emphatically No! "No one takes my life from me, but I lay it down of my own accord. I have power to lay it down and I have power to take it again" (John 10:18). The Father did not begrudge the gift of his Son and the Son did not begrudge the gift of his life. It was the Father's pleasure to bruise him (Isaiah 53:10). Therefore "He who did not spare his own Son, but gave him up for us all, how will he not also give us all things with him?" (Romans 8:32). It is the Shepherd's pleasure to give the kingdom—all things—to his flock.

Happy to Be Little

Fifth, consider the word "little." "Fear not, *little* flock, for it is your Father's pleasure to give you the kingdom." Jesus is at pains to choose every word that will help us see God the way he really is. Why does he say "*little* flock"? I think Jesus means it to have two effects. First, it's a term of affection and care. If I say to my family when they are in danger, "Don't be afraid, *little* family," what I mean is this: "I know you are in danger and that you are small and weak, but I will use all my power to take care of you because you are precious to me." So "little flock" has the effect of helping us feel the affection and care of Jesus and his Father.

It also implies that God's goodness to us is not dependent on our greatness. We are a *little* flock—little in size, little in strength, little in wisdom, little in righteousness, little in love. If God's goodness to us depended on our greatness, we would be in big trouble. But that's the point. It doesn't. So we aren't. "Fear not *little* flock, it is the Father's pleasure to give us the kingdom."

Just the Kingdom, That's All

Finally, consider the word "kingdom." "Fear not, little flock, it is your Father's pleasure to give you the kingdom." The unrestrained gladness of God in giving to his children is proved by the greatness of his gift. He does not promise to give us wealth in this world. In fact, he says, "It is easier for a camel to go through the eye of a needle than for a rich man to enter the kingdom of God" (Luke 18:25). He does not promise popularity or fame or admiration among men. In fact, he says, "Blessed are you when men hate you, and when they exclude you and revile you, and cast out your name as evil, on account of the Son of man!" (Luke 6:22). He does not even promise security in this life. In fact, he says, "You will be delivered up even by parents and brothers and kinsmen and friends, and some of you they will put to death; you will be hated by all for my name's sake" (Luke 21:16).

All he promises to give us is the kingdom of God.

The magnitude of this gift is felt when we realize that the unspeakable privileges of it are secondary to the main reward. In the kingdom we will inherit the earth and the world, but this is secondary (Matthew 5:5; Romans 4:13). In the kingdom we will judge angels, but this too is secondary (1 Corinthians 6:2-3). In the kingdom we will reign on earth with Christ and possess power over the nations (2 Timothy 2:12; Revelation 2:26-28); we will eat of the tree of life, which is in the Paradise of God (Revelation 2:7); the wolf shall dwell with the lamb, the lion shall eat straw like an ox; the little child shall play over the hole of the asp and put his hand on the adder's den (Isaiah 11:6-8); we will beat our swords into plowshares, and our spears into pruning hooks, nation shall not lift up sword against nation, neither shall they learn war any more (Micah 4:3); justice shall roll down like waters and righteousness like an ever-flowing stream (Amos 5:24); our bodies will be made new, and God will wipe away every tear from our eyes, and death shall be no more, neither shall there be crying or pain or guilt or fear any more (Revelation 21:4); and we will sit on the very throne of the King of kings (Revelation 3:21)—but all these are secondary privileges of the kingdom.

The Soul's End: The Pleasure of God in God—in Us

The main reward of the kingdom, the reward *above* all others and *in* all others, is that in the kingdom we will behold the glory of God and enjoy that glory with the very pleasure of God. One of the great frustrations of this life is that even when we are granted a glimpse of the glory of God, our capacities for pleasure are so small that we groan at the incongruity between the revelation of heaven and the response of our heart. Therefore the great hope of all the holiest people is not only that they might see the glory of God, but that they might somehow be given a new strength to savor it with infinite satisfaction—not the partial delights of this world, but, if possible, with the very infinite delight of God himself.

And this highest of all hopes is exactly what Jesus prays will happen to his little flock in the kingdom. "Father, I desire that they also, whom you have given me, may be with me where I am, to behold my glory which you have given me in your love for me before the foundation of the world. . . . I made known to them your name, and I will make it known, *that the love with which you have loved me may be in them and I in them*" (John 17:24,26). Jesus asks the Father that we might see his glory. But more than that! He asks that the very love that the Father has for the Son might be in us. Jesus prays for the highest imaginable privilege and pleasure—that we might be so filled with the fullness of God that the pleasure of God in the beauty of his Son might fill us and be our pleasure in the Son. He prays that the Son himself might be in us and thus fill us with the infinite delight he has in his Father. This is the soul's end—the blessing beyond which no better can be imagined or conceived: an infinite, eternal, mutual, holy energy of love and pleasure between God the Father and God the Son flowing out in the Person of God the Spirit, and filling the souls of the redeemed with immeasurable and everlasting joy.

Surely this is the river of God's delights (Psalm 36:8). This is the water of life that wells up to eternal life and satisfies forever (John 4:10,14). And the river is free. It is our Father's pleasure to give it. "The Spirit and the Bride say, Come. Let him who is thirsty come, let him who desires take the water of life without price" (Revelation 22:17). Let this be the greatest and final incentive to drink—that God is most glorified in us when we are most satisfied in him. And so may the end of all our meditation, all our hope, all our prayer, all our obedience, be this great discovery: that our satisfaction in God will be infinite when, by his gift and in his kingdom, it becomes the pleasure of God in God.

Notes
1. *John G. Paton, Missionary to the New Hebrides,* ed. James Paton (Edinburgh: Banner of Truth Press, 1965, originally published 1891), 85.
2. Ibid., 83.

Letter to a Friend

Concerning the So-called "Lordship Salvation"

*with a list of Scripture passages
on the necessity of obedience*

Explanatory Note: In the February 1989 issue of *The Standard*, the journal for news and comment of the Baptist General Conference, I published a very affirming review of John MacArthur's book, *The Gospel According to Jesus* (Zondervan, 1988). One respected and effective minister of our fellowship responded to me with serious concern about what I was saying. The gist of his concern is seen in a few excerpts from his letter. I am going to change a few details so as not to draw attention to any one individual, because my friend speaks for many.

He said, "Near the age of fifteen I accepted Christ as my Savior. As I look back on my life, I can see He had powerful influence during my late teen years and early twenties. In my late twenties I began to be aware of the concept of Christ as Lord. As I investigated that concept and struggled with it, I realized that for Christ to be Lord, I had to submit everything to Him. In my early thirties I did just that. The concept of 'lordship salvation' that you support would mean that had I died at age twenty-two, that is, before Christ was Lord, I would not have gone to Heaven."

Dear Friend!

Thank you for taking time and interest to respond to my review of John MacArthur's book, *The Gospel According to Jesus*. I have heard of your love for Christ and your faithfulness in evangelism and discipling. This is plain also from your response. And I thank God for it. I hope these things can be discussed in a way that will minimize widespread misunderstanding. If you see any misrepresentations of your thinking please let me know.

Interpreting Two-stage Experiences

Do you know what I think the biggest problem is between the way I see things and the way you see things? It is not so much that I deny your *experience*, but rather that I disagree with the way you describe it or interpret it. I can accept that you received Christ as your Savior near the age of fifteen, and that you were at that moment savingly converted. I praise God that he opened your eyes like Lydia (Acts 16:14) and that he drew you to his Son (John 6:44) and took out the heart of stone and put in a heart of flesh (Ezekiel 36:26) and granted you to repent (2 Timothy 2:25) and believe (Philippians 1:29) and be saved totally by grace apart from any works (Ephesians 2:8).

Not only that, I can accept that some years later, when you were in your early thirties, you had another remarkable experience with Christ in which you made a decisive commitment to him as Lord and submitted everything in your life to him. This *experience* or something like it, is told again and again in my church as people give their testimonies.

I highlight the word *experience*, because my guess is that your *description* of it has been significantly influenced by a popular, contemporary paradigm which, in my judgment, is not fully biblical. I think I can show this from Scripture. But the hundreds of testimonies I have listened to over the years also bear this out.

One can tell pretty quickly the people who have been taught to describe their experience in this two-stage, Savior-Lord sequence. As I have queried some of these people it has become clear to me that the secondary nature of the *description* sometimes is so tied in with the genuineness of the *experience* that to question the description is like calling into question the experience, which I hesitate to do. God alone is the final judge of a person's true experience of salvation. But the Bible is the judge of how we should describe it.

When I have suggested to others another way of describing what has happened to them, they have often seen truth in what I say and dropped the two step, Savior-Lord paradigm as sub-biblical and misleading.

A Converted Catholic Monk

I recall one fellow in particular from South Africa, a converted Catholic monk. He was converted remarkably by the sovereign work of God one night during his evening prayers in the monastery. He knew he was a new person the next morning when, instead of getting angry at the bothersome 3:00 A.M. prayers of his aged neighbor, he felt pity and compassion for him.

His life, typically had its ups and downs as he discovered more and more fully the meaning of belonging to Jesus. Having left the monastery he joined a ministry in South Africa. Through this ministry he learned to interpret his experience and give his testimony in a two-stage, Savior-Lord sequence. He spoke of conversion to Christ as Savior and of a later submission to him as Lord.

But as he sat at our dinner table one Sunday after service, telling his story, I could tell that things simply did not jive. The paradigm did not work. His experience, as it came out in his longer interaction with us, simply did not fit. So I said to him, (what I think I would say to you if I were talking to you now), "You know, Bill (not his real name), I think Jesus was your Lord before that later act of submission. I think he was your Lord the night you were converted and since then your experience has been one of more and more yieldedness to his sovereign rights as Lord over your life. And I don't think that you have bowed to his lordship consistently since that time you 'made him Lord'. You are not fully yielded now or you would be sinless. But he is still your Lord now. And you were not fully yielded then, but he was your Lord then."

Bill was dumbfounded that I would call his testimony into question. No one had ever spoken to him like this. He had only heard one paradigm for describing his experience. He sat in silence for a few minutes, and then said, "You know, I think you're right." And he went on to say that it had never felt quite right and that what I said seemed to make more sense out of the Scriptures as well as his experience.

My Father, the Evangelist

My own father is a full-time evangelist and has led thousands of souls to Christ over the last fifty years of faithful gospel ministry. I just called him in Easley, South Carolina, to have him rehearse for me his experience and give me a reading as an evangelist on the two step, Savior-Lord paradigm.

He said that he used to talk that way but has given it up in recent years (he just turned seventy-two) because of how much damage he saw it doing to the churches as it encouraged people who were not saved to think they were. He quoted Romans 10:9 on the phone and said, "If a person does not have Jesus as Lord he does not have him at all."

He himself received Christ at the age of six at his mother's knee. Then as a teenager in 1934 during special services at his dad's church in Reading, Pennsylvania, he was brought under deep conviction of the weakness of his life and the cowardice of his witness. He went forward and "surrendered totally to the Lord." That was the first time, he said, that he knew the fullness of the Spirit in his life, and he became powerfully courageous, even standing up the next day in his public high school and preaching for twenty minutes.

But he does *not* say Jesus was not his Lord before that experience of deeper surrender. Rather he talks of coming more fully to submit to his lordship which had reigned savingly over his life for the past ten years but had allowed him to have many struggles and come to a crisis of commitment.

Then at about the age of thirty there was another crisis. He was drowning in debt and experiencing depression and insomnia. He began to read a book by James McConkey about submission to God. The basis of the book was Psalm 37:4-5, and the author spoke of committing all to God and submitting to God's sovereign plan for your life and resting in him. My father said that he realized at that point, in spite of the great power in his life for saving souls, he was not totally submitted to God. He bowed and gave up all to the Lord again. He said he found a peace beyond anything he had ever known.

His point was, and my point is, that from the time of our first saving acceptance of Christ, he is our King and Lord and Savior and Priest and Prophet and Counselor. All that he is, he is for those who are his. And then begins a life of faltering and growing yieldedness to Christ in all that he is. This can come in the form of decisive crises, or in the form of gradually growing commitment, or in the form of daily surrenderings. The lordship of Christ, in reality, is something that is not discovered and yielded to once, but thousands of times. It is yieldedness to his lordship that is at stake every time we are tempted to sin—every day.

He Was My Lord, Then I "Made Him Savior"

I have another friend who tells his testimony like this: I received Jesus as my *Lord* when I was a child but it was many years before I discovered how much he wanted to *save* me from my sins of lust and greed and pride. Then I had a powerful encounter with Jesus and discovered this great *saving* intention and "made him my Savior" in a new and powerful way.

That has as much to say for it as the reverse paradigm. We would probably want to admonish him that he *must* have received Jesus as Savior at the beginning *in some sense*. He would have to admit that, I think, just as I think you would have to admit that you received Jesus as Lord *in some sense* when you were first saved.

There are even indications in your response to me that Jesus was the Lord of your life before the crisis experience in your early thirties. One indication is your statement that Christ "had a *powerful* influence during my late teen years and early twenties." Could we not say that this word "powerful" means that Jesus had a *"lordly"* influence in your life in those years? Was he passive or was he exerting the power of his reign as Lord? If you were being powerfully influenced by the risen Jesus, it was the *Lord* who was influencing you, for only as Lord does Christ reign and work among his people.

You may say, "But I did not relate to him as Lord in those years." I wonder if that is exactly true? I wonder about this because something may be real even when we don't understand it fully or even use the right language to describe it. For example, is a person not "born again" just because he has never heard the term "born again" and does not relate to Jesus in those terms but only in terms of faith and forgiveness and atonement? No. A person is just as born again if he believes in Jesus, even if he has never heard of the word "regeneration" or the term "born again." Many have been born again and saved through gospel tracts which say nothing about the term "rebirth."

So I reckon it is possible that many people "have Jesus as their Lord" who don't think much about that term (as evidently you didn't for ten years after your conversion). If you were not dealing with Christ as one who authoritatively calls for newness of life, you would probably have been changed very little. But your testimony is that Christ "had a powerful influence" on your life in those early days. I believe you were dealing with him as your Lord even though that may not have been a title you fully understood. I'm sure I didn't in my earliest days as a believer.

In fact none of us yet understands the full implications of the lordship of Christ on our lives. I am struggling every day to know what the Lord is requiring of me in specific choices among good options. I am learning every day the extent of his lordly control of the world and his mysterious ways of fulfilling his promises as Lord of my life and my church. Submitting to the lordship of Christ is a lifelong activity. It must be renewed every day in many acts of trust and obedience. Submission to Christ's lordship is not merely a once-for-all experience.

Rejecting Christ as Lord and Still Saved?

I say "not merely" because in a sense it *is* a once for all experience. I believe this is conversion. And if I understand the main difference between us it is right here. You seem to say that a person can be converted and saved even if they *reject* the claim of Jesus to be their Lord. I may be wrong here. But that seems to be the implication of what you are saying. For if you are only saying that a person can be saved and not know fully the implications of Christ's lordship, then we have no argument on this point.

But your response goes further than that, I think, and says that people *"do not have Christ as Lord"* and yet are saved. I take the phrase, "do not have Christ as Lord," to mean "reject his lordship." Otherwise you would only be saying that all saved people own Jesus as Lord of their lives but live out that submission in greater or lesser degrees of consistency. But that is what I am saying. There would be no dispute.

So I take it that you are saying something much more extreme, namely, that people can actually be presented with the claims of Christ as Lord and say, "No, I don't want to bow to him as Lord, and I do not accept his claim on my life as authoritative Guide and Teacher," but still be saved (if they believe that he died for them!). If that is what you are saying, then there is a great difference between us indeed. And not only between you and me, but between you and centuries of Christian orthodoxy.

No Assurance While Intent on Sin

The Bible makes it plain, I believe, that people who persistently refuse the command of Jesus' lordship have no warrant for believing that they are saved. Such people should not be comforted that they are saved simply because there was a time when they "believed" gospel facts or walked an aisle or signed a card or prayed a prayer. In fact, Jesus seems far more eager to explode the assurance of false "professions of faith" than he is to give assurance to people who are intent on living in sin. Where does he ever bolster the "eternal security" of a person unwilling to forsake sin?

I am not saying that only perfect people are saved. There are no perfect people on this earth. We sin every day and every good work we do is tainted with sinful remnants of corruption. I am saying that a person who goes on willfully rejecting the commands of Jesus for his life has no warrant for salvation. The evidence for this is found in the passages of Scripture listed at the end of this letter.

To clear up just what I think the Bible teaches about salvation by faith I'd like to respond to some other specific points in your letter that seem to reflect either a misunderstanding of what I am saying, or a rejection (without sufficient warrant) of what I am saying.

If I Died before Making Jesus Lord

1. You say, "The concept of 'lordship salvation' would mean that had I died at age twenty-two, that is, before Christ was Lord, I would not have gone to Heaven."

I think I have said enough above to assure you that my interpretation of your experience is a very hopeful one. I do think you would have gone to heaven. But, oh, how I wish you could feel how St. Paul and Jesus and all the great, godly spokesmen of Christian orthodoxy for 1900 years would cringe at hearing the words, "Before Christ was Lord"!

Where in the New Testament can you find anything close to such a description of a true believer? This way of talking about an immature believer has no warrant in the New Testament. And it is *so* misleading!

It is misleading because Christ *is* Lord whether we acknowledge that or not (Acts 2:36; Philippians 2:11). And it is misleading because he is the Lord *of every true believer* whether we grasp this fully or obey him fully or not.

Just consider these few observations. Dozens of times in writing to all the believers of a church Paul refers to Jesus as "our Lord." Some of these places have to take in *all* the believers, not just those who are more mature in their devotion to Christ. For example, Romans 8:39 is a text you would probably want to use to encourage a faltering believer that he was secure in the arms of God. Yet the verse says that nothing will separate us from "the love of God in Christ Jesus *our Lord.*"

If the verse is to comfort the reader, the reader has to see himself in the "our." Paul has no intention here of saying that there are some Christians who do not have Jesus as Lord and thus do not have security. All true Christians can say "our Lord" and be included here. (The same thing could be said of Romans 6:23.)

Romans 10:9 says, "If you confess with your lips that *Jesus is Lord* and believe in your heart that God raised him from the dead, you will be saved." It is a frightening thing, in view of this verse, to tell people that they do not have to confess Jesus as Lord in order to be saved. That is just the opposite of what scripture says. (Romans 10:13 is just as strong.)

In Romans 14:7-8 Paul says, "*None of us* lives to himself and none of us dies to himself. If we live we live to *the Lord*, and if we die we die to *the Lord*; so then whether we live or whether we die, we are *the Lord's.*" Notice the phrase, "none of us." There is no group of Christians who do not live to the Lord. We may do it imperfectly and haltingly. But to belong to the Lord is to live to the Lord.

Paul simply identifies Christians in 1 Corinthians 1:2 as "all those who in every place call on the name of our *Lord* Jesus Christ, both their Lord and ours." He can do this because becoming a Christian *means* confessing Jesus as Lord (Romans 10:9) and calling on the name of the Lord (Romans 10:13).

Paul described the content of his gospel preaching like this: "For what we preach is not ourselves, but Jesus Christ *as Lord*" (2 Corinthians 4:5). And in 1 Thessalonians 1:8 he says that the spreading of this gospel by the churches is the sounding forth of "the *Word of the Lord.*" This is not a second stage "discipleship" message. This is what he preached as the gospel.

You Did Not Receive a Half-Christ

In Colossians 2:6 Paul says, "As therefore you received Christ Jesus *the Lord*, so live in him." This is the way we should speak to new believers: you received Jesus in all his offices when you received him for salvation. You did not receive a half-Christ. He is Prophet, Priest and King—and he is this for you. This is the One you received. Now live in him in a way that befits his offices. If you reject him in any of his offices you reject the Christ and are left with one of your own making who cannot save.

There are many other uses of the term "Lord" in the New Testament that show that Paul and the others never conceived of the possibility of saying that a person could be saved and "not have Jesus as Lord." It is not a biblical way of talking and it is dangerously misleading.

2. You say with regard to equipping people for evangelism, "We must have a concept that is transferable. If we have to develop the concept of 'lordship salvation,' the task becomes impossible. It will be difficult enough to equip our people to communicate salvation by faith." There is one serious misunderstanding of "lordship salvation" in this quote and one questionable attitude to Scripture.

Lordship Salvation Is *Salvation by Faith*

2.1 The misunderstanding is the implication that lordship salvation is anything other than "salvation by faith." Paul said to the Philippian jailer, "*Believe on the Lord* Jesus Christ and you will be saved." He said, "Believe." And he said, "Believe on the *Lord.*" Now that is lordship salvation *and* salvation by faith—*both*. The question is not whether salvation is by faith. It is (Ephesians 2:8). The question is first, What is faith? and second, Whom do we have faith in?

Paul's answer is that we have faith in the *Lord*. This does not turn salvation into salvation by works. It simply means we have to know whom it is we are trusting.

The answer to the question, What is faith? is the most basic one in this whole controversy. It is not a simple mental assent to facts—not lordship facts and not Savior facts. It is a heartfelt coming to Christ and resting in him for what he is and what he offers. It is an act of the heart that no longer hates the light but comes to the light because a new set of spiritual taste buds have been created and Christ now tastes satisfying to the soul. This notion of faith is taken mainly from the Gospel of John where Jesus says, "I am the Bread of Life; he who comes to Me shall not hunger, and *he who believes in Me shall never thirst*" (John 6:35). (See the texts at the end of this letter under the title "The Nature of Faith in the Gospel of John." [Also see the discussion of saving faith in chapter 9, pp. 250-257 of this book.])

This view of faith implies that faith itself will inevitably wean a person away from sin because faith is a resting in what Jesus has to offer, namely, the pathway of life. Obedience is not something artificially added to saving faith later after a second discovery in the Christian walk. It is what faith does because faith is the soul's cleaving to Jesus for the forgiveness and guidance and hope it needs to be happy. If you don't do what the doctor says, you don't trust him.

So lordship salvation is *not*—emphatically *not*—anything other than salvation by faith (true faith) in the *Lord* Jesus Christ.

Does Experience or Scripture Define the Gospel?

2.2 Your quote also contains a questionable attitude to Scripture. I say questionable because I don't think you really want to say what I hear you saying, namely, that our definition of evangelism and of the gospel must fit in with what we decide is effective and workable (transferable) whether or not it is out of sync with Scripture.

You say, "If we have to develop the concept of lordship salvation, the task becomes impossible." Do you know what I hear in that sentence? I hear the words of the disciples after Jesus has turned the rich young ruler away unsaved because he would not submit to the demand of Jesus to stop loving his money. They say, "Who then can be saved?" And Jesus says, "With men it is impossible."

It does not seem to me that your rejection of "lordship salvation" (because it would be "impossible" to teach) is in line with the attitude of Jesus. It is *your* judgment call that this is "impossible," not the Bible's. The Bible does not say that this kind of evangelism is impossible and Jesus, and the apostles demonstrate with their lives that it is not.

Jesus said that the way is hard that leads to life and few there be that find it (Matthew 7:14). Could it be that we are so bent on having immediate, measurable results that we have defined the gospel and evangelism in a way that enables people to understand and respond even without spiritual comprehension and heart change? I fear this is largely why we are so weak as a church. The very foundations have been laid wrongly.

Staggeringly Unbiblical

3. You say, "One of my primary objectives [in discipling four men] is to bring them to a point where Christ becomes Lord. That is a primary task of discipleship."

I find these words staggeringly unbiblical! Nowhere! Nowhere in the New Testament, can you find such an idea, that mature Christians should suggest to newer believers that Christ is not their Lord. Do you honestly think the apostle Paul would allow a new convert to say to him: "Jesus is not my Lord, but I am saved"?

Now let me see if I can cool down here and be conciliatory. Again I believe that you are in essence teaching something true, namely that very often a person is converted without realizing the full implications of the lordship of Christ for their lives.

It is like deciding to join the army and knowing that there will be a commander but not realizing all that he may tell you to do and all the rebellion that still remains in your heart. But that is very different from saying that you can join the army while rejecting the very right of the commander to tell you what to do.

So I agree that discipling is "teaching them to observe all that I commanded you" (Matthew 28:19). But I do not agree that Jesus is not the Lord (commander) of true Christians. No one is a Christian who does not, in principle (i.e. even if he does not know all the specifics), bow the knee to Jesus as Lord and say one way or another, I reckon myself dead to sin and alive to God. "Those who belong to Christ (*all* of them!) have crucified the flesh" (Galatians 5:24).

How Do You Preach to Disobedient, Professing Christians?

4. You ask, "Could we dare say that they [the unconcerned, apathetic, stingy, uncommitted professing believers] do not have salvation?"

I believe that our unwillingness to take this possibility seriously is one of the things that makes preaching across our country anemic. If you measure by the preaching of Jesus and by the epistles of Paul the way to preach to disobedient, professing Christians, it means saying things like: "I warn you, as I warned you before, that those who do such things *shall not inherit the kingdom of God*" (Galatians 5:21; cf. 1 Corinthians 6:9-10). "Would that you were cold or hot! So, because you are lukewarm, and neither cold nor hot, *I will spew you out of my mouth*" (Revelation 3:15-16). "*Strive to enter by the narrow door*, for many, I tell you, will seek to enter and will not be able" (Luke 13:24). "*If you live according to the flesh you will die*" (Romans 8:13).

The absence of this kind of preaching—with such urgency *to professing believers*—is one of the weaknesses of the evangelical pulpit. I am puzzled that you are so hesitant to consider that thousands of professing Christians are not saved, when that is what Jesus very strongly suggests was true in his day (Matthew 7:13-14) and will be true at the end of the age—our day (Matthew 24:12-13).

MacArthur is right when he says that Jesus far more often calls people's false assurance into question than he tries to give security to any willfully disobedient beginner. And yet we seem to have just the opposite concern. We shrink back from calling anyone's assurance into question if they are a professing believer. And we shrink back from telling new believers anything about the demands of Jesus that would cause them to wonder if they are really saved. We are not in sync with Jesus or the epistles at this point.

Labor On for the Lord of Glory

Well, I hope that what I have said will help us both to be as biblically effective as possible in the immensely important cause of evangelism and world missions. My great burden is that we know what the evangel *is*. I think it has been watered down in some presentations to the point where it is not the robust, powerful, life-changing message that I hear in the New Testament.

I hope the lines will be open between us for further conversation. These things are immensely important. There will not be any lasting and deep revival apart from a radical commitment to the full-orbed truth of all that the Bible teaches (Acts 20:20,27).

I praise God for how he has used you in his service. Let nothing I say be heard as diminishing the great way in which God is blessing your life and work. May great grace continue to crown all your labors for the Lord of glory!

Your partner in the Great Work,

John Piper

P.S. Here are the texts I referred to in the letter.

Texts that point to the necessity of yielding to Christ as Lord in order to inherit eternal life.

NOTE: None of these texts means that salvation can be earned by works of the law. Salvation is by grace through faith; it does not come from ourselves; it is the gift of God (Ephesians 2:8). What these texts teach is that the faith which justifies also sanctifies (Acts

15:9). All the obedience of believers necessary for final salvation is obedience that comes from faith (1 Thessalonians 1:3; 2 Thessalonians 1:11; Galatians 5:6; Hebrews 10:35-36; 11:8). If it does not come from faith it is legalism and gains nothing but deeper condemnation (Romans 9:32). What is being taught in all these texts is this: "By my works I will show you my faith . . . faith apart from works is barren . . . faith apart from works is dead" (James 2:18,20,26). Salvation is by grace through faith. But saving faith is no fruitless mental assent to gospel facts. These texts point to the truth that the faith that saves is a feeding on Jesus with such satisfaction that we are gradually weaned away from the enslaving addictions to sin (John 6:35; Hebrews 11:24-26). [For more on how faith necessarily produces obedience, see chapter 9, pp. 253-257.]

The Necessity of Doing Good

Matthew 7:21-23, "Not everyone who says to me, 'Lord, Lord,' shall enter the Kingdom of Heaven, but he who does the will of my Father who is in heaven. On that day many will say to me, 'Lord, Lord, did we not prophesy in Your name, and cast out demons in Your name, and do many mighty works in Your name?' And then I will declare to them, '*I never knew you. Depart from Me, you evildoers.*'"

John 5:28-29, "Do not marvel at this; for the hour is coming when all who are in the tombs will hear His voice and come forth, *those who have done good, to the resurrection of the life*, and those who have done evil, to the resurrection of judgment."

Romans 2:6-10, "For He will render to every man according to his works: *to those who by patience and well-doing seek for glory and honor and immortality He will give eternal life*; but for those who are factious and do not obey the truth, but obey wickedness, there will be wrath and fury. There will be tribulation and distress for every human being who does evil, the Jew first and also the Greek, *but glory and honor and peace for everyone who does good*, the Jew first and also the Greek."

Galatians 6:9, "And let us not grow weary in well-doing, for in due season we shall reap, if we do not lose heart."

First Timothy 5:8, "If anyone does not provide for his relatives, and especially for his own family, he has disowned the faith and is *worse than an unbeliever*."

James 2:17,26, "Faith by itself, *if it has no works, is dead . . .* For as the body apart from the spirit is dead, *so faith apart from works is dead.*"

The Necessity of Obedience

Matthew 7:24-27, "Everyone then who hears these words of mine *and does them* will be like a wise man who built his house upon the rock; and the rains fell and the floods came and the winds blew and beat upon that house but it did not fall, because it had been founded on the rock. And everyone who hears these words of mine and *does not do them* will be like a foolish man who built his house upon the sand; and the rains fell and the floods came, and the winds blew and beat against that house, and it fell; and great was the fall of it."

Matthew 12:48-50, "But Jesus replied to the man who told him, 'Who is my mother, and who are my brothers?' And stretching out his hand toward his disciples, he said, 'Here are my mother and my brothers! For *whoever does the will of my Father in heaven is my brother,* and sister, and mother.'"

Luke 13:6-9, "And He told this parable: A man had a fig tree planted in his vineyard; and he came seeking fruit on it and found none and he said to the vinedresser, 'Lo, these three years I have come seeking fruit on this fig tree, and I found none. Cut it down; why should it use up the ground?' And he answered him, 'Let it alone, sir, this year also, until I dig about it and put on manure. And *if it bears fruit next year, well and good but if not you can cut it down.*'"

Luke 8:11-15, "Now the parable is this: The seed is the word of God. The ones along the path are those who have heard; then the devil comes and takes away the Word from their hearts, that they may not believe and be saved. And the ones on the rock are those who, when they hear the Word receive it with joy; but these have no root, they believe for a while and in time of temptation fall away. And as for what fell among the thorns, they are those who hear, but as they go on their way they are choked by the cares and riches and pleasures of life, and their fruit is not mature. And *as for that in the good soil, they are those who, hearing the Word, hold it fast in an honest and good heart, and bring forth fruit with patience.*"

John 14:15, "If you love me *you will keep my commandments.*"

John 15:2, "*Every branch of mine that bears no fruit, he takes away*, and every branch that does bear fruit he prunes, that it may bear more fruit." John 3:36, "He who believes in the Son has eternal life; *he who does not obey the Son shall not see life*, but the wrath of God rests upon him."

Romans 6:12,14, "Let not sin therefore reign in your mortal bodies, to make you obey their passions . . . *For sin will have no dominion over you*, since you are not under law but under grace."

First Corinthians 6:9-10, "Do you not know that the unrighteous will not inherit the Kingdom of God? Do not be deceived, neither the immoral nor idolaters nor adulterers nor sexual perverts nor thieves nor the greedy nor drunkards nor revilers nor robbers will inherit the Kingdom of God."

Hebrews 5:8-9, "Although He was a Son, He learned obedience through what He suffered; and being made perfect *He became the source of eternal salvation to all who obey Him.*"

Hebrews 10:36, "For you have need of endurance, so that you may *do the will of God and receive what is promised.*"

First John 2:4, "He who says 'I know Him,' but *disobeys his commandments* is a liar, and the truth is not in him." (See 1 John 3:1-10.)

First John 2:17, "And the world passes away, and the lust of it; but *he who does the will of God abides forever.*"

The Necessity of Holiness

Second Thessalonians 2:13, "But we are bound to give thanks to God always for you, brethren beloved by the Lord, because God chose you from the beginning to be *saved through sanctification by the Spirit* and belief in the Truth."

Hebrews 12:14, "Strive for peace with all men, and for *the holiness without which no one will see the Lord.*"

The Necessity to Forgive Others

Matthew 6:12-15, "And forgive us our debts, as we also have forgiven our debtors; and lead us not into temptation but deliver us from evil. For if you forgive men their trespasses, your heavenly

Father also will forgive you; but *if you do not forgive men their trespasses, neither will your Father forgive your trespasses.*"

NOTE: The eternal significance of this forgiveness in Matthew 6 is made plain in the parable of the unforgiving servant in Matthew 18. Jesus is not merely talking about losing fellowship. He is talking about losing God if we go on through life with an unforgiving spirit.

Matthew 18:32-35, "Then his lord summoned him and said to him, 'You wicked servant! I forgave you all that debt because you besought me; and should not you have had mercy on your fellow servant as I had mercy on you?' And in anger his lord delivered him to *the torturers,* until he should pay all his debt. *So also my heavenly Father will do to every one of you, if you do not forgive your brother from your heart.*"

The Necessity Not to Live According to the Flesh

Romans 8:12-14, "So then, brethren, we are debtors not to the flesh, to live according to the flesh—*for if you live according to the flesh, you will die,* but if by the Spirit you put to death the deeds of the body you will live. For *all who are led by the Spirit of God are sons of God.*"

Galatians 5:19-21, "Now the works of the flesh are plain: immorality, impurity, licentiousness, idolatry, sorcery, enmity, strife, jealousy, anger, selfishness, dissension, haughty spirit, envy, drunkenness, carousing, and the like. I warn you, as I warned you before, that *those who do such things will not enter the Kingdom of God.*"

Galatians 5:24, "*Those who belong to Christ Jesus have crucified the flesh* with its passions and desires."

Galatians 6:8, "For he who sows to his own flesh will from the flesh reap corruption; but *he who sows to the Spirit will from the Spirit reap eternal life.*"

The Necessity of Being Free from the Love of Money

Luke 14:25-33, "Now great multitudes accompanied Him; and He turned and said to them, 'If anyone comes to me and does not hate his own father and mother and wife and children and brothers and sisters, yes, and even his own life, he cannot be my disciple. Whoever does not bear his own cross and come after me cannot be my disciple . . . so therefore *whoever of you does not renounce all that he has cannot be my disciple.'"*

Luke 18:18-22, "And the ruler asked him, 'Good Teacher, *what shall I do to inherit eternal life?'* And Jesus said to him, 'Why do you call me good? No one is good but God alone. You know the commandments: "Do not commit adultery, do not kill, do not steal, do not bear false witness, honor your father and mother."' And he said, 'All these I have observed from my youth.' And when Jesus heard it, he said to him, 'One thing you still lack. *Sell all that you have and distribute to the poor, and you will have treasure in heaven; and come follow me.'"*

The Necessity of Love to Christ and God

Matthew 10:37-39, "*He who loves father or mother more than me is not worthy of me;* and he who loves son or daughter more than me is not worthy of me; and he who does not take his cross and follow me is not worthy of me. He who finds his life will lose it, and he who loses his life for my sake will find it."

Matthew 24:12-13, "And because wickedness is multiplied, most men's *love* will grow cold. *But he who endures to the end will be saved.*"

John 8:42, "Jesus said to them, '*If God were your Father, you would love me*, for I proceeded and came forth from God.'"

Romans 8:28, "All things work together for good *for those who love God* and are called according to His purpose."

First Corinthians 2:9-10, "As it is written, 'What no eye has seen, nor ear heard, nor the heart of man conceived, what God has prepared *for those who love Him*,' God has revealed to us through the Spirit."

First Corinthians 8:3, "But *if one loves God, one is known by Him.*"

First Corinthians 16:22, "*If anyone does not love the Lord let him be accursed.*"

Second Thessalonians 2:9-10, "The coming of the lawless one by the activity of Satan will be with all power and with pretended signs and wonders, and with all wicked deception for those who are to perish because they *refuse to love the truth and so to be saved.*"

Second Timothy 4:8, "Henceforth there is laid up for me the crown of righteousness which the Lord, the righteous Judge, will award to me on that day, and not only to me, but also to *all who have loved His appearing.*"

James 1:12, "Blessed is the man who endures trial, for when he has stood the test he will receive the crown of life which God has *promised to those who love him.*"

James 2:5, "Listen, my beloved brethren. Has not God chosen those who are poor in the world to be rich in faith and heirs of *the Kingdom which He has promised to those who love Him?*"

First Peter 1:8, "Without having seen Him *you love Him*; though you do not now see Him you believe in Him and rejoice with unutterable and exalted joy."

First Peter 2:7, "To you, therefore, who believe, *he is precious.*

First John 2:15, "Do not love the world or the things in the world. *If anyone loves the world, love for the Father is not in him.*"

The Necessity to Love Others

Matthew 25:40-46, "And the King will answer them, 'Truly, I say to you, as you did it to one of the least of these my brethren, you did it to Me.' Then He will say to those at His left hand, 'Depart from me, you cursed, into the eternal fire prepared for the devil and his angels; for I was hungry and you gave me no food; I was thirsty and you gave me no drink; I was a stranger and you did not welcome me; naked and you did not clothe me; sick, and in prison, and you did not visit me.' Then they also will answer, 'Lord, when did we see you hungry or thirsty or a stranger or naked or sick or in prison, and did not minister to you?' Then He will answer them, *'Truly, I say to you, as you did it not to one of the least of these, you did it not to me.' And they will go away into eternal punishment,* but the righteous into eternal life."

Luke 10:25-28, "And behold a lawyer stood up to put Him to the test, saying, 'Teacher, *what shall I do to inherit eternal life?*' He said to him, 'What is written in the law, how do you read?'

And he answered, 'You shall love the Lord with all your heart, and with all your soul, and with all your strength, and with all your mind; and *your neighbor as yourself.*' And He said to him, '*You have answered right; do this, and you will live.*'"

Galatians 5:6, "For in Christ Jesus neither circumcision nor uncircumcision is of any avail, but *faith working through love.*"

First Peter 3:9, "Do not return evil for evil or reviling for reviling; but *on the contrary bless, for to this you have been called, that you may obtain a blessing.*"

First John 3:14, "*We know that we have passed out of death into life, because we have loved the brethren. He who does not love remains in death.*"

First John 4:8,20, "*He who does not love does not know God;* for God is love . . . . If anyone says, 'I love God,' and hates his brother, he is a liar for he who does not love his brother whom he has seen, cannot love God whom he has not seen."

The Necessity to Love the Truth

Second Thessalonians 2:10, "[They] are to perish because *they refused to love the truth and so be saved.*"

The Necessity of Being Childlike

Matthew 18:2-3, "And calling to Him a child, He put him in the midst of them, and said, 'Truly, I say to you, *unless you turn and become like children, you will never enter the Kingdom of Heaven.*'"

The Necessity to Bridle the Tongue

James 1:26, "If any one thinks he is religious and *does not bridle his tongue but deceives his heart, this person's religion is vain.*"

The Necessity of Perseverance

Mark 13:13, "You will be hated by all for My name's sake. But *he who endures to the end will be saved.*"

Luke 9:62, "Jesus said to him, '*No one who puts his hand to the plow and looks back is fit for the Kingdom of God.*'"

First Corinthians 15:1-2, "Now I would remind you, brethren, in what terms I preached to you the gospel, which you received, in which you stand, *by which you are saved, if you hold it fast—* unless you believed in vain."

Colossians 1:21-23, "And you, who once were estranged and hostile in mind, doing evil deeds, He has now reconciled in His body of flesh by His own death, in order to present you holy and blameless and irreproachable before Him, *provided that you continue in the faith,* stable and steadfast, not shifting from the hope of the gospel, which you heard, which has been preached to every creature under heaven, and of which I, Paul, became a minister."

Second Timothy 2:11-12, "This saying is sure: If we have died with Him, we shall also live with Him; *if we endure, we shall also reign with Him;* if we deny Him, He also will deny us."

Hebrews 3:6, "Christ was faithful over God's house as a Son. And we are His house *if we hold fast our confidence and pride in our hope.*"

Hebrews 3:12-14, "Take care, brethren, lest there be in any of you an evil, unbelieving heart, leading you to fall away from the living God. Exhort one another every day, as long as it is called today, that none of you may be hardened by the deceitfulness of sin. *For we have shared in Christ, if we hold our first confidence to the end.*"

Hebrews 6:11-12, "We desire each one of you to show the same earnestness in *realizing the full assurance of hope until the end,* so that you may not be sluggish, but imitators of those who *through faith and patience inherit the promises.*"

Hebrews 10:36, "For *you have need of endurance, so that you may do the will of God and receive what is promised.*"

The Necessity of Walking in the Light

First John 1:7, "*If we walk in the light,* as He is in the light, we have fellowship with one another, and *the blood of Jesus His Son cleanses us from all sin.*"

The Necessity of Repentance

Luke 3:3, John the Baptist "went into all the region about the

Jordan, preaching a *baptism of repentance for the forgiveness of sins.*"

Mark 1:14-15, "Now after John was arrested, Jesus came into Galilee preaching the gospel of God, and saying, 'The time is fulfilled, and the Kingdom of God is at hand; *repent and believe in the gospel.*'"

Luke 3:8, "*Bear fruits that befit repentance,* and do not begin to say to yourselves, 'We have Abraham as our father'; for I tell you, God is able from these stones to raise up children of Abraham."

Luke 5:32, "I have not come to call the righteous, but *sinners to repentance.*"

Luke 13:1-3, "There were some present at that very time who told Him of Galileans whose blood Pilate had mingled with their sacrifices. And he answered them, 'Do you think that these Galileans were worse sinners than all the other Galileans, because they suffered thus? I tell you, no; but *unless you repent you will all likewise perish.*'"

Luke 15:7, "Just so, I tell you, there will be *more joy in heaven over one sinner who repents* than over ninety-nine righteous persons who need no repentance."

Luke 24:46-47, "Thus it is written, that the Christ should suffer and on the third day rise from the dead, and that *repentance and forgiveness of sins should be preached in His name to all nations,* beginning from Jerusalem."

Acts 2:38, "And Peter said to them, '*Repent, and be baptized every one of you in the name of Jesus Christ for the forgiveness of your sins,* and you shall receive the gift of the Holy Spirit.'"

Acts 3:19, "*Repent therefore, and turn again, that your sins may be blotted out,* that times of refreshing may come from the presence of the Lord."

Acts 5:31, "God exalted Him at His right hand as Leader and Savior, *to give repentance to Israel and forgiveness of sins.*"

Acts 11:18, "When they heard this they were silenced. And they glorified God, saying, 'Then to the Gentiles also, God has granted *repentance unto life.*'"

Acts 20:21, "Testifying both to Jews and to Greeks of *repentance to God and faith in our Lord Jesus Christ.*"

The Necessity of Warfare Vigilance

First Timothy 6:12, "Fight the good fight of faith; *take hold of eternal life* to which you were called when you made the good confession in the presence of many witnesses."

Matthew 7:13-14, "*Enter by the narrow gate;* for the gate is wide and the way is easy that leads to destruction, and those who enter by it are many. For the gate is narrow and *the way is hard that leads to life* and those who find it are few."

Luke 13:24, "*Strive to enter by the narrow door;* for many, I tell you, will seek to enter and will not be able."

Hebrews 3:12-14, "*Take care brethren lest there be in any of you an evil, unbelieving heart,* leading you to fall away from the living God. *Exhort one another every day,* as long as it is called today, that none of you may be hardened by the deceitfulness of sin. For we share in Christ, if we hold our first confidence to the end."

Hebrews 12:14, "*Strive for peace with all men, and for the holiness without which no one will see the Lord.*"

First Corinthians 9:24-27, "Do you not know that in a race all the runners compete, but only one receives the prize? *So run that you may obtain it.* Every athlete exercises self-control in all things. They do it to receive a perishable wreath, but we an imperishable. Well, I do not run aimlessly, I do not box as one beating the air, but I pommel my body, and subdue it, *lest after preaching to others I myself should be disqualified.*"

Second Timothy 4:7, "I have *fought the good fight,* I have *finished the race,* I have kept the faith."

God's Promise of Preservation in Holiness

NOTE: In chapter 5, pp. 146-148, I tried to show that part of the good news of God's sovereign grace is that "This truth enables us to own up to the demands for holiness in the Scripture and yet have assurance of salvation." The key to assurance is not to reduce commands from requirements to options, but rather to magnify grace as a power to obey as well as a pardon for sin. This essential truth of grace as power as well as pardon is developed in chapter 9 under the heading, "God's pleasure in obedience is good news because the obedience he loves is the obedience of faith" (pp. 250-257). The following passages express the certainty of what God's gracious power will achieve for the child of God.

Mark 13:22, "False christs and false prophets will arise and show signs and wonders, to lead astray, *if possible*, the elect."

Luke 22:31-32, "Simon, Simon, behold, Satan demanded to have you that he might sift you like wheat, but *I have prayed for you that your faith may not fail*; and when you have turned again, strengthen your brethren."

John 10:27-30, "My sheep hear my voice, and I know them, and *they follow Me*; and I give them eternal life, and *they shall never perish*, and no one shall snatch them out of My hand. My Father, who has given them to Me, is greater than all, and no one is able to snatch them out of my Father's hand. I and the Father are one."

Romans 8:30, "And those whom He predestined He also called; and those whom He called He also justified; and *those whom He justified He also glorified*."

First Corinthians 1:8-9, "*He will sustain you to the end*, guiltless in the day of our Lord Jesus Christ. God is faithful, by Whom you were called into the fellowship of His Son, Jesus Christ our Lord."

Philippians 1:6, "I am sure that *He who began a good work in you will bring it to completion* at the day of Jesus Christ."

Philippians 2:13, "*God is the one who is at work in you, both to will and to work for His good pleasure*."

First Thessalonians 5:23-24, "May the God of peace Himself sanctify you wholly; and may your spirit and soul and body be kept sound and blameless at the coming of our Lord Jesus Christ. *He who calls you is faithful and He will do it*."

Second Timothy 1:12, "I am not ashamed, for I know whom I have believed, and *I am sure that He is able to guard until that Day what has been entrusted to me*."

Hebrews 13:20-21, "Now may the God of peace who brought again from the dead our Lord Jesus, the Great Shepherd of the sheep, by the blood of the eternal covenant, equip you with everything good that you may do His will, *working in you that which is pleasing in His sight* through Jesus Christ; to whom be glory forever and ever. Amen."

First Peter 1:5, "*Who by God's power are guarded through faith for salvation* ready to be revealed in the last time."

The Nature of Faith in the Gospel of John

John 3:19-21, "And this is the judgment, that the light has come into the world, and *men loved darkness rather than light*, because their deeds were evil. For everyone who does evil *hates the light*, and does not come to the light, lest his deeds should be exposed. But he who does what is true comes to the light, that it may be clearly seen that his deeds have been wrought in God."

NOTE: *Coming* to the Christ is one way John describes faith (John 6:35). But no one comes to the light if they hate the light (John 3:20). So before there can be the coming of faith there must be the deeper transformation that brings us to love the light and not hate it. This means that saving faith in John's Gospel is the act of a new heart and not merely the mental assent of an old one that does not love the light. Love is implicit in John's view of saving faith. And this is why he says in 1 John that if we don't love we don't even know God and have not passed from death to life (1 John 3:14; 4:8,20).

John 3:36, "He who *believes* in the Son has eternal life; He who does not *obey* the Son shall not see life, but the wrath of God rests upon him."

NOTE: Saving faith implies (and includes) an obedient spirit to the Son of God.

John 4:14, "Whoever drinks of the water that I *will give him will never thirst;* the water that I shall give him will become in him a spring of water welling up to eternal life."

NOTE: Saving faith is spoken of here as a drinking of water that satisfies the deepest longings of the soul. This satisfaction is what gives faith its life-changing power. It replaces sin with "the expulsive power of a new affection" (the title of an old sermon by Thomas Chalmers).

John 6:35, "I am the Bread of Life; he who *comes* to Me shall not hunger, and he who *believes* in Me shall never thirst."

NOTE: This confirms that coming is a way of talking about believing. It also confirms that John 4:14 was talking about faith. It also shows that faith is a feeding and drinking from the presence and promise of Jesus to the degree that we are not dominated by the alluring pleasures of sin (Romans 6:14).

John 5:41-44, "I do not receive glory from men. But I know that you have not the love of God within you. I have come in my Father's name and you do not receive Me; if another comes in his own name, him you will receive. *How can you believe, who receive glory from one another and do not seek the glory that comes from the only God?*"

NOTE: Faith is impossible for a person who is in love with the praise of men. So faith is of such a nature that it excludes the bondage to applause. It includes a love for God that makes the praise of men pale by comparison to what God is.

John 8:45-47, "But, because I tell you the Truth you do not *believe* Me. Which of you convicts Me of sin? If I tell you the Truth, why do you not *believe* Me? He who is of God hears the words of God; the reason why you do not hear them is because you are not of God."

NOTE: You cannot even hear the word of God (in a compliant way) if you are not "of God," that is, not born anew by the free-blowing Spirit (John 3:8; 1:12-13). Therefore faith is a fruit of God's work in the soul and comes from a heart regenerate and drawn to Christ. This is what Jesus means in John 6:44 when he says, "No one can come to me unless the Father draws him." The drawing enables the coming, which we have seen is faith. The drawing corresponds to being "of God" in John 8:47 and being Jesus' sheep in John 10:27.

John 10:25-28, "Jesus answered them, 'I told you, and you do not *believe.* The works that I do in my Father's name, they bear witness to me; but *you do not believe, because you do not belong to my sheep.* My sheep hear my voice, and I know them and they follow Me.'"

NOTE: You do not become a sheep by believing. You can believe only because you are a sheep. This is the way Jesus taught the doctrine of election as John records it. The teaching is also found in John 6:44,65; 8:47; 18:37; 3:8; etc. But the point for faith is that it comes from a certain heart—a heart of a sheep of Jesus which is described like this: My sheep hear my voice . . . and follow me. Faith therefore must be of such a nature that it produces that following.

John 12:25, "He who loves his life loses it and *he who hates his life in this world will keep it for eternal life.*"

NOTE: Hating the life in this world means being willing to suffer in obedience to Jesus' command of love, just like he suffered for the sake of love. This shows that eternal life cannot be inherited by a faith that is fruitless and leaves the heart loveless and selfish.

John 15:2, "*Every branch of mine which bears no fruit, He takes away*, and every branch that does bear fruit He prunes, that it might bear more fruit."

NOTE: Fruitless faith is not saving faith and results in being cut off from Jesus (like Judas). As verse 6 says, "He is cast forth as a branch and withers; and the branches are gathered and thrown into the fire and burned." (Ponder John 13:8-10.)

Scripture Index

Reference	Page
Genesis	
1:2	97n5
1:4	83
1:12	83
1:21	83
1:25	83
1:31	83
4:1	152n5
6:7	74n14
8:1	63
12:3	229
15:6	167
15:13	73n6
15:16	73n6
18:17-19	127
18:19	141
18:25	165
34:8	152n7
40:8	72n6
49:10	229, 234
50:20	75n16, 154n16, 191

Reference	Page
Exodus	
3:19	73n6
4:22	36
4:22-23	129
9:16	107
14:21	63
15:10	63
17:8-16	242
19:4	128
27:17	152n7
32:11-12	119n4
33:12	152n4
33:18	47
34:6	192
34:6-7	249
34:29	48
38:17	152n7
38:28	152n7

Reference	Page
Numbers	
13:30	237
14:13-16	119n4
14:21	55, 84

Reference	Page
Deuteronomy	
4:20	128
4:37-39	128
6:24	249
7:6-8	132, 133
7:7	152n7
8:17-18	152n6
9:4-5	152n6
9:27-29	119n4
10:12-13	249
10:14-15	122, 129-130, 133, 158n38

10:15 . . . . 152n7
14:2 127
18:10 246
21:11 . . . . 152n7
23:5 . . . . 158n38
25:17-19 242
28:63 . . . . 65, 67
29:2-4 . . . . 154n16
30:6 . . . . . . 147, 202, 225, 226
30:9 191
30:11 249
31:16 . . . . 73n6, 129
31:36 129
32:39 64

Joshua
2:10-11 107
7 108
7:8-9 108
24:2-3 127

Judges
21:25 102

1 Samuel
2:6 64
5 104
8 102
8:5 . . . . 102, 103
8:7 103
8:9 103
8:17 103
8:19,20 103
9:21 246
10-12 103
11:15 243
12:14 244
12:19 103
12:20-21 103
12:22 . . 100, 102-105, 106, 108
12:23 243
12:24 244
14:32 245
15 242
15:2-3 242
15:6 243
15:9 243
15:11 . . 74n14, 243, 244, 265n1
15:12 245

15:13 243
15:15 243
15:17-18 246
15:19 245
15:21 245
15:22 . . . . 240, 242
15:22-23 246
15:23 247
15:24 . . . . 243, 244
15:29 . . . . 265n1
16:7 218
23:10-13 . . . . 73n6

2 Samuel
7:23 106
24:1 . . . . 75n16

1 Kings
9:19 . . . . 152n7
13:2 . . . . 72n6

2 Kings
13:19 . . . . 73n6

1 Chronicles
21:1 . . . . 75n16
29:14 49

2 Chronicles
7:14 221
8:6 . . . . 152n7
16:9 191

Ezra
1:1 . . . . 74n16
6:22 . . . . 74n16

Nehemiah
9:7 127
9:10 108

Job
1:11-12 63
1:19 63
1:21 63
1:22 63
38:4-7 84
38:16, 25-26 90
39:1 90

39:19-25 208
42:2 . . . . 155n16

Psalm
1:2 51
1:6 . . . . 152n4
2:4-5 209
2:11 209
3:3 25
3:7 25
4:5 221
7:11 66
8 . . . . 118n3
8:3 94
9:8 165
16:3 51
16:8 47
19:1 . . . . 118n3
19:1-2 . . . . 86, 140
20:7 208
22:18 . . . . 73n6
22:27 229
22:27-28 55
23 275
23:3 112
23:6 191
25:11 . . . . 39, 110, 112, 241
25:15 47
27:4 . . . . 96n2
27:8-9 47
31:3 241
32:1 221
32:1-2 167
32:10-11 . . . . 221, 222
33:10-11 . . . . 75n16
33:17 208
34:20 . . . . 72n6
35:27 192
36:8 278
37:4 190
37:4-5 282
37:18 . . . . 152n4
48:3-5,7 89
50:10-15 207
50:13-15 223
51:17 221
60:5 . . . . 158n38
65:2 229
66:4 . . . . 116, 229

67:3 234
71:4-6 207
71:14 207
73:25-26 . . . . 96n2
78:26 63
79:9 . . . . 110, 241
84:11 189
86:8-9 229
86:9 116
89:27 36
91:14 . . . . 152n7
102:15 116
103:22 89
104 86
104:14 92
104:24 . . . . 91, 92
104:25-26 91
104:31 . . . . 78, 83, 84, 86
104:31-34 94
106:7-8 . . . . 108, 133
107:10-13 209
107:25 63
115:1-3 51
115:3 . . . . 51, 52, 57, 69
119:67 189
119:68 190
119:71 189
127:2 . . . . 158n38
135 . . . . 61, 64
135:1-6 50
135:6 . . . . 46, 51, 58, 65
135:6-11 65
135:6, 8-10 64
135:7 61
138:2 142
147:4-5 205
147:10 207
147:10-11 . . . . 186, 204
147:11 . . . . 20, 222
147:16-17 205
147:18 61
148:7 . . . . 89, 90
148:8 63
149:4 . . . . 66, 193

Proverbs
1:24-26 65
3:12 . . . . 158n38
8 28

8:30 . . . . 43n23
8:27,30 28
8:31 . . . . 41n4
10:1 28
11:1 . . . 240, 258, 259, 260, 261
15:8 . . . 210, 217, 218, 220, 222
15:20 28
16:4 . . . . 154n16
16:9 . . . . 154n16
16:11 262
16:33 . . . . 154n16
17:15 166
19:21 . . . . 154n16
20:14 259
20:17 261
21:1 . . . . 74n16, 154n16
21:31 208

Ecclesiastes
3:4,7 62

Isaiah
1:11 163
1:13 219
1:15-16 219
6:9 . . . . 73n6
8:12-13 244
11:6-8 276
11:15 63
12:4 116
24:15-16 117
30:31-32 65
38:17 . . . . 152n7, 189
40:26 . . . . 92, 93
40:28 92
42:1 . . . . 20n6, 26
42:9 55
43:1 128
43:4 . . . . 158n38
43:7 133
43:13 . . . . 75n16
43:15 128
43:21 . . . . 106, 133
44:1-2 128
44:28 . . . . 72n6
45:7 64
45:11 129
46:9-10 . . . . 51, 55, 57
46:10 . . . . 154n16

48:9-11 . . . . 110, 265
48:14 . . . . 158n38
51:12-13 244
53 162
53:4 175
53:5 165
53:6 . . . . 164, 165, 175
53:8 . . . . 163, 165, 175
53:9 165
53:10 . . 56, 160, 163, 164, 166,
   175, 176, 275
53:11 . . . . 164, 176
53:12 . . . . . . 163, 164, 165, 175
55:4 234
55:10-11 228
57:15 198
62:4 . . . . 51, 163
62:4-5 194
63:12-14 108
63:17 . . . . 154n16
64:1-2 116
64:4 . . . . 216, 250
64:7-8 129
65:17-18 187
65:19 194
66:2 221
66:3 220
66:4 220
66:19 116

Jeremiah
1:5 141
2:11 40
2:12-13 40
10:23 . . . . 154n16
13:11 . . . . 105, 126
14:7,9 110
31:2-3 149
31:31-34 188
32:39-41 188
32:40-41 189
32:40 . . . . 154n16
32:41 . . . . 20n6, 191, 194
38:17-20 . . . . 73n6

Lamentations
3:37-38 . . . . 75n16, 154n16
3:38 64

Ezekiel
3:6-7 .... 73n6
5:13 65
11:19 .... 225, 226
11:19-20 .... 59, 202
11:20 147
18 65
18:23 61
18:30 61
18:31 .... 61, 64
18:32 .... 61, 65, 144
20:5 127
20:9 108
33:11 144
36:20-23 .... 109, 265
36:26 280
36:27 ... 56, 59, 147, 202, 225, 227, 264
39:25 109

Daniel
2:20-21 .... 74n16
4:34-35 .... 74n16
4:35 .... 155n16
7:18 237
7:22 237
7:27 237
9:15 108
9:19 110
12:2 .... 180n10

Hosea
11:1 129
14:4 .... 158n38

Amos
3:2 .... 127, 141
3:6 .... 64, 75n16
5:24 .... 264, 277

Jonah
1:4 63
4:8 63

Micah
4:3 277

Habakkuk
2:14 .... 84, 232

Zephaniah
2:8 198
2:10 198
3:12 .... 199, 200
3:15 .... 197, 198
3:17 .... 186, 197, 198
3:19 .... 198, 199

Zechariah
12:10 .... 72n6, 134

Malachi
1:1-5 .... 152n8
1:2-3 .... 158n38
1:6 129
2:10 129

Matthew
1:21 143
3:9 131
3:12 .... 180n10
3:16-17 26
3:17 .... 42n10
5:3-11 .... 41n2
5:5 276
5:16 .... 20, 242, 261
5:23-24 .... 183n13
5:24 .... 183n13
5:43-47 263
5:44-45 148
5:45 202
5:48 38
6 .... 233, 295
6:9 29
6:9-10 265
6:10 236
6:11 232
6:12-15 .... 292, 294
6:13 .... 231, 236
6:24 209
7:11 274
7:13-14 .... 290, 301
7:14 .... 148, 289
7:21 .... 154n16
7:21-23 292
7:24-27 293
8:25 .... 181n10
8:29 .... 75n16

9:17 . . . . 181n10
9:38 . . . . 232, 236
10:6 . . . . 181n10
10:28 . . . . 20n6, 181n10
10:37-39 296
11:21 . . . . 73n6
11:26 . . . . 153n12
11:27 . . . . 29, 202
11:28-30 250
11:30 148
12:14 . . . . 181n10
12:18-20 26
12:28 . . . . 42n10
12:32 . . . . 181n10
12:48-50 293
12:50 . . . . 154n16
13:38 234
13:43 193
13:55-58 199
16:18 . . . . 75n16
17 24
17:2 25
17:5 . . . . 22, 25, 27, 42n10
17:6 25
18 295
18:2-3 298
18:8 . . . . 180n10
18:32-35 295
19:29 117
21:43 133
22:10 263
22:14. 154n13, 155n18, 155n19
22:37 16
23:37 . . . . 74n14, 154n16
24:12-13 . . . . 290, 296
24:14 . . . . 55, 228, 235
25:21 20
25:23 23
25:40-46 297
25:41 . . . . 75n16, 181n10
25:46 . . . . 181n10
26:24 . . . . 181n10
26:64 32
28:19 290

Mark
1:11 . . . . 42n10
1:14-15 300
2:10 32

3:29 . . . . 181n10
4:39 . . . . 32, 61
6:41 32
9:43-48 . . . . 180n10
10:15 274
10:27 289
13:13 . . . . 237n6, 298
13:22 302
14:24 188

Luke
1:34-35 32
2:14 . . . . 153n12
2:7 36
3:17 . . . . 180n10
3:22 . . . . 42n10
3:3 299
3:8 300
4:5-7 . . . . 74n16
5:31-32 248
5:32 300
6:13 . . . . 154n13
6:22 276
7:30 . . . . 154n16
8:10 274
8:11-15 293
8:54 32
9:62 298
10:17-18 . . . . 75n16
10:19 60
10:21 . . . . 134, 153n12
10:22 135
10:25-28 297
11:21-22 . . . . 75n16
11:46 250
12:4-5 . . . . 181n10, 234
12:3 . . . 242n10, 237, 268, 271,
272, 276
13:1-3 300
13:6-9 293
13:16 62
13:24 . . . . 290, 301
14:7 . . . . 154n13
14:24-33 295
15:7 . . . . 195, 300
15:7,10,23 66
15:10 195
15:11-32 195-196
16:14-15 215

16:26 . . . . 181n10
18:7f 236
18:18-22 296
18:25 276
19:41-42 144
21:12-19 235
21:16 276
21:24 133
21:36 231
22:3 . . . . 74n16
22:31 . . . . 75n16
22:31-32 302
22:32 . . . . 75n16
23:46 177
24:46-47 300

John
1:1 37
1:1,3 88
1:1-2 36
1:1-3 28
1:12 29
1:12-13 304
1:14 . . . . 29, 32, 36
1:18 . . . . 29, 36
3:8 304
3:16 . . . . 29, 36, 144
3:18 . . . . 29, 36, 202
3:18-19 . . . . 266n7
3:19-21 303
3:20 303
3:34-35 30
3:35 26
3:36 . . . . 294, 303
4:10 . . . . 255, 278
4:14 . . . . 255, 278, 303
5:1-4 . . . . 266n7
5:18 29
5:20 30
5:28-29 292
5:41-44 304
5:43 . . . . 111, 200
6:35 . . . . 254, 288, 292, 303
6:37 . . . . 139, 154n113, 202
6:37-39 138
6:39 . . . . 139, 154n13
6:44 . . . . 202, 280, 304
6:44 55
6:44-45 . . . . 155n17

6:53 . . . . 266n6
6:64 . . . . 73n6
6:64-65 . . . . 266n6
6:65 . . . . . 55, 155n17, 202, 304
7:17 . . . . 154n16
7:37-38 . . . . 266n6
8:42 296
8:44 62
8:45-47 304
8:47 304
8:58 32
10:3 139
10:3-4 56
10:4-5 139
10:11 139
10:14 139
10:15 139
10:16 . . 155, 150, 151, 154n13, 155n17, 202
10:17 . . . . 30, 33, 177
10:18 . . . . 67, 275
10:25 111
10:25-26 137
10:25-28 304
10:26 . . . . 138, 154n13
10:27 . . . . 139, 149, 304
10:27-29 138
10:27-30 302
10:28 139
11:15 . . . . 153n11
11:43 32
11:52 . . . . 150, 202
12:25 304
12:26 30
12:27-28 . . . . 111, 168
12:28 200
12:31 . . . . 74n16
13:1 . . . . 149, 274
13:18 . . . . 154n13
13:31 169
13:8-10 305
14:14 . . . . 200, 223
14:15 294
14:9 . . . . 32, 274
15:2 . . . . 294, 305
15:6 305
15:11 23
15:13-14 149
15:16 . . . . 154n13

15:19 . . . . 154n13
17 169
17:4 169
17:5 30
17:6 . . . 111, 138, 139, 154n13,
    200
17:9 . . . . 154n13, 155n17
17:10 139
17:12 . . . . 181n10, 200
17:13 23
17:15 . . . . 75n16
17:22-23 149
17:24 . 28, 33, 154n13, 155n17,
    277
17:26 . . . . 24, 26, 111, 277
18:37 304
18:9 . . . . 155n17
19:10-11 . . . . 74n16
19:24 . . . . 73n6
19:36-37 . . . . 72n6
20:17 29

Acts
2:23 . . . 56, 74n16, 154n16, 164
2:36 286
2:38 300
2:47 58
3:19 300
4:12 200
4:27-28 . . . . 75n16, 154n16
4:28 56
5:31 300
7:51 . . . . 154n16, 155n19
9:16 . . . . 113, 117
10 117
10:38 62
11:18 300
13:1-3 231
13:48 . 56, 58, 150, 154n16, 202
14:16 59
14:16-17 134
14:17 148
14:22 194
15:14 117
15:9 292
16:1 112
16:14 . . . . 55, 150, 154n16,
    155n19, 202, 225, 227, 280
16:9 230

17:25 . . . . . . 10, 49, 53, 64, 241
17:30 . . . . 59, 134
18:9-10 150
18:10 202
19:10 113
20:17 113
20:20 291
20:21 300
20:27 291
21:13 113
26:17-18 . . . . 266n3
26:18 . . . . 75n16

Romans
1:5 113
1:16 228
1:18 . . . . 118n3, 174
1:19-23 . . . . 87, 89
1:23 . . . . 168, 178n1
1:24-32 174
2:3 174
2:5 174
2:6-8 . . . . 182n10
2:6-10 292
2:8-9 174
2:16 174
2:29 188
3:6 174
3:19 174
3:23 . . . . 162, 178n1
3:23-26 . . . . 165, 166
3:24 . . . . 166, 176
3:24-26 174
3:25 . . . . 166, 167
3:25-26 . . 111, 119n5, 166, 168,
    174, 176, 178n3, 203
3:26 167
4:5 . . . . 166, 167
4:6-8 167
4:7 . . . . 41n2
4:13 276
4:20-21 218
5:1 140
5:3 . . . . 42n10
5:8-9 . . . . 179n4
5:9 . . . . 183n13
5:9-10 174
5:10-11 . . . . 183n13
6:12 294

6:14. . . . . 294, 303
6:23. 286
8:1. 193
8:7. 149
8:7f 174
8:12-14 295
8:13. 290
8:15-17 273
8:19. 273
8:19-22 265
8:21. 193
8:28. . 75n16, 154n16, 189, 296
8:28-30 141
8:28-32 139
8:28-33 . . . . 154n13
8:29. 140, 141, 152n4, 253, 264
8:29-30 . . . . 156n19
8:30 . . . . . . 140, 141, 143, 147,
    203, 302
8:31. 273
8:32. . . . . 31, 275
8:35-37 191
8:35-39 117
8:37-39 . . . . 75n16, 117
8:39. . . . . 141, 286
9-11. . . . . 75n19, 179n4
9:6-8 . . . . 153n10
9:8. 131
9:10-13 131
9:11. 148
9:14-23 . . . . 154n16
9:16. 226
9:17. 107
9:22-23 . . . . 67, 75n19
9:31-32 251
9:32. 292
10:1 . . . . 75n19, 76n19,
    153n12, 224
10:9. . . . . 282, 286, 287
10:13. . . . . 286, 287
10:13-17 228
11:4-7 . . . . 154n13
11:6. 251
11:12. 134
11:15. 134
11:20. . . . . 75n19
11:24. 134
11:24-36 . . . . 154n16
11:25. . . 55, 75n16, 76n19, 133

11:28. 174
11:32. 134
11:33-36 146
11:34-36 48
11:36. 203
12:19. 174
13:1. . . . . 74n16
13:11. 253
14:7-8 286
14:22. . . . . 41n2
14:23. . . . . 218, 262
15:7. 200
15:9. 200
15:15-18 55
15:18. 148
15:20. 113
15:26-27 . . . . 42n10
15:31. 236
16:19-20 . . . . 75n16
16:20. . . . . 75n16

1 Corinthians
1:2. 287
1:8-9 302
1:18. 252
1:21. . . . . 41n9, 42n10
1:23-24 . . . . 155n19
1:24. . . . . 155n19
1:26-31 . . . . 135-136, 142
1:27-28 . . . . 154n13
1:31. 203
2:9. 146
2:9-10 296
2:14. 149
2:23-24 202
4:7. 49
5:5. . . . . 182n10
6:2-3 276
6:9-10 . . . . 290, 294
8:3. 296
8:5-6 53
8:6. 88
9:24-27 301
9:26-27 . . . . 238n6
10:5. . . . . 42n10
11:25. 188
15:1-2 299
15:10. . . . . 55, 148, 252
15:25f 174

16:22 296

2 Corinthians
3:6 188
3:14-15 . . . . 21n10
3:18 . . . . 17, 21n10
4:3-4 . . . . 21n10, 74n16
4:4 . . . . 40n1, 41n1, 75n16, 234
4:4-6 . . . . 155n19
4:5 287
4:6 38
5:4 203
5:8 . . . . 42n10
5:9 214
5:10 174
5:18-20 . . . . 183n13
5:19 . . . . 183n13
8:2 . . . . 42n10
10:3-5 . . . . 234, 238n6
11:3 . . . . 75n16
12:10 . . . . 42n10

Galatians
1:15 . . . . 41n9, 42n10
3:10 174
3:13 177
3:29 188
4:4-5 29
5:6 . . . . 256, 292, 298
5:19-21 295
5:21 290
5:22 193
5:24 . . . . 290, 295
6:8 295
6:9 292

Ephesians
1:3-5 . . . . 153n13
1:4 . . . . 154n13, 202, 265
1:4-6 137
1:5 . . . . 50, 153n12
1:6 203
1:9 . . . . 153n12
1:11 . . . . 154n13, 154n16
1:11-12 137
1:14 137
1:17f 236
2:2 . . . . 74n16
2:3 174

2:4-5 149
2:5 174
2:7 193
2:8 . . . . 252, 280, 288, 291
3:6 188
3:17-19 254
3:18 236
4:29-30 66
5:1 38
5:2 175
5:16 234
5:25-27 265
6:10-13 . . . . 75n16
6:10ff. 234
6:12-13 . . . . 238n6
6:19 . . . . 231, 236

Philippians
1:6 302
1:11 236
1:15 . . . . 153n12, 272
1:17 272
1:29 280
2:6 37
2:9 . . . . 30, 177, 200
2:11 . . . . 200, 286
2:12-13 . . . . 56, 154n16
2:13 . . . . 147, 153n12, 302
4:6 232
4:19 . . . . 193, 216

Colossians
1:4-5 265
1:12 174
1:13 . . . . 31, 75n16
1:15 . . . . 34, 35, 36, 37
1:15-16 33
1:16 . . . . 35, 36, 88
1:18 . . . . 42n17
1:19 . . . . 32, 33, 42n10
1:21-23 299
2:6 287
2:9 . . . . 32, 33
2:15 . . . . 75n16
3:6 174
3:12 149
3:17 112
4:3 . . . . 231, 232, 236

1 Thessalonians
1:3.................... 292
1:4.................... 149
1:4-5 202
1:8.................... 287
2:8.................... 42n10
3:1.................... 42n10
3:5.................... 237n6
3:12................... 236
4:3.................. 154n16
4:7-8 253
5:17-19 .... 154n16
5:23-24 302

2 Thessalonians
1:9......... 181n10, 182n10
1:11............ 153n12, 292
1:11-12 252
2:8................ 174
2:9-10 296
2:10................... 298
2:12................. 42n10
2:13...... 147, 149, 202, 294
2:13-14 253
3:1........... 231, 232, 236
3:1-2 227

1 Timothy
1:3.................... 113
1:11 .... 9, 23, 40n1, 41n1,
    41n2, 53
2:4.................... 144
4:10................... 148
5:8.................... 292
6:1.................... 112
6:9................. 182n10
6:12......... 234, 237n6, 301
6:15-16 52

2 Timothy
1:12................... 302
2:11-12 299
2:12................... 276
2:19.................... 56
2:24-26 .... 75n16, 154n16
2:25............. 202, 280
2:25-26 .... 56, 225, 227
2:26................... 235
4:7.............. 237n6, 301

4:8.................... 297

Titus
2:14................... 265

Hebrews
1:2.................... 88
1:3................ 37, 87
1:5.................... 30
1:6.................... 30
1:13................... 30
1:14................... 85
2:9................. 30, 177
2:13.................. 176
2:14-15 .... 75n16
3:6................... 299
3:12-14 .... 299, 301
4:15............... 66, 199
5:8-9 294
6:1-2 .... 182n10
6:11-12 299
8:6-13 188
10:6................. 42n10
10:8................. 42n10
10:10................. 265
10:29.................. 30
10:32-36 256
10:34-36 265
10:35-36 292
10:36............. 294, 299
10:38............... 42n10
11:1.................. 255
11:4............. 167, 218
11:6.................. 218
11:7.................. 167
11:8.................. 292
11:24-26 .... 255, 292
12:2.................. 199
12:9-10 273
12:14...... 147, 148, 294, 301
12:23.................. 36
13:3.................. 256
13:5-6 .... 265n2
13:20................. 147
13:20-21 .... 154n16, 302
13:21.................. 56

James
1:5-6 209

1:12. 297
1:26. 298
2:5. . . . . . 154n13, 154n14, 297
2:17. 293
2:18. 292
2:20. 292
2:26. . . . . 292, 293
4:4. 174
4:6. 202
4:7. . . . . 75n16
4:8. 202
4:13-16 64
5:16. 232

1 Peter
1:2. 253
1:5. . . . . 253, 302
1:8. 297
1:23. 228
2:7. 297
2:9. . . . . 106, 203
3:14-15 244
3:9. 298
4:11. . . . . 148, 219, 252
5:8-9 . . . . 75n16

2 Peter
1:10. 147
1:17. . . . . 42n10
1:17-18 25
3:9. 144

1 John
1:7. . . . . 201, 299
1:9. . . . . 111, 201
2:4. 294
2:12. . . . . 39, 112, 201
2:14. . . . . 75n16
2:15. 297
2:17. . . . . 154n16, 294
3:1-10 294
3:8. . . . . 75n16
3:14. . . . . 298, 303
4:8. . . . . 298, 303
4:9. . . . . 29, 36
4:20. . . . . 298, 303
5:3. 250
5:18. . . . . 75n16

3 John
5-8. 113

Jude
12-13. . . . . 182n10

Revelation
1:16. 25
2:3. 112
2:7. 276
2:26-28 276
3:15-16 290
3:21. 277
5:2. 27
5:5. 27
5:5-6 27
5:6. 27
5:8. 223
5:9. . . . . 117, 150, 235
7:9. 117
12:12. 234
12:17. . . . . 238n6
14:11. . . . . 182n10
17:14. . . . . 238n6
17:17. . . . . 154n16
18:20. 65
19:3. . . . . 182n10
20:10. . . . . 75n16, 182n10
21:3. 254
21:4. 277
22:17. . . . . 148, 278

Person Index

Alexander, Bishop 33-34
Alford, Henry. 40n1, 41n9, 42n18
Andre, Major 145
Anselm, St. 179n4
Aristotle 97n11
Arius 33-37, 42n13, 42n14
Augustine 71n6, 96n2, 147
Barrett, C.K. 179n3
Barrett, David .. 121n10, 121n12
Bauer, Arndt & Gingrich. . 41n10
Bergin, G. Fred .. 151n1, 209n1, 209n2, 209n3,
Bettenson, Henry. . 42n15, 96n2, 158n36
Brainerd, David. 14, 49-50, 69n2, 101, 118, 231
Bridges, Charles 261,267n8
Briggs, C. 152n7
Brown, F. 152n7
Bryant, David. . . 232-233, 238n8
Bryant, Robyne 233
Bunyan, John 125
Burnet, Bishop Gilbert 14

Calvin, John 142
Carey, William 58-60, 61, 73n6, 229, 230
Carre, Captain E.G. ... 212-214, 237n3

Charnock, Stephen 72n6
Chauncy, Charles 143
Chrysostom. 36
Colson, Charles. 267n9
Constantine. 34
Cranfield, C.E.B. .. 141, 156n20
Cromwell, Oliver. 72n6
Cunningham, William 41n8

Dabney, Robert L. 145-146, 156n26, 156n27, 156n28, 156n29, 156n30, 156n31, 156n32, 156n33
Dallimore, Arnold 20n4, 156n20, 156n21
Darwin, Charles 97n11
Denney, James 175
Driver, S.R. 152n7
Duewel, Wesley L. 238n7
Duff, Alexander. 231
Dwight, Sereno.... 41n3, 74n15

Eastman, Dick .. 225-226, 237n4
Edwards, Jonathan ... 27, 31, 42, 41n3, 41n7, 42n21, 42n23, 62-63, 69n2, 73n6, 75n17, 75n18, 88, 94, 96n3, 96n4, 118n1, 121n16, 143, 171, 175, 184n16, 184n17, 266n7,
Edwards, Sarah 62-63

Eliot, John 230, 231

Forster, R.T. . . . 153n13, 154n16

Gerstner, John 75n18
Gray, Thomas 89-90
Grounds, Vernon 183n15
Guiness, Os. 260

Harrison, Everett F. 183n14
Hein, Rolland 180n6
Helm, Paul 41n7
Holtzen, Ellen. 97n6
Hudson, Winthrop S. 20n4
Hyde, John 212-214

Johnstone, Patrick . . . 60, 74n12,
  74n13, 236, 238n11
Judson, Adoniram 231

Keil and Delitzsch 41n4
Kevengere, Festo. 56
Kilby, Clyde 69n3, 69n4 95,
  96n1, 97n11
King, Mary 152n3
Kuyper, Abraham 260

L'Engle, Madeleine 179n4,
  180n9
Lewis, C. S. . . 36, 42n20, 52, 53,
  69n5, 71n6, 82, 170, 180n4,
  180n5
Lightfoot, J.B. 42n16
Livingstone, David. 150-151, 231
Lucian. 33
Luther, Martin. . 253-254, 266n4

MacArthur, John. 279, 290
MacDonald, George . . . 170-175,
  180n6, 183n13, 184n16
MacDonald, William G. . 153n13
Marshall, Chief Justice. 145
Marston, V.P. . . 153n13, 154n16
Martyn, Henry 14
Mather, Cotton. 230, 237n5
McCheyne, Robert Murray . . . 14
McConkey, James 282
Metzger, Bruce 42n19
Moody, Dwight L. 211

Mueller, George. . 124, 125, 142,
  151n1, 189-191, 209n1, 209n2,
  209n3, 209n4, 211-212, 237n2
Mueller, Lydia. 189
Mueller, Mary 190
Murray, Iain. 74n8, 156n23,
  158n39, 158n40

Newton, John 58
Nicole, Roger . . . 179n3, 183n13

Oehler, Gustav F. 118n2,
  152n4, 158n37

Packer, J.I. 73n6
Pate, Larry 119n7
Paton, John G. . . . 231, 269-270,
  278n1, 278n2
Paton, Mary Ann. 270
Pettit, Norman 69n2
Pierson, A.T. 236, 238n10
Pinnock, Clark H. . . 70n5, 70n6,
  75n19, 153n13, 156n23
Powell, Louisa. 170

Quayle, William. 92, 97n7

Reapsome, Jim 238n9
Rice, Richard. 70n5
Robinson, William Childs. . . 174,
  183n14
Robson, Mary Ann. 269-270
Ryland, John. 74n9, 74n10
Ryland, Jr., John 74n9

Sabellius the Libyan. 34
Schaff, Philip. 42n11, 72n6
Scott, John 151
Scott, Peter Cameron 151
Scougal, Henry. 12, 13-17,
  20n1, 20n2, 20n3, 20n4, 20n5,
  20n7, 20n8, 20n9, 39, 266n7
Socinius 71n6
Socrates. 34
Spurgeon, Charles. 125-126,
  151n2, 151n3, 156n23, 156n24
Stevenson, J. 41n8

Talbott, Thomas 179n4,

180n9, 183n13, 184n16
Theodotus 41n8
Thornton, Henry 264
Toplady, Augustus 58
Tozer, A.W. 31, 41n6, 73n6
Tucker, Ruth. 158n41

Washington, George . . . 67, 145,
  157n32
Wells, Tom 74n11
Wesley, Charles. 15
Wesley, John. 142, 264
Whitefield, George 14-15,
  20n4, 58, 73n6, 142
Wilberforce, William . . . 263-264
Williams, Charles. 98n11
Winter, Ralph . . 115-116, 119n9,
  120n10, 121n15

Subject Index

Arianism, 33-38
Arminianism, 69-74
  prelude to Universalism,
    143, 156
Assurance of salvation
  and the demand for holiness,
    146-148
  none while intent on sin, 285
  rooted in election, 146-148
  texts to encourage, 301-302
Atonement
  George Macdonald's view,
    172-175
  how the death of Christ achieves
    it, 165-169
  Madeleine L'Engle's view, 179
Beholding
  as a way of becoming, 15-17
Bible
  its central drama, 162
  most important paragraph,
    165-166
Blessed
  meaning "happy," 41
Call of God
  two kinds of call, 155-156
Calvinism
  Charles Spurgeon's discovery,
    125-126
  George Mueller's discovery, 124

Spurgeon identifies with the
  gospel, 156
William Carey's, 58
Childlikeness
  necessity for final salvation, 298
Comfort of Christian hearts
  being loved by God from
    eternity, 148-149
Command of God
  as good news for sinners,
    204-207
Compassion
  God's on all people, 143-145
Controversy
  can controversial teaching
    edify?, 123
Conversion
  God sovereign in, 225-226
  God's work, 56
  not a two-step event, 280-285
  not at risk, 56
  Whitefield's, 15
Creation
  expresses glory of God, 86-87
  God's delight in, 79-96
Death of Christ
  how it vindicates God and
    justifies sinners, 168-169
Election
  a biblical truth, 142

and prayer, 224-227
basis of infallible salvation, 139
Charles Spurgeon's discovery,
125-126
confounding man-centered
expectations, 135-136
corporate view examinined,
153-154
George Mueller's discovery, 124
God's delight in electing love,
129-130
holiness and assurance of
salvation, 146-148
humbles sinners and exalts God,
142-143
not based on foreknown faith,
139-141
of Israel, 126-128
preserves from false
philosophies, 143
to the glory of God's grace,
137-139
unconditional, 130-132
Eudokeo- (Greek), 41-42, 153
Evangelism
hope in election, 150-151
Faith
foreknown faith not basis of
election, 139-141
how it produces obedience,
253-257
Jonathan Edwards's definition,
266-267
lordship salvation is by faith,
287-288
nature of in John's gospel,
303-305
source of obedience, 218
Fame of God
goal of missions, 112-113
prayer in his name to spread his
fame, 227-228
Fear of God
and hope at the same time,
204-206
Foreknowledge
election not based on foreknown
faith, 139-141
God's limited?, 69-74

Forgiveness of others
necessity for final salvation,
294-295
Freedom of God, 51-52
in electing Israel, 128-129
in election, 130-132
Galaxies, 93-94
Glory of God
election for God's glory,
137-138
expressed in creation, 86-87
God's love for it central theme,
162
gone public, 105-106
God (see Trinity)
a mountain spring not a
watering trough, 241
a risk-taker?, 53-58
as shepherd, 275
complex emotional life, 66
delight demonstrates greatness,
192-194
delight in me or in himself,
199-200
excellency measured by his
pleasures, 16-17
freedom of in election, 128-129
his compassion on all people,
143-145
happy in fellowship of Trinity,
48
he loves to give not sell, 274
his favorite food, 223
his goodness in Mueller's
tragedy, 189-191
his happiness as his glory, 23
his love as the root of election,
132-133
his repentance, 265
his secular interests, 260-263
how he is like George
Washington, 145-146
in a class by himself, 52-53
need of the world to know him,
18
never bored, 192
not forced by situations, 57
Paul's unmodern problem with
God, 167-168

pleasure in his Son, 24-40
reconciled to us, 183
self-sufficient, 48-50
should he be impeached?,
    166-167
the sound of God singing, 187
what is the true Father like?,
    272-274
who effectively saves, 226-227
works for those who wait for
    him, 216-217
Gospel
    defined by Bible not experience,
        288-290
    God's value is driving force,
        19, 203
    grounded in God's plesure in
        himself, 39
    is demand for obedience good
        news?, 248-250
    of the glory of the happy God,
        23
    what kind of command is good
        news?, 204-207
Grace
    definition, 19, 203
    God-centered, 9
    power not just pardon, 252
    sovereign, 58
Great Commission
    not at risk, 55
Hell
    can we still be happy?, 75
    George Macdonald's view, 172
    its justice, 183
    Madeleine L'Engle's view,
        179-178
    texts showing its eternal
        duration, 180-182
Holiness
    and the assurance of salvation,
        146-148
    necessity for final salvation, 294
Holy Spirit
    divine person of Trinity, 43
Hope
    a command that is good news
        for sinners, 206-207
    and fear of God at the same

time, 204-206
    basis in God's delight in God,
        39
    God-centered ground, 102-105
    why it glorifies God, 222
Humility, 220-221

Image of God
    in unbelievers, 261-263
Incarnation
    not a risk, 56
Intimacy
    between Father and Son, 29-30
Israel
    election of, 126-128
Jealousy
    should Jesus be jealous of
        creation?, 85-86
Jesus
    as perfect ideal of the Father,
        42-43
    begotten not made, 33-38
    Co-creator with the Father,
        27-29, 87-88
    combines paradoxical attributes,
        27, 184
    deity, 31-38
    forsaken but loved by the
        Father, 176-177
    how could God delight in his
        death, 175-176
    intimacy with the Father, 29-30
    jealous of creation?, 85-89
    the name of God, 200
    what his death achieved,
        168-169
    who killed Jesus?, 164-165
Justice
    pleasure of God in public justice,
        257-258
Justice of God (see righteousness
    of God)
    George Macdonald's view,
        171-172
Kingdom of God
    God loves to give it, 276-277
Lordship salvation, 279-306
    texts showing its truth, 291-305
Love

as delight or pleasure, 16
Love of God
  unconditional in election,
    132-133
  God's love as passion, 16
Love of God
  experience of being loved by
God, 148-149
Love of others
  necessity for final salvation,
    297-298
Love to Christ and to God
  necessity for final salvation,
    296-297
Mercy of God
  flows from his pleasure in his
    name, 110-112
  its God-centered ground,
    107-109
Missions
  goal is the fame of God,
    112-113
  Paul-type missionaries, 112-115
  secured in election, 150-151
  sovereignty of God over Satan,
    60
  table of unreached peoples, 114
  table showing the task is
    finishable, 115
  third-world missionary force,
    114, 119
  Timothy-type missionaries,
    112-115
  why missionaries did not come
    sooner, 59
  will not fail, 55
Money
  necessity to be free from love of
    it, 295-296
Name of God, 101-102
  meaning according to Oehler,
    118
Necessity of doing good
  texts, 292-293
Nicene Creed, 34-35
Obedience
  all God's pleasures lead here,
    264-265
  how faith produces it, 253-257

is the demand good news,
    248-250
  necessity for final salvation,
    293-294
  why God delights in it, 243-248
Omniscience of God
  limited?, 69-74
Operation World, 60
Pardon
  flows from God's pleasure in his
    fame, 110-112
Passion
  for God, 11
Perfection
  upright but not perfect,
    221-222
Perseverance
  necessity for final salvation,
    298-299
  God's promise of preservation,
    301-302
Plan of the book, 18-19, 47
Pleasures of God
  how do we please God,
    201-202, 214-216
  in all he does, 50-69
  in bruising the Son, 161-185
  in creation, 79-96
  in death of the wicked?, 60-69
  in destruction?, 65-69
  in doing good to those who
    hope in him, 187-209
  in election, 123-159
  in God--in us, 277-278
  in himself not vanity, 38-39
  in his fame, 101-122
  in his Son, 24-40
  in obedience is good news,
    248-250
  in persevering political
    engagement, 263-264
  in personal obedience and public
    justice, 241-267
  in the prayers of the upright,
    211-238
  in us or in himself?, 199-200
  in us, 40
  where they are all leading,
    264-265

Political engagement
  God's pleasure in, 263-264
Prayer
  a weapon wielding the word,
    212, 231-232
  and election, 224-227
  and pains will do anything, 231
  appeal for wartime praying,
    233-237
  definition from catechism, 211
  express God-exalting hope, 222
  in God's name to spread his
    fame, 227-229
  materialistic evangelical praying,
    232-233
  patience in, 211-212
  preparation for each pentecost,
    236
  wartime walkie-talkie, 231-232
Preaching
  to disobedient professing
    Christians, 290
Preservation in holiness
  God's promise of preservation,
    301-302
Propitiation
  defined, 167, 178-179
Puritan hope, 229-230
Ranger Rick, 90
Reconciliation
  God must be reconciled to us,
    183
Religion
  Abominable, 217-219
Repentance
  necessity for final salvation,
    299-300
Repentance of God, 265
Resolutions of Clyde Kilby, 95,
    97-98
Righteousness
  its essence, 39
  of God defined, 165, 178
Risk
  definition, 55
  God a risk-taker?, 53-58
  take risks for Christ, 57
Salvation
  effected not just offered, 143

lordship of salvation is by faith,
    287-288
  the two-stage experience,
    280-281
Sanctification
  saved through it, 252-253
Satan
  limited rule of the world, 74-75
Schizophrenia in heaven?,
    162-164
Secular interests of God, 260-263
Self-sufficiency of God, 48-50
Sin
  opposed to glory of God,
    161-162
Son of God (see Jesus)
Sovereign grace
  according to William Carey, 58
Sovereignty of God, 51-52
  and suffering, 60-69
  can he make something too
    heavy to pick up?, 69-70
  in conversion, 225-226
  in my church, 67-68
  in my mother's death, 68
  texts on God's unstoppable
    purpose, 154
Spiders, 90-91
Suffering
  does God delight in it?, 60-69
  George Mueller's tragedy,
    189-191
  in my church, 67-68
  loss of my mother, 68
  Paton's loss of wife and child,
    269-270
  prayers and pains, 231
Times of the gentiles, 133-134
Trembling at the word of the
  Lord, 220-221
Trinity
  described, 38, 42-44
Unbelief
  Jesus battles it, 271
Unbelievers
  their honest work, 261-262
Universalism
  George Macdonald's view,
    172-174

Madeleine L'Engle's view, 179
result of Arminianism, 143, 156
texts showing eternal duration
   of hell, 180-182
Unreached peoples,
   definition, 119-120
   table on relation to missionaries,
      114-115
   table on how the task is
      finishable, 115
Upright
   not the same as perfect,
      221-222
   why God delights in prayers of
      upright, 222-223
Vanity of God?, 38-39
Warfare
   life is warfare, 231-232,
      237-238
   necessity of vigilance, 301
Works
   obedience not "by works,"
      251-252